PRECARIOUS HO

PRECARIOUS HOPE

Migration and the Limits of

Belonging in Turkey

AYŞE PARLA

STANFORD UNIVERSITY PRESS
STANFORD, CALIFORNIA

Stanford University Press
Stanford, California

© 2019 by the Board of Trustees of the Leland Stanford Junior University.
All rights reserved.

Printed in the United States of America on acid-free, archival-quality paper

Library of Congress Cataloging-in-Publication Data
Names: Parla, Ayşe, author.
Title: Precarious hope : migration and the limits of belonging in Turkey / Ayşe Parla.
Description: Stanford, California : Stanford University Press, 2019. | Includes
    bibliographical references and index.
Identifiers: LCCN 2019009009 (print) | LCCN 2019009649 (ebook) | ISBN 9781503609440
    (e-book) | ISBN 9781503608108 (cloth : alk. paper) | ISBN 9781503609433 (pbk. : alk.
    paper)
Subjects: LCSH: Immigrants—Turkey—Social conditions. | Turks—Bulgaria—Social
    conditions. | Citizenship—Turkey. | National characteristics, Turkish. | Emigration
    and immigration law—Turkey. | Turkey—Emigration and immigration. |
    Bulgaria—Emigration and immigration.
Classification: LCC JV8745 (ebook) | LCC JV8745 .P37 2019 (print) |
    DDC 305.9/0691209561—dc23
LC record available at https://lccn.loc.gov/2019009009

Cover design: Kevin Barrett Kane
Cover photograph: Behiç Günalan
Typeset by Motto Publishing Services in 10/14 Minion Pro

For my parents, Jale and Taha

CONTENTS

ACKNOWLEDGMENTS

This book had its origins at the Boğaziçi University Library in Istanbul, where I met the inspiring women who, in addition to sharing their expertise as librarians, shared with me such amazing stories of their journey across the Bulgarian-Turkish border that they pulled me in like a magnet. In particular, I would like to acknowledge my gratitude to Nazmiye Ademoğlu and Mensiye Dahil; their stories do not appear in the book, but they are the original influence behind it. During the long journey that brought the book to this point, I was blessed to have as my guardian angels the legendary administrative team at Boğaziçi Library—Zeynep Metin, Sema Taşal, and Hatice Ün.

I was introduced to anthropology in an undergraduate class at Harvard, taught by Ken George, who gave me the first alluring glimpse of the ethnographic and theoretical richness of the field through his own work and his phenomenal teaching. He also introduced me to the anthropology of emotions and the groundbreaking work of Lila Abu-Lughod, who would become the kind of mentor one could only dream of. She supported me at every step along the way during graduate study at New York University. And she continues to inspire me by her dedication, her generosity, and her unique ethnographic style, which combines the most sophisticated theory with a novelist's sensitivity to the details of individual lifeworlds. At New York University, I am also most indebted to Theresa Caldeira, Michael Gilsenan, Fred Myers, Susan Rogers and Bambi Schieffelin for all they have taught me. I consider myself especially lucky to have had Jessica Catellino in my cohort: after that first exchange in front of Rufus D. Smith Hall, I knew we would be great friends, but I did not yet realize just how much I would come to admire her intellectual grace over the years and how invaluable her support would prove to be.

The field research and writing for this book were made possible through the support of grants no. 106K162 and no. 108K522 from the Scientific and Technological Council of Turkey (TÜBİTAK), an Exceptional Young Scholar

Grant from the Turkish Academy of Sciences (TUBA), and a membership at the Institute for Advanced Study (IAS) in Princeton, New Jersey.

The activists and colleagues I met at the Migrant Solidarity Network taught me much about engagement and endurance. I benefited from the discussions, which frequently extended beyond the meetings and the protests and into late—and often musical—evening hours. I would especially like to thank Ufuk Ahıska, Ayşe Akalın, Begüm Özden Fırat, Ezgi Güner, Deniz Özgür, Ceren Öztürk, Muhsin Kemal Şimşek, and Kerimcan Yıldırım for thinking with me, challenging me, and broadening my perspective. Fırat Genç and Zeyno Pekünlü deserve special thanks: they not only provided me with a most comfortable couch to crash on but even set aside a drawer where I stored some of the earliest scribbles of the manuscript.

Feedback from audiences and participants at various workshops have helped me immensely to think through my ideas and sharpen my analyses: the Rapoport Center for Human Rights and Justice at the University of Texas, Austin; the UCLA Center for the Study of International Migration; the Anthropology Department at UCLA; the Political Science Forum at Vassar College; the Hagop Kevorkian Center for Near Eastern Studies at New York University; the European Studies Center at the University of Florida; the Center for the Study of Social Difference at Columbia University; and the Department of Anthropology at Boston University. I would particularly like to thank Can Açıksöz, Güldem Baykal Büyüksaraç, Başak Can, Jessica Catellino, Joanna Davidson, Andy Davison, Eva-Marie Dubuisson, Karen Engle, Ilana Feldman, Ken George, Saygun Görarıksel, Akhil Gupta, Sondra Hale, Zeynep Korkman, Bailey Miller, Kirin Narayan, Esther Romeyn, Susan Rottman, Maria Stoilkova, Anoush Suni, Miriam Ticktin, Roger Waldinger, Rob Weller, Lale Yalçın-Heckman, and Berna Yazıcı. Saygun Görarıksel and Kirin Narayan get to take credit for the main title of the book, *Precarious Hope*—I think they announced it in unison during our delightful ethnographic writing workshop in Istanbul in 2016.

Most of the manuscript was completed at the Institute for Advanced Study, Princeton, where I was a Member in 2016–17 and a Visitor in 2017–18. The Institute was an exceptional space that combined the best of solitude with the best of intellectual engagement. I want to thank especially Lori Allen, Fadi Bardawil, Ruha Benjamin, Céline Bessire, Amy Buroway, Peter Coviello, Anne-Claire Defossez, Andrew Dilts, Thomas Dodman, Karen Engle, Sara Farris, Bernard Harcourt, David Kazanjian, Paul di Maggio, Pascal

Marichalar, Reuben Jonathan Miller, Silvia Pasquetti, Peter Redfield, Shatema Threadcraft , Emily Zatkin, and Andrew Zimmermann, who have provided invaluable insights over formal discussions but also over lunch, three p.m. tea, late-night rehearsals of the "New Orientalists" band, and during walks in the Institute Woods, where an ephemeral sighting of a red fox may turn into a lasting thought. It is hard to put into words the gratitude and admiration I feel for Didier Fassin and Joan Scott, brilliant scholars and exceptional mentors, who lead by example and make the School of Social Science at IAS the piece of paradise on earth that it is. I cannot thank Linda Cooper, Jennifer Hansen, Laura McCune, Donne Petito, and Marcia Tucker enough for their expertise and tireless assistance. At Princeton, I reunited with dear old friends and priceless colleagues whose support was indispensable: Emine Fetvaci, Keena Lipsitz, and Grigore Pop-Eleches—thank you. I know I will never quite be able to return the favor.

I feel fortunate to have a transnational group of colleagues from whose wisdom this work has benefited across the years: Çağla Aykaç, Evren Balta, Banu Bargu, Jacqueline Bhabha, Kristen Biehl, Didem Danış, Mine Eder, Sumru Erkut, Bruce Grant, Alexander Kiossev, Esra Özyürek, Umut Türem, Zachary Whyte, and Noah Zatz have offered insights that have stayed with me. I owe Bailey Miller and Ararat Şekeryan huge thanks for helping me with the bibliography and to Emily (Max) Coolidge Toker for stepping in on such short notice. Lori Allen, Ateş Altınordu, Yelena Baraz, Elizabeth Ann Davis, Elizabeth Harman, Ahmet Faik Kurtulmuş, Pascal Marichalar, Esra Özyürek, Peter Redfield, and Merav Shohet read parts of the manuscript in its latest stages and offered invaluable feedback, although I am afraid I have not been able to do justice to their insights. The manuscript was completed at Boston University, and I am grateful for the warm welcome and collegiality of my fellow faculty in the Department of Anthropology.

At Stanford University Press, I was most fortunate to be working with the legendary Kate Wahl, whose support and editorial acumen were priceless. The two reviewers' excellent and sharp comments have been very useful in guiding my revisions of the text. I also want to thank Gretchen Otto and Leah Pennywark for their assistance and patience and Jan McInroy for her meticulous copyediting and superb attention to detail.

Sabancı University, the institution where I worked for more than a decade and one that I left not entirely of my own volition but because of the increasing impingement on academic freedoms in Turkey, will always remain a special place. Among the outstanding students I met there, I would like thank in particular Bürge Abiral, Rahime İsmetova, Oya Nuzumlali, and Ayşe Şanlı. Zeynep Kaşlı deserves special mention as an exceptional assistant for two research grants. Ayşe Kadıoğlu, former President of the University, was a beacon of integrity, steering the community with care and courage in politically turbulent times. And above all, I am most fortunate to have found colleagues at Sabancı who are also among the closest friends I have in life. Ateş Altınordu, Çağla Aydın, Gürol Irzık, Sibel Irzık, and Ahmet Faik Kurtulmuş sustained me with their sharpness and depth, compassion, and (not least) distinctively sardonic brand of joie de vivre, especially during these last two years of writing away from "home." I consider them my analytic and moral compass in things intellectual, political, and beyond.

The stamina and faith to complete the book also came from those who have taught me year after year that chosen kinship revels in converging paths but is invincible in the face of distance and difference. I am grateful beyond words for the family I have in them: the brilliant Amanda Schaffer, who makes magic with words and who already knew how to tread gently on dreams, hopes, and convictions as we wondered about life on the steps of Widener Library in college; Cumhur Kuşçuoğlu, who can make me laugh at the most dismal of moments, who has a heart of gold, and who will finally get to boast after chiding me for all the years of delay that he (rightly) refused to understand; *kuyrıgıs* Nora Tataryan, the bright and caring *bızdig* sister I always yearned for; Hilmi Luş, for all that he has unostentatiously done; my *sladkiy*, Natalya Nesterova, a constant inspiration because of her talents and also for her demonstration of what a woman can accomplish through sheer will; and my wise, beautiful Sis, Ece Alakoç, part of the household since we met at age eleven, aunt to my son, and who knows my heart and soul.

I imagine Turhan Alpan, doting grandfather and always the perfect gentleman, including the very last time I saw him conscious before his sudden ailment took him away much too quickly and much too soon, taking a copy of the book to Bizimtepe to show his buddies. I will cherish his memory and the gentle, generous care he lavished on us until the very end.

As for the gang at home, they'd rather go unnamed, but they go on naming the world for me for all that I could want it to be.

PRECARIOUS HOPE

INTRODUCTION

Shielding Hope

NEFIYE, AN ADMINISTRATIVE WORKER in her native Ruse, Bulgaria, first migrated to Istanbul, Turkey, in 2003 and took a job as a nanny. Slim and agile, she had a sprightly gait that made it hard for others to keep up, and she dressed in the latest fashions, even while having to pinch pennies. When I first met her, in 2008, she was nearly fifty years old and still working as a nanny. By then, she was fed up with her uncertain legal status, which involved crossing the Bulgarian-Turkish border on a tourist visa that granted a three-month stay; after the visa expired she would typically lapse into illegality until the government issued another amnesty, which forgave overstay but granted only another temporary residence for a few more months. Despite making multiple trips across the border to maintain her visa and taking advantage of every amnesty, she still often ended up working without a permit.

Nefiye thrived on order and clarity, whether it was maintenance of her employer's sweaters and shirts in color-coordinated, nifty piles or the meticulous categorization of files that she set up for her own legal documents. Thus the structural ambiguities of bureaucracy and the unpredictable promises and disappointments of the legalization process that she encountered in Turkey frayed her nerves. She had to navigate a complex bureaucracy that imposed opaque and ever-shifting application criteria. She also worked for unpredictable and exploitative employers who might demand that she iron a dress after midnight or prohibit her from using the shower after five o'clock in the afternoon. But none of these difficulties dampened Nefiye's hope of success in her quest for citizenship, or *kimlik*—literally "identity"—as citizenship is colloquially called among migrants.

Over the course of four years, from 2008 to 2012, I stood in various queues with Nefiye. These queues typically involved filing a petition at one of the Balkan migrant associations, which advocate on behalf of ethnically Turkish migrants, getting one more document translated and authorized by a notary, rushing to make the deadline at the police station for an amnesty that would allow for another temporary stay, or waiting at the Foreigners' Department of Istanbul Police Headquarters to have "days counted" to see if she had accumulated the two years required for a citizenship application.

On a scorching day in July 2011, Nefiye and I stood in yet another line at the Foreigners' Branch to inquire about what appeared to be an exceptional amnesty. Like the previous short-term amnesties, this one too was available only to those who were from Bulgaria and who, like Nefiye, could claim Turkish ethnicity. But this amnesty promised to be different from the others because it offered more than temporary residence status. Instead, it promised a fast track to citizenship for currently undocumented migrants from Bulgaria who had overstayed their visas.[1]

Sorting through the documents she had accumulated over the years, Nefiye turned to me and said, "I have hope that finally this time, this citizenship matter will be resolved. Don't you think?"

By now, I had learned that Nefiye's questions regarding hope were not just queries but also claims. The reassurance she sought was less about whether she had done things right—she was always confident in her way of going about things and rarely asked for guidance. Rather, she wanted to confirm my participation in her hopeful stance. I was anxious, however, about what appeared to be too good a promise on the part of the government. Since the late 1990s, the policy pattern had been implicit but consistent: tolerate irregular migration from Bulgaria through the practice of granting intermittent, temporary amnesties, but discourage citizenship. The current offer seemed like an aberration, and I found myself turning into a killjoy. "Let's not get too hopeful—who ever knows in this country? Who knows what excuse they might come up with to reject your application after all this trouble?" Nefiye was displeased and, being the straightforward person that she is, took no pains to hide it. "Do not kill my hope," she admonished me. Yes, she agreed, of course something might go wrong. "But," she added pointedly, "if I persist, I will eventually get this *identity*. I am, after all, *soydaş* [racial kin]." I will shortly elaborate on the significance of Nefiye's identification as "racial kin." For now, let me conclude this vignette by noting that Nefiye's hope proved well founded. She ended up receiving citizenship through this last application.

The path would prove to be far more tortured for İsmigül and her family, whose quest for citizenship lasted longer than a decade. İsmigül had worked as a chemist in the city of Razgrad in Bulgaria. Now, in Istanbul, she was employed as a domestic worker six days a week. By the time I met her, she was forty-eight years old and had already made several attempts to gain citizenship on behalf of herself, her husband, and their two children, ages twelve and fifteen. So far, she and her husband had managed to avoid undocumented status by obtaining "companion permits." These were residence permits that ethnically Turkish migrants received by enrolling their children in school. Those who could prove Turkish origins were allowed to apply for citizenship after two years of continuous residence rather than five years, which is the minimum for all other migrants. İsmigül and her husband hoped that they had accumulated enough days to be eligible. However, companion permits came with complications. Because they were granted through children, who do not go to school during the summer holidays, there would always be an interruption in the residence record.

As İsmigül, her husband, and I waited in line for what İsmigül hoped would be the final stage in the application process, she was basking in the affirmation she had received at our previous stop, the Ministry of National Education's community center. There, applicants are usually tested for proficiency in Turkish, but İsmigül was gratified to have been recognized for "who she was." She had already recounted her triumphant moment to me and her husband, although we had both been present at the event. Now, she addressed another ethnically Turkish migrant who had just joined us in the line, as if to include her in this hopeful state of anticipation: "See, the clerk did not make us take language exam. He waived the language exam for us. He could tell who we are the moment we came through that door, let me tell you. They understand it from the way we walk and carry ourselves, the way we dress, our expressions. I have this hope inside me that everything else will go just as well."

I nodded my assent and, in this instance, kept my reservations to myself, lest any comments from me might "kill hope." However, things did not go well, at least not right away. The clerk who reviewed İsmigül's file became visibly impatient as she examined each document. Finally, when she reached the critical *soy belgesi*, a document of origins that is required for proof of Turkishness, she threw up her arms in exasperation and said, "There are too many different spellings here. One spelling in the Turkish translation, another in the Bulgarian document. I can't process this file. Every single name on every single document has to match."

On the ferry back to the Asian side of Istanbul, İsmigül was frustrated by the weight of an entire workday gone to waste, not to mention the money spent on the documents, most of which had to be notarized both in Sofia, the capital of Bulgaria, and then again in İstanbul. She protested, "Even if we figure out the money, when will I have time to go back to Bulgaria again to start all over? We wait and wait. There is no way these children are going back. But still . . . no citizenship, no work permit. We, too, have Turkish blood in our veins."

The swift move into racial identification as the grounds for claiming belonging was not unique to İsmigül. It was a strategy that Bulgaristanlı migrants often used in their appeals to officials to mark their distinction from other undocumented migrants. "Once, I confronted them," İsmigül said. "'Those Filipino are getting work permits now,' I said to the clerk at the Foreigners' Branch. "Why not us? And we are Turks," she protested, voicing her resentment this time for my benefit. "But you cannot question things too much. Because if you overdo it, they [the police] can always say, 'That's it! We are deporting you.'"

Within three months, İsmigül had redone all of the documents and sorted out the discrepancies. But when she submitted the revised application, she and her family were again refused. They were told, at the very end of the process, that the companion permit was no longer a valid basis for the residence requirement. The unexpected (and unannounced) shift in the regulation was particularly frustrating because it coincided with another major change in Citizenship Law No. 403/1964: whereas until 2009, those of Turkish descent had had a reduced residence requirement, the revised Citizenship Law (No. 5901/2009), passed in 2009, sought to eliminate overtly ethnicist biases in the law in part by equalizing the terms for citizenship. This meant that like non-Turkish migrants, İsmigül and her family would now have to fulfill five years of uninterrupted residence instead of the two that they had previously been striving for. Still, as we were having a picnic with all the children—and for once not waiting in line—İsmigül declared that she was not about to lose hope: "You know me, I am not one to give up. Also, I could see it, the chief, he felt bad for us, I could see it. He said to my cousin, you know the doctor, who tried to help, 'Of course I, too, would prefer citizens like these.'" İsmigül went on, "Naturally, he does not want all those people coming from here and there; of course he wants us instead."

It took another three years and several more amnesties for İsmigül's family to eventually obtain citizenship, that object of desire that had governed their lives for so long. But it is not just the uncertainty and the arduousness of the bureaucratic processes that render the hope of İsmigül and other migrants precarious. It is also whether citizenship, which the majority of my interlocutors eventually obtain, delivers on its promises.

*   *   *

This book explores the degrees and limits of migrant privilege and the terms of belonging in contemporary Turkey by tracking the constant fluctuations that İsmigül, Nefiye, and other migrants from Bulgaria experience between expectation and uncertainty, entitlement and refusal. The vacillations that characterize the precarious hope I depict are not only "waverings of the mind that increase or diminish one's capacity to act," as Spinoza ([1677] 2000) famously described emotions. The hope for legalization that circulates among Bulgaristanlı migrants is also a "collective structure of feeling," in the felicitous phrasing of the Marxist cultural theorist Raymond Williams (1977), one that varies according to social class and is shaped by migration bureaucracies, laws, and their criteria of differentiation.

Although some individuals may be of a more hopeful disposition than others, my approach to hope as an emotion is not one that examines emotions as inner states that reside in the individual. Rather, I follow the classic scholarship on the anthropology of emotions to attend to hope's historical, political, and legal production (Abu-Lughod 1986; Briggs 1971; Lutz 1988; Myers 1986).[2] Within the wide semantic range of hope, which covers a vast spectrum from fear to doubt to anticipation, the hope for legalization that I discuss here veers closer to expectation. In that sense, my analysis partially aligns with the rationalist thinking on hope.[3] My focus, however, is not just on propositional attitudes by single individuals regarding the probability of things they hope for to be realized. Rather, I am most interested in explicating what feminist legal scholar Patricia Williams (1991) has called a "structured expectation," in which members of a certain group, class, or race can take hope for granted in their encounters with the law.[4]

The hope described in this book is not hope against the odds. Nor is it a "radical hope" that is cultivated regardless of what is structurally possible.[5] Compared to the majority of other undocumented migrants living in Turkey, my interlocutors were not among the most vulnerable. They had a reasonable expectation that they would fare better than other migrants, even though they were still subject to the whims of opaque and ever-changing legal regulations, as well as to the exploitative labor market.

The ethnographic challenge I pose, then, is this: What happens to hope as a category of analysis and experience when we shift the lens away from the increasingly visible figure of the downtrodden migrant or the suffering refugee who risks potentially fatal journeys across borders in inflatable boats or airless containers and who hopes against hope? What happens when we instead attend to those migrants whose hope oscillates between a sense of entitlement and the threat of instability, a hope that holds ethnic privilege in tension with economic and legal vulnerability? The theoretical question I ask, in turn, is this: What happens when we read hope in relation to structures of privilege, while also exploring how structures of privilege are not immune to states of precariousness?

"I am *soydaş*." This is the plea to which Nefiye and İsmigül resort in cultivating their hope of legalization and in shielding it from possible assault, whether from migrants they deemed less worthy or from the ethnographer. This plea also constitutes the historical and structural conditions of possibility on which their hope rests. A cultural identification with legal ramifications, *soydaş* indexes those who are considered to be "of Turkish origin." Translated in the scholarship most frequently as "ethnic kin," *soydaş* is an agglutinated word that derives from the root *soy*, which covers a range of meanings, from race, ethnicity, lineage, and blood to family, ancestry, kin, and descent, and the suffix -*daş*, meaning having something in common or being a fellow. But there is an emotional component of belonging inherent in the suffix -*daş* as well, which functions as a crucial landing point for the structures of feeling that are associated with this word for Turkish speakers. It also covers a range of affiliations, such as "sharing," as in *kardeş* (sibling), "having in common," as in *dindaş* (of the same religion), or "fellowship," as in *yoldaş* (comrade) or *vatandaş* (citizen). Depending on which meaning of the root one selects, the term *soydaş* may be translated variously as "of the same ancestry," "of the same blood," "of the same lineage," and so on. "Ethnic kin" is a frequently deployed translation in the migration scholarship on Turkey. However, I prefer the term "racial kin," for two reasons. One, the root of the earlier iteration of *soydaş*, namely *ırkdaş*, corresponds strictly to the word for "race."[6] Two, the term "racial kin" captures the nationalist preoccupation with sharing the same blood and thus better delineates the ethnoracial underpinnings of Turkey's citizenship and migration regime that I explore in this book.[7]

In addition to indexing a collective structure of feeling, *soydaş* has legal underpinnings. As stipulated by the successive Settlement Laws (No. 885/1926; No. 2510/1934; No. 5543/2006), which constitute the key body of legislation that has regulated migration since the founding of the Turkish nation-state, Turkey accepts as a migrant only an individual who is of "Turkish race/lineage and who has ties to Turkish culture." Article 4 of Settlement Law No. 5543/2006 explicitly prohibits the migration of those who are not of Turkish origin. Since the original Settlement Law formulation in 1926, and through each iteration, the law has retained this racial definition of who qualifies as a migrant.[8] The claim to being *soydaş*, then, is both a cultural and a legal appeal that upholds migrants' insistence on hope and is validated by history, particularly among those from Bulgaria. Indeed, even as migrants of Turkish origin from other regions in the Middle East or Central Asia have occasionally been granted citizenship, those from the Balkans constitute by far the greatest number of immigrants who have succeeded in becoming Turkish citizens, both during the founding years of the republic and throughout the twentieth century.[9]

AN UNLIKELY MIGRATION
FROM EUROPE TO TURKEY?

Who are these migrants who undertake sometimes permanent, sometimes circular migrations across the Bulgarian-Turkish border? And what motivates them to go against the grain of conventional south-north migrations and instead leave Europe, where they hold EU citizenship, to migrate eastward to Turkey, a non-EU country?

The ethnic Turkish minority that currently resides in Bulgaria and is concentrated in the southeastern and northeastern regions[10] traces its ancestry back to the Muslim populations that were settled in strategic border areas during the expansionist phases of the Ottoman Empire. As the empire sought to expand westward toward Europe, the conquest of the Balkans went hand in hand with the colonization of this critical region. The ruling strategy of the empire was known as *şenlendirme*. Literally "jollification," *şenlendirme* involved settling Turkish and Muslim groups amid "foreign elements" in newly conquered territory. The term *evlad-ı-fatihan* (children of the conquerors), a

military-nationalist Ottoman term, is still used to refer to contemporary migrants from the Balkans, evoking this history of conquest and the ancestry of
these migrants as Ottoman raiders.

In the late nineteenth century, as the Ottoman Empire began to disinte-
grate, these Muslim-Turkish populations ended up on the wrong side, as it
were, of the new world order of nation-states. After Bulgaria's liberation from
Ottoman rule in 1878, the Muslim Turks in that territory became a minority.
Following the Russian-Turkish War of 1878, and then, in greater numbers, after the Balkan War of 1912–13, Muslim Turks fled from these areas, back into
the fold of the retreating Ottoman Empire. They were settled in the region of
Thrace, which in turn caused the displacement of the local Greek population,
who were forced to flee, their property seized and transferred to the arriving
refugees.[11] This confiscation of land became a recurring pattern in the aftermath of the Armenian Genocide and into the first three decades of what became the Republic of Turkey in 1923. In fact, migrants from the Balkans were
actively summoned to bolster areas that had been decimated by the Armenian Genocide and World War I and to reconfigure the nation toward the
ideal of ethnic and cultural homogeneity.

Muslim-Turkish refugees from the Balkans were received enthusiastically
not only because they helped to replace a depleted population but also because they were perceived as *kurucu unsur* (constituent elements) of the new
nation-state. That is, they were regarded as the "true and unique inheritors
of the Ottoman Empire," given the critical role they had played in defend-
ing territory and extinguishing rebellions against the empire in the Balkans[12]
(Karpat 2004, 283). In the first fifteen years of the Turkish nation-state, the
825,000 migrants from the Balkans accounted for nearly 10 percent of the
population. They were also qualitatively significant in that many were re-
cruited into the military and bureaucratic cadres, holding elite positions that
allowed them to influence future policy regarding migration. This included
the provision that those from the Balkans who could prove they were of Turkish origin would be granted citizenship. Additionally, until the 1960s, they
were also given property for settlement.

The special status of migrants from the Balkans began to wane in the fifties, with a gradual shift in perception and policy toward them. Over time,
they became regarded less as constituent members of the nation-state who
should be reintegrated into its territorial boundaries and more as *dış Türkler*,
or "distant Turks"—that is, Turks who should continue to live outside of Tur-

key as citizens of other states and who could promote the nationalist cause beyond Turkey's borders. Even with this shift in perception, however, the nationalist narrative continued to extol the ways in which the Turkish minority in Bulgaria preserved its identity, culture, and traditions despite all attempts at assimilation by the Bulgarian state. This feat was considered all the more valiant in the Cold War era, when Bulgaria became the communist enemy.

In actual experience, the degree of belonging and attachment to either Turkey or Bulgaria has varied significantly among the Turkish minority in Bulgaria across regions, generations, and proximity to and identification with the Communist Party. Especially during my visits to northern Bulgaria, I met people in their fifties and older who were unabashed in their identification as citizens of Bulgaria and in their allegiance to communism. Even as they recalled some of the excesses of the Communist regime, people were often affectionate in their sarcasm and full of admiration for the regime's commitment to uniform access to health care and education. In reference to the final years of communism, however, from 1984 to 1989, when the Bulgarian government turned totalitarian and violently assimilationist, my interlocutors would qualify their comments, their jovial tone turning somber and their previously mirthful expressions darkening. A recurrent collective sentiment in relation to the "Revival Process" (in Bulgarian, Văzroditelen process), the official name and the euphemism given to the forced assimilation of Bulgaria's Muslim minorities, went as follows: "They opened our eyes with this 'Revival Process.' We were becoming Bulgarized anyway, but by forcing Bulgarian names upon us, they actually awakened us to our [Turkish] origins." I was also told that the enthusiastic identification with Bulgaria would already have been far more ambivalent in the southern region of Kırcalı even before the assimilation campaign, since that was a region where the Turkish minority was typically more isolated—or, depending on one's perspective, stayed more true to what was upheld as Turkish traditions and culture.

But regardless of whether they viewed Bulgaria or Turkey as their real homeland and regardless of which nation-state they pledged ultimate allegiance to, the identification of this minority in Bulgaria as ethnically Turkish tended to be unanimous and resolute. In fact, the first thing that I learned in the field was never to refer to migrants from Bulgaria as Bulgar Türkleri (Bulgarian Turks) or, equally jarring, as Bulgar göçmenleri (Bulgarian migrants). To the dismay of Turkish migrants from Bulgaria, these phrases today represent the two most common ways of referring to them in Turkey. "It makes me cringe to my bones when I get referred to as Bulgarian," was the friendly warning I received after my first and last faux pas on this score, which was followed by an informative lecture on the history of this minority in Bulgaria that was intended to settle once and for all the question of ethnic origins. Later, I listened to numerous protestations on the injurious effect of the terms "Bulgarian migrant" and "Bulgarian Turk." Even when the speaker may not have held any specific intention of attributing a particular ethnic designation, my interlocutors made clear, they would recoil with pain at being called Bulgarian and feel contempt for the speaker's ignorance. "We are allergic to that phrase—Bulgarian Turks," was how a 1989 immigrant once put it to a public audience.[13]

Such visceral reactions have their roots in the still-fresh memory of the violent assimilation campaign that the Turkish minority experienced in Bulgaria between 1984 and 1989. During that time, speaking Turkish was banned, along with all religious rituals, and Turkish names were forcibly changed to Slavic/Bulgarian ones. The phrases my interlocutors use in referring to themselves are Bulgaristanlı (of/from Bulgaria), *Bulgaristan göçmeni* (migrant of/ from Bulgaria), and Bulgaristan Türkü (Turkish from/in Bulgaria). What all of these preferred designations have in common is that they assiduously avoid the term "Bulgar" (Bulgarian), with the latter's implication of ethnic identity, and retain instead a reference to Bulgaria as a geographical location. In keeping with the emic designation, I use the term "Bulgaristanlı" throughout the book.

Just as there is significant diversity among the Turkish minority in Bulgaria with regard to political identification and cultural practice, there is also internal variation among the Bulgaristanlı in Turkey in terms of political leaning, religiosity, and intensity of their attachment to Bulgaria. Although a few devoted former members of the Communist Party explicitly stated that they were atheists, the Bulgaristanlı did not on the whole disavow Islam. To the contrary, they were sensitive to accusations that their religiosity was not good enough or that it was compromised, especially since the Bulgarian government's assimilation campaign targeted religious as well as cultural practices.

Still, the Bulgaristanlı took a decisively secularist stance with regard to expressions of religion in the public sphere. Though I have met a few women who were covered, the veil was anathema for the overwhelming majority. Once, at a Balkan music concert in Sultanbeyli, an area in which Bulgaristanlı mix with a more devout local population, I asked my companions if the person who had just passed our seats was Bulgaristanlı. Emine, a friend who had come to Istanbul for a master's degree while she worked as an accountant and who had a penchant for dancing (which she managed to display even within our narrow seats at the concert), proclaimed, "How can you even think that? A covered Bulgaristanlı?!" Another friend in the group said with a grave expression, "Emine, you say that, but you know we are getting this veil more and more in Bulgaria now. Mostly among the Pomak, but still . . . "[14]

In Turkey's landscape, where the majority of the population abstains from pork, the Bulgaristanlı made it a point of pride, expressed only after a certain intimacy had been established, to admit that they enjoyed consuming pork—except, they would often add, during the religious holidays—and that back in Bulgaria they liked to brew their own *rakıya*, a strong and delicious alcoholic drink that resembles vodka and is made from apricots or other seasonal fruit picked from their own gardens. Women in particular also boasted of egalitarian gender relations in their homes and communities, explicitly contrasting the freedom and sense of power they have as women to what they deemed to be the generally sad state of affairs in Turkey in terms of women's subservience. If their legacy as *evlad-ı-fatihan* (children of the conquerors) is promoted by the religious-nationalist perspective of most migrant associations to boost their legalization demands, Bulgaristanlı women's culinary habits, sleeveless shirts, and ease in mixed-gender company are deemed as progressive by the secular elite in Turkey, who prefer to employ Bulgaristanlı women as domestic workers precisely because they are both Turkish and secular.

More pertinent to this book, however, is how internal differentiation among the Bulgaristanlı is enacted not by cultural and political markers of difference but by the law. At the same time as perceptions shifted, so too did legal policy. After the 1960s, the privilege of being settled with property, although still a legal possibility, was almost never bestowed, while citizenship continued to be granted with ease until 1990. A major wave of migration to Turkey took place following the collectivization of land in Bulgaria in 1951. This was followed by intermittent migrations, usually aimed at uniting separated families. The final mass exodus from Bulgaria to Turkey took place in 1989, following the violent assimilation campaign of the Bulgarian government. In Turkey, this migration of more than 300,000 people was officially cheered as the great homecoming of *soydaş*, who had ensured the survival of Turkish identity despite persecution at the hands of the Bulgarian state. Furthermore, in 1989, at the level of state policy, the Bulgaristanlı still held a special status as migrants, in that they all were granted citizenship. But there were already signs of cultural disapproval. To older residents, the migrants did not seem sufficiently Turkish. Their difference was especially pronounced in terms of the gender roles, moral codes, and public behavior of women who worked full time and dressed less conservatively (Parla 2009). During earlier fieldwork among the 1989 migrants, I frequently heard what has become something of a mantra: "In Bulgaria we were persecuted because we were Turkish. Here in Turkey we are persecuted because we are seen as too Bulgarian."[15] Indeed, within a year after the fall of the Communist government in Bulgaria, approximately one-third of the more than 300,000 migrants returned to Bulgaria (Eminov 1997; Vasileva 1992), complicating the nationalist narrative of homecoming (Parla 2003, 2004).

The waning of the Bulgaristanlı's privileged status, in both legal and cultural terms, has become far more marked since 1990. Unlike the 1989 immigrants, who were formally welcomed and granted citizenship, no official fanfare accompanied the routine border crossings of post-1990 labor migrants. The borders between Bulgaria and Turkey, once porous for *soydaş*, became more formidable, starting with restrictions on travel in the early 1990s. These included an unannounced policy of allowing only one visa per family, a policy that led to clandestine border crossings in which children were sometimes entrusted to smugglers. Starting in 2001, and after this opaque rule was no longer enforced, migrants from Bulgaria could enter Turkey by virtue of a liberal policy that required only sticker visas, obtainable at the border. However, unlike their predecessors, they could not count on legalization or citizenship. Described by scholars as "circular migrants," the emic term the Bulgaristanlı use to characterize their periodic border crossings is "three-monthers" (*üç aylık*). The term alludes to the requirement that they cross the Bulgarian-Turkish border every three months in order to renew their visas. These periodic crossings ensured that their residence status was regular. Yet they still lapsed into illegality because they worked on tourist visas, a testament to the murky nature of the line between legality and illegality. Nefiye, for example, like hundreds of thousands of other migrants working in the informal labor market, was a "legal" resident so long as she exited and entered the country every three months; she was "illegal" insofar as she worked without a permit.

Despite the weakening of their privileged treatment as the preferred migrants of the Turkish nation-state, the Bulgaristanlı have continued to expect legal exceptions, amnesties for temporary legalization, and favorable discretionary treatment in the formal and informal spheres of the law after 1990, situating them at what I call the fraught intersection of ethnonational appropriation and labor market exploitation. On the basis of historical precedent and through the racial kinship clause still retained in the Settlement Law of 2006, legalization for the post-1990 Bulgaristanlı labor migrants is a continuing promise. But the delivery of the promise resides with the Council of Ministers in Turkey, the final authority, which has the discretion to make decisions on a case-by-case basis. Therefore, although the Bulgaristanlı can still benefit from the favored treatment that the status of being *soydaş* accords them, this privilege is no longer as secure and evident as it was before 1990, when *soydaş* were settled with land and integrated into the regular market economy soon after their arrival. This book pursues, on the one hand, what endures and what has waned of the *muhacirlik kurumu*, or the "institution of being a (privileged) migrant," in Sema Erder's apt phrasing (Erder 2014), and on the other hand, the affective universe that the law fosters, one in which past entitlement continues to bear on present precarity. Both historical precedent and the remnants of legal privilege continue to provide the basis of hope for legalization among the Bulgaristanlı, a hope that is meticulously cultivated as a collective structure of feeling and a hope that other migrants in Turkey cannot rely on in the same, institutionally structured way.

TURKEY'S MIGRATION AND CITIZENSHIP REGIME

Migration to Turkey has garnered a great deal of international attention, as Turkey has abruptly become the country that hosts the greatest number of migrants in the world.[16] Since 2011, of the nearly six million Syrians who fled the civil war in their nation, more than three million have arrived in Turkey.[17] But in fact Turkey's transformation into a country with high immigration dates back to the late 1980s, long before the Syrian crisis. Migrations unprecedented in terms of numbers and geographical scope reversed Turkey's historical record as a country of emigration, turning it into one of immigration. This change resulted from a constellation of factors: the liberalization of the Turkish economy; a concomitant demand for cheap, informal labor; and geopolitical turmoil in neighboring regions.

With the collapse of the Soviet bloc in the early 1990s, a predominantly feminized migration wave from the former Soviet republics began, with women migrants working as "shuttle traders" who brought goods to sell in their suitcases, as sex workers, and most commonly, as domestics and care providers. Initially these migrants hailed from Moldova, Bulgaria, and Ukraine; later they came from Uzbekistan, Azerbaijan, Turkmenistan, Georgia, and Armenia.[18] Starting in the 2000s, civil and international wars in Iran, Iraq, and Afghanistan led migrants to flee to neighboring countries, including Turkey, usually with the goal of eventually reaching Europe; however, they often ended up living in limbo, with conditions of transit turning into permanent stays.[19] Finally, poverty or simply the prospect of better opportunities is increasingly driving migrants from sub-Saharan Africa to seek work in Turkey.[20] By 2012, even before the arrival of Syrian refugees, the unofficial estimate for undocumented migrants from these diverse geographical regions to Turkey was between 1 and 1.5 million.[21]

The nearly nonexistent path to citizenship for these undocumented migrants sets them apart from my Bulgaristanlı interlocutors. Whether they struggle to reach Europe or to survive in Turkey, whether they have fled war and poverty or are in search of better opportunities, the majority of refugees and labor migrants, who cannot claim *soydaş* status, have virtually no prospect of long-term legalization in Turkey, let alone citizenship.[22] The scarcity of paths to legalization for undocumented migrants to some extent replicates the dynamics seen in other national contexts. That is to say, as is the case in other neoliberal capitalist countries around the world, the rhetoric of migration deterrence goes hand in hand with tacit tolerance in order to accommodate a labor market in need of a flexible and disposable workforce; migrants are excluded as legal subjects but included as workers in this precarious market. While it replicates to some extent such global patterns of late capitalist migration governance and their mechanisms of inclusive exclusion, Turkey's contemporary migration regime also displays its own particularities.[23]

The first distinction of Turkey's migration governance is the coexistence of restrictive rules for permanent legalization and porous national borders. Since the 1990s, Turkey has adopted an increasingly neoliberal, laissez-faire approach to borders, providing unfettered entry through visa sticker agreements with numerous countries. While there has been no official call to receive migrants as laborers, the liberalization of the border through visa waiver agreements has allowed migrants to come in with relative ease and to overstay their visas. However, aside from marriage to a Turkish citizen, the key requirement for obtaining citizenship is five years of continuous residence, which, in turn, requires securing a long-term, renewable residence permit.[24] In order to obtain this type of residence permit, migrants must submit a work permit, a work contract, or an account balance equal to three hundred dollars for every month of stay. These requirements are not feasible for the overwhelming majority of the undocumented, whether they are street vendors from Nigeria, domestic workers from Georgia, or refugees from Congo. Despite a comparatively flexible border policy, therefore, legislation that would allow "foreigners" to obtain permanent residence or grant them access to work permits is extremely restrictive, and in Erder and Kaska's apt assessment, "reflective of the characteristics of a closed society" (2012, 115). Whereas conventional wisdom often describes borders as being soft on the inside but hard on the edges, Turkey's borders have been soft on the edges but hard on the inside.

A second and related measure that restricts legalization is a limitation to the 1951 Geneva (refugee) Convention, which Turkey has followed since it became a signatory to the convention in 1961. Unlike other countries that have since removed any geographical limitation to the scope of refugees that they will accept from around the world, Turkey continues to grant its protection only to refugees coming from Europe, as defined by the borders of the European Council.[25] Therefore, virtually none of Turkey's current migrant population qualifies for refugee status, even though migrants from non-European countries are often escaping civil wars or ethnic or political persecution.[26]

The third key feature that distinguishes Turkey from the otherwise common logic of neoliberal migration governance is the near lack of regulation and coherent legislation related to migration, especially before the implementation in 2014 of the Law on Foreigners and International Protection No. 6458/2014. Without a unified body of law, lawyers and officials alike used to patch together ad hoc interpretations of disparate pieces of the Citizenship Law and the Settlement Law when making arguments and decisions about specific cases. An assortment of eclectic circulars was drawn up as needed, but the public has no access to these documents. As legal scholar Bertan Tokuzlu has pointed out, the legal system in Turkey relies on circulars to an extent that undermines the rule of law, and this was especially true when it came to the field of migration.[27]

Such fragmented regulation has been applauded by some as allowing migrants more agency, freedom, and mobility; it has even been held up as an example to be emulated by the rest of Europe (see, for example, Tolay 2010). However, the overwhelming evidence provided by critical migration scholarship points to the opposite conclusion. Far from being a model for ease of mobility, the Turkish case stands out as an unbridled version of the neoliberal migration governance common in Europe and the United States. The tenuous life circumstances that migrants face are exacerbated by a lack of reliable information and a high degree of arbitrariness in the practices of governmental officials and the police, who exercise enormous discretion in matters related to custody, duration of detention, and deportation. While lack of regulation may offer flexibility to some undocumented migrants, it often also intensifies labor exploitation, especially for those working in jobs that involve physical danger.

Turkey began to regulate its borders more strictly in the 2000s to meet the requirements for its accession to the European Union,[28] which included synchronization with EU policy in terms of visa systems, readmission agreements, border control, refugee status determination, and reception conditions. These eventually led to the implementation of the first comprehensive migration law that Turkey has ever had: the Law on Foreigners and International Protection No. 6458/2014. The ostensible goal of the law was to systematize policy internally and align it with the international human rights standards for the protection of refugees and migrants.

Indeed, the new law did offer some improvements in terms of clarifying and standardizing the basic rights of asylum seekers. On paper at least, it minimized residence fees, promised access to emergency health care, and placed a limit on the duration of detention, whereas previously there had been none. However, most activists, NGO representatives, and critical scholars of migration have been cautious about whether the law is making an actual difference for asylum seekers.[29] Kristen Biehl (2015a) has characterized the asylum system in Turkey before the acceptance of the new law as one of "protracted uncertainty." That system has remained largely intact, since implementation of the new law has also been marked by "improvisation, unpredictability and irregularity" (Sarı and Dinçer 2017, 69). Finally, and most importantly for my purposes, the new law does not address the rights of undocumented migrants, including the basic right of access to education for undocumented children.[30]

The fourth and final distinctive feature of Turkey's migration regime speaks to the central concerns of this book and to the relative privilege of Bulgaristanlı migrants. Turkey's response to the influx of migrants in the 1990s also reflects a fact that, I would argue, has not received sufficient attention: that is, an actual migration policy has always existed and become historically entrenched, even if it has not been explicitly advertised. Though it was referred to rather euphemistically as a "national" stance (Kirişçi 1996), I would gloss this as an ethnoracial and religious policy vis-à-vis migration; historically, the Turkish nation-state has not simply preferred but also endeavored to limit legal citizenship to those migrants who are considered Turks and Muslims. Since its founding in 1923, the Turkish state has restricted immigration to those "of Turkish descent and with affinities to Turkish culture," as stipulated by the first Settlement Law, passed in 1926, and as reiterated by the subsequent Settlement Laws of 1934 and 2006.

It is indeed the case that all nation-states develop explicit or implicit criteria favoring migrants who are deemed to be most easily assimilated, even if the state describes its nationalism in civic rather than ethnic terms or purports to abide by the principle of *jus solis* (territorial citizenship) rather than *jus sanguinis* (blood-based citizenship). Migration policy around the globe thus tends to involve a certain favoritism toward those deemed more desirable or deserving, whether in terms of skills or ethnic/cultural background. Viewed from this broader perspective, the preference for Sunni Muslim and ethnically Turkish migrants is not unusual. However, what still distinguishes the Turkish nation-state from a comparative angle is that the preference for those migrants deemed more desirable is reflected in the legal definition of the term for "migrant" itself. Because all Settlement Laws in Turkey have defined *göçmen* (migrant) by making Turkish descent and culture a *prerequisite* (and not, for example, a more desirable feature), the word *göçmen* in effect becomes synonymous with *soydaş*.

To say, therefore, that Turkey has never had a rights-based or inclusive migration policy framework, a verdict increasingly pronounced in critical migration scholarship on Turkey, is important and true, but does not quite capture the distinctiveness of Turkey's migration regime in comparative terms. Navigating between the Scylla of exceptionalism and the Charybdis of normalization, one may posit this distinctiveness as the degree to which Turkey's migration governance leans toward the ethnoracial end on the spectrum of criteria for migrant inclusion as well as the fact that this ethnoracial conception of migrant is written into the law. What we have here is more than simply the usual discrepancy between the principle of equality upheld by formal law and the actual practices of discrimination and differential inclusion that occur during the law's implementation.[31] What we additionally have in Turkey is the legal codification of ethnonationalist sentiment, or de jure discrimination, in which the wording of the law itself does not feign or attempt neutrality.

This exceptionally restrictive definition of who qualifies as a migrant was consolidated over a century, as part of a process of population engineering that began during the transition from the Ottoman Empire to the Turkish nation-state and endured beyond it. The statistics alone give a chillingly straightforward indication of the remaking of the population into an ethnically and religiously homogeneous national body. At the beginning of World War I, in what was still the Ottoman Empire, the total population was 16 million, of which 20 percent were non-Muslim. Within this group, the great majority were Greeks and Armenians, with some members of other Christian communities as well (Courbage and Fargues 1997). In 1915, the Armenian Genocide decimated the Armenian population. In 1924, one year after the founding of the Turkish republic, the forced exchange of the Greek population in Turkey with the Muslim population in Thrace virtually eliminated the Greek presence in Turkey. By 1927, the total population, now reduced to 13 million, was less than 3 percent non-Muslim. That the processes of Muslimification and Turkification continued well after the founding of the republic is reflected in the fact that by 1950 the number of non-Muslims in Turkey had dropped below 1 percent of the population. (By 1980, it was 0.2 percent. As of 2018, it was around 0.01percent.)

The ideal of a homogeneous Sunni and Turkish citizenry was achieved not only through genocide and displacement but also through active recruitment of other populations that were regarded as desirable. Between 1923 and 1950, when the non-Muslim population decreased to less than 1 percent of the total, more than 800,000 Muslim-Turkish migrants from the Balkans, nearly 10 percent of the entire population, arrived in the new Turkish nation-state and were granted citizenship.[32] They were mostly settled on the properties of those Armenians and Greeks who had been massacred or exiled, as well as those who were dispossessed by virtue of laws that confiscated the properties of those who managed to survive.[33]

The dominant ideology of the modern Turkish republic, Kemalism, named after its founding father, Kemal Atatürk, has been enormously successful in enshrining itself as a secular and civic nationalism based on democratic principles. But a growing body of scholarship is increasingly confronting the enduring and vexed legacy of Kemalism and the terms of belonging it has dictated.[34] Kemalism fostered a state tradition of highly centralized power, one in which the state is the unitary actor and is largely unchecked by civil society. It is a tradition, in Banu Bargu's concise description, of "elitist republicanism combined with authoritarian pragmatism" (2014, 94). This has led to a political culture in which any opposition to the state, whether from leftist movements, religious minorities, or ethnic groups that refuse to accept the oppressive terms of their assimilation, is regarded as an internal security threat and summarily quashed. Turkey has had four military coups and interventions since 1960, each undertaken with the purported goal of preventing what the army deemed to be deviations from the precepts of Kemalism. But even during periods of democratic government, the "privileging of raison d'etat over political contestation" (96), to cite Bargu again, has prevailed in Turkey, drastically narrowing the space of oppositional politics.

Scholars have also been increasingly challenging the official view of Kemalism as civic and inclusive. The justification advanced by a Member of Parliament for the 1934 Settlement Law as it was debated in the Parliament is emblematic of the underlying if subsequently veiled ethnoracial vision of the newly founded Turkish republic: "The Turkishness of any person who calls himself a Turk in the Turkish Republic, should be clear and transparent to the state. Here, the state does not want to harbor the slightest suspicion of the Turkishness of any Turk" (TBMM Zabıt Ceridesi 1934, 8). On the basis of a study of the entire speeches and declarations of Kemal Atatürk, Taha Parla (1991) has called Turkish nationalism Janus-faced: it proclaims inclusiveness at the same time as it posits supremacist ethnoracial characteristics for the Turkish people as a collectivity. Subsequent scholarship that explores the discursive construction of Turkishness by Turkey's founding intellectuals and politicians insists on the racialized underpinnings of Turkish nationalism in even more unqualified terms (see, for example, Ergin 2017; Maksudyan 2005).

If its claim of inclusiveness is one of the overstated aspects of Kemalism,[35] the claim that it eliminated religion from the public domain and from national identity is another. Most scholars concur that Kemalism did indeed establish a new framework for belonging in which religious allegiance was to some extent replaced by national allegiance and that the Ottoman index of religious belonging was subordinated to the ethnonational identity of Turkishness. However, the core definition of national identity, even under Kemalist ideology, never abandoned Sunni Islam as a key feature of the Turkish nation-state. In Cihan Tuğal's formulation: "The Turkish nation was unambiguously defined against non-Muslims. This implicit Islamic definition of

Turkishness enabled the state to assimilate several ethnic groups of various sizes" (Tuğal 2009, 39).

Within this nationalist cosmology that defined belonging in ethnoracial and religious terms, the regulation of any remaining religious and ethnic diversity has been stamped by its own internal hierarchy of otherness. This hierarchy of otherness includes, on the one hand, state practices of violence and assimilation, and on the other hand, minority groups' acquiescence or resistance to the terms of belonging imposed on them. Survivors of the Armenian Genocide are bound to carry on in a post-genocidal geography defined by the institutionalized denial of genocide (Ekmekçioğlu 2016; Suciyan 2015). As Turkey's "tolerated minority" (Brink-Danan 2011),[36] the Jews have had to routinely enact what Paul Silverstein (2004) calls "performative citizenship": unlike the unmarked majority, the Jewish minority is called upon to demonstrate in overtly visible ways that their allegiance to the values of the Turkish state is absolute. The Muslim yet non-Sunni Alevi population has been subjected to a strict policy of domestication (Tambar 2014). As for the mostly Sunni Muslim Kurdish population, who have been deemed troublesome but still assimilable, the Turkish state refused until the 1990s to acknowledge them as a separate ethnicity, using the designation "mountain Turks" to identify them and refusing their demands for cultural rights such as education in their native language. Only when Kurds are willing to be assimilated into or to prioritize Sunni Islam (an option never available for Alevi Kurds) have they been welcomed into the fold of Islamic religiosity and ethnic nationalism. And when they have refused Turkification and chosen to pursue the path of struggle instead, the Kurds have been banished from the category of "prospective citizens" and relegated to the category of "pseudo-citizens" (Yeğen 2009), facing some of the most brutal punitive measures and massacres enacted in the name of the Turkish state since the Armenian Genocide.

It is only within this hierarchy of otherness produced by Turkey's citizenship regime that the full significance of the cultural and politico-legal category of *soydaş* and how it has been operationalized in the creation of a homogenized national populace through migration management can be understood. By restricting the legal definition of "migrant" to people who are considered racial kin, the Settlement Laws of 1926, 1934, and 2006 have legitimized only the migration of those who are Turkish and Muslim and have rendered suspect the migration of anyone else. Bulgaristanlı migrants in Turkey, who could historically claim the category of *soydaş*, have embedded themselves in this nationalist narrative of belonging in their legalization quest. Given the deep legacy of the alliance between religious identity (Sunni-Islam) and ethnonational identity (Turkishness), which continues to define the legal and affective structures of belonging in Turkey, Bulgaristanlı migrants, even in their undocumented status, have been able to claim the most desirable combination in their bid for belonging.

Bulgaristanlı migrants, then, are not the migrants in crisis that haunt the media and a good deal of scholarship. In depicting the hope for legalization sustained by the Bulgaristanlı, I work against the narrative of the desperate migrant. I do so not because that narrative is superfluous; desperation indeed marks the lives of many displaced people around the globe. But here I attend to another, more ordinary migrant experience that slips through the cracks when the focus is only on crisis and desperation. I also suggest that ordinariness reveals just as much about power, privilege, and entitlement. And I approach the question of privilege and its lack not through the lens of those marginalized within national borders for being irreducibly different, but instead through the lens of those on the outside who are beckoned into national borders as *almost* the same. This book thus invites the reader to rethink the limits of belonging in contemporary Turkey from the perspective of those to whom legal and cultural privilege is intimated, promised, and occasionally delivered.

Political scientist Barış Ünlü has defined "Turkishness" in Turkey as a universe of privileges. He is inspired by critical whiteness studies and Charles W. Mills's notion of the "racial contract," which assures the privilege of whiteness through written and unwritten codes, including an entire legal system that favors whites and punishes blacks. Ünlü, in turn, conjures an unwritten "Turkishness contract," which implicitly stipulates that "in order to be able to live in safety and privilege in Turkey, *and to have the hope of such a life*, one needs to be Turkish or to be Turkified" (Ünlü 2014, 49, my translation and italics). This book suggests that the hierarchies of otherness that govern difference in contemporary Turkey can be read in terms of who can have such hope and what kinds of complicities, contradictions, and consequences that hope entails. Hope governs the legal and social universe of migration in contradictory ways: at the same time that the hope for legalization motivates Bulgaristanlı migrants to persevere in their quest, it also dovetails with the logic of a broader migration regime that selects, rewards, discriminates, and deports according to a rigid hierarchy of belonging that is based on ethnic and religious kinship.

ANTHROPOLOGIES OF HOPE

"Hope" is the thing with feathers
That perches in the soul,
And sings the tune without the words,
And never stops at all

Emily Dickinson (1830–1886)

There is a renewed fascination with hope in anthropology, critical theory, progressive politics, and activism alike. One particularly enthusiastic perspective seeks to discover or recover hope in everyday life or in the hidden recesses of the imagination in order to make possible alternative ways of being and becoming. Examples from politics include Barack Obama's best-selling *Audacity of Hope* and presidential campaign framed around hope. Other instances, such as Rebecca Solnit's *Hope in the Dark*, are found in the works of public intellectuals in the Anglo-Saxon world who ask us to reclaim hope in these sinister times of late capitalism, which try to convince us that there is no hope of an alternative to the capitalist system. A 2017 issue of *Cultural Anthropology*, one of the signature journals of the field, is titled "Reclaiming Hope." In addition, an entire field of "hope studies" now aims to produce the conditions for scholarly hope by exploring the hopes of "ordinary people" as they go about their everyday lives and then replicating them on academic terrain in order to counter a loss of confidence in the missions of social theory.[37]

In these affirmative reclamations, which draw heavily on the legacy of Ernst Bloch's magnum opus, *The Principle of Hope* ([1947] 1986), hope acquires a nearly sacrosanct quality. Associated intimately with becoming, dynamism, transcendence, and open-endedness, the cultivation of hope is proposed as remedy or panacea to left-wing melancholy (Brown 1999), to political apathy (Harvey 2000; Zournazi, Mouffe, and Laclau 2003), or to epistemological uncertainty and loss (Lear 2006; Miyazaki 2004). Of course, I do not wish to equate all reclamation of hope as being driven by exactly the same logic. The endorsement of hope as future potential in the work of cultural theorist José Esteban Muñoz (2009), the cultivation of hope as a method for self-knowledge proposed by anthropologist Hirokazu Miyazaki, and the radical hope posited by philosopher Jonathan Lear as a way of surviving extreme situations of cultural loss are among the most sophisticated elaborations, each with its own nuances, of reclamations of hope as a normative category. Still, there is something common to these projects in that they go beyond analyzing hope and elevate it to the status of a principle, a virtue, or a method. The analysis itself is meant to become, in Nicholas H. Smith's words, "a source of hope, a 'hope-maker'" (2008, 6).

This ethnography tracks everyday hopes of migrants for legalization, without, however, the accompanying commitment to elevate hope to a principle or a central category that informs in a fundamental fashion all other ways of knowing and understanding. Hope here is not understood to be an all-encompassing category. I take to heart Vincent Crapanzano's (2003) avoidance of an overarching and timeless definition of hope. In addition to acknowledging its historical contingency and cultural variability, I am particularly interested, following Ghassan Hage (2003, 2016), in the unequal distribution of the grounds for hope among groups who are differentially positioned vis-à-vis legal and cultural resources for inclusion.

Indeed, the history of philosophical engagements with hope since antiquity offers a counterpoint to the more buoyant, Blochian perspective that either treats hope as a political instrument for transformative politics or ontologizes it as an instrument for radical potentials of becoming. In ancient Greek philosophy, hope was primarily associated with inadequate knowledge of facts or with wishful thinking and was thus viewed as likely to lead to detrimental action.[38] The Stoic philosopher Seneca deemed the relation of hope to fear to be fundamental.[39] A strongly negative nineteenth-century pronouncement on hope is found in Nietzche's interpretation of the myth of Pandora in *Human, All Too Human* ([1878] 1986). Nietzsche designated hope as the worst of all evils because it "prolongs the torments of man." And in perhaps one of the worst indictments of hope, Schopenhauer, in his *World as Will and Representation*, ([1844] 2010) viewed it as a fundamentally flawed relationship to the world characterized by the inability to withstand hardships at the heart of existence.

Other thinkers and poets who did not come down so hard on hope nevertheless recognized it as a fundamentally ambivalent emotion, one that exists on a continuum with doubt or dread. "Nor dread nor hope attend / a dying animal / a man awaits his end / dreading and hoping all," wrote W. B. Yeats, evoking the inextricable mixture of hope and dread as humankind's distinctive trait. For Spinoza, the philosopher who perhaps most deeply pondered the ambivalence of hope, it is doubt that distinguishes hope from confidence. In a justly famous formulation, Spinoza defined hope as an "inconsistent pleasure" that he contrasted with fear, which, in turn, he described as "inconsistent pain." The operative word regarding hope (and fear) in Spinoza's grammar of affect is "inconsistent." It is a term that captures the element of doubt that is intrinsic to hope (Spinoza [1677] 2000, 215). If doubt were removed, hope would turn into confidence (and fear into despair.)[40]

Indeed, hope seems to have been singled out as *the* ambivalent emotion in mythology. Recall the myth of Pandora's box: as all the other vices escape, does hope remain in the box because it is the only virtue or because it would go on to plague humankind in perpetuity? The mythological ambivalence is beautifully reinscribed by the poet Emily Dickinson, who refers to hope as "the thing with feathers / That perches in the soul, / And sings the tune without the words, / And never stops at all."[41] More recently in cultural theory, in one of the most influential contemporary interpretations of hope as cruel optimism, Lauren Berlant (2011) posits that while a certain degree of optimism is necessary for the act of living, late capitalism breeds a form of optimism that is (more) cruel because the objects we desire and attach ourselves to in fact prevent us from flourishing as individuals.

This book, too, seeks to reckon with the fundamentally ambivalent nature of hope as it informs the legalization quest of Bulgaristanlı migrants. The hope for legalization that they firmly hold on to enables them to endure the seemingly endless mazes of bureaucracy and waiting. Hope enables them to persist despite all the uncertainties of legal regulations governing migration: the whimsical amnesties, the exceptions and the arbitrary implementation of the law. At the same time, hope may lead to a certain idealization of its object: citizenship, even if attained, often fails to deliver the anticipated economic security. The justifications entertained by the Bulgaristanlı for their hope can also have unintended consequences that are troubling when the predicament of other migrants in Turkey is taken into account. To the extent that their hope emerges from circumstances that reinforce a flawed system, the Bulgaristanlı's hope for legalization may unwittingly reinforce the existing hierarchy of migrant desirability.[42] Engaging with the ambivalent aspects of even "positive" feelings, Jason Throop (2015) writes of the ambiguities that mark the existential possibilities of happiness: for example, "our own happiness may actually diminish possibilities for happiness in others" (47). Adapting Throop's formulation, I focus less on existential considerations and more on the structural conditions that lead to the unequal distribution of hope as a desired good. I suggest that in the contemporary migration regime in Turkey, the hope of the Bulgaristanlı migrants for legalization, inclusion, and belonging may come at the expense of the hope of other undocumented migrants who are not able to make their claims of legalization on the basis of shared kinship.

My equivocal approach is inspired as well by brilliant anthropological work that captures the paradoxes of hope. In her exploration of the practices of hope among people struggling with chronic or terminal illness, Cheryl Mattingly (2010, 3) depicts hope as a resource diligently cultivated by ailing patients and their caretakers at the same time as it is always "poised for disappointment" because it asks for more than life often delivers. Laurence Ralph (2014) describes how lifelong bodily injury imparts a renegade quality to the dreams of black youth in Chicago, who often recognize that their dreams, which may be as modest as hope for affordable housing or a stable job, are nearly impossible, even as they continue working toward them. But my ethnography is also distinct from these poignant and sophisticated depictions of hope under extremely constrained circumstances in that I attend to hope in relation to conditions of relative privilege. Although I recognize that hope is a powerful category in probing the possibilities for self-knowledge and self-becoming, my greater interest in this book is in deciphering the structural and historical production of hope as well as its unequal distribution.

Although the Bulgaristanlı who migrated after 1990 were often undocumented, they were not the most vulnerable migrants within the broader migrant landscape in Turkey. Instead, they had a reasonable expectation that they would fare better than others, in terms of both how they were treated by officials in bureaucratic encounters and how likely they were to obtain legalization. This expectation was not merely wishful thinking but historically informed and structurally reinforced, given the Turkish state's preference for *soydaş*.

Against the more prevalent engagement with hope in the face of improbability or impossibility—the notion of "hoping against the odds"—the hope entertained by the Bulgaristanlı migrants thus echoes a different line of thinking, one that locates the kernel of hope in rationality and attainability. Such a focus resonates both with economistic approaches in which hope is defined through its attainability (Swedberg 2017) and, perhaps less intuitively, with certain theological approaches to hope as well. For instance, Aquinas's emphasis on attainability and expectation provides an alternative grammar in which "only something that is attainable elicits hope" (Cessario 2002, 232–33). From a secular perspective, Emil Durkheim, too, would explain hope in empirical and rational terms—namely, as evidence of "relative bounty of life" ([1893] 1960, 267). For Durkheim, hope exists not because it is cultivated in the absence of fortune or wielded as a shield against misfortune. Rather, hope exists because on the basis of our past experiences we can recall enough moments of good fortune and well-being to cultivate hope as a collective sentiment.

As resonant as Durkheim's depiction of hope as a sentiment learned through experience is with my depiction of it as a collective structure of feeling, Durkheim's generalization of the existence of "relative bounty" to all people rests on his assumptions of societal stratification and class inequality. In the Durkheimian vision, hope emerges as a blanket category of experience, available to all in the same manner, a vision consistent with Durkheim's general indifference to critical concern for the existence of (class) inequality that routinely hampers the experience of relative bounty for all. What would happen to Durkheim's definition of hope as evidence of life's bounty if we took seriously the reality of inequalities in wealth, status, and life chances? In this book, I trace the hopes of those who have privileged access to legal and cultural inclusion, even if that privilege is not absolute. But rather than generalizing that experience to embody the definition of hope, I instead specify hope based on relative privilege as "entitled hope." Taking my cue from Raymond Williams's exploration of the "complex relation of differentiated structures of feeling to differentiated classes" (1977, 134), I also shed light on how hope as a collective structure of feeling varies in relation to legally and culturally differentiated migrant groups.

I do not have an investment in salvaging hope as a normative category of analysis.[43] Nor do I have an interest in condemning it as delusion or wishful thinking that gets in the way of radical action. What I aspire to is an equivocal approach to hope that seeks to capture its ambiguities: hope has the potential to enable or to disable, to inspire or to obscure, depending on the context, its object, and its justifications. In my reading, approaching hope as a moral stance is not incompatible with identifying ways in which practices of hope can become complicit in exclusionary acts. Given the structural constraints of non-egalitarian societies, hope, too, can become a scarce good that one keeps for oneself and shields from others.

THE EVER-EXPANDING
CONCEPT OF PRECARITY

But if entitlement is a key constituent of hope for the Bulgaristanlı, so, too, is precariousness: the Bulgaristanlı are not entirely secure in their legal, economic, or cultural belonging. Their legal status rests on temporary permits with lapses into undocumented existence. Residence permits do not mean work permits; migrants often reside legally but work illegally. The work itself that Bulgaristanlı migrant women engage in, as domestic workers and nannies without work contracts, is dependent on the whims of employers and thus imbued with uncertainty. Cultural acceptance is not uncomplicated. The Bulgaristanlı's identification as Turkish and Muslim places them on the ladder of familiarity, and yet in a citizenship regime in which the historical norm is sameness rather than diversity, even *soydaş* are regarded with suspicion if they fail to exhibit the right markers of ethnic kinship and proper religiosity. The women in particular are subject to disapproval for having been drawn into overly European lifestyles, compromised by loose morals, or tainted by communist ideas and upbringing. My interlocutors felt these suspicions acutely, as they had expected wholehearted acceptance upon their arrival in Turkey, the symbolic homeland. Recall İsmigül's assessment, which captures perfectly the mix of bravery and caution. She questioned authority figures, but added, "You cannot question too much. They might deport you." Unlike most other migrants, who would not challenge a police officer in the first place while pressing for a residence or work permit, İsmigül dared to do so. Up to a point.

If the term "entitled hope" is intended to highlight the expectation and possibility, I use the term "precarious hope" as its counterpoint in order to capture the uncertainty, unpredictability, and insecurity that also mark the experiences of Bulgaristanlı migrants. But I do not simply show how the everyday lives of the Bulgaristanlı in Turkey provide yet another example of precarity. Heeding the ever-present tension between privilege and precarity in the legalization quests of migrants who are neither entirely exposed nor entirely protected in their legal and economic status, I also wish to rethink the concept of precarity itself, circumscribing a term that risks losing its analytic edge through ever-expanding deployment. What are the analytic consequences when we consider precarity in tandem with relative privilege?

Precarité was once a rather provincial and specific coinage, used primarily in France, Italy, and Spain in reference to contingent, irregular work conditions and adopted by labor movements of the 1970s as a political rallying cry to foster solidarity and highlight common grievances. The term was then adopted in a more limited, specific context with regard to scholarship on neoliberal capitalism to describe the increasing scarcity of long-term, protected labor (Ong 2006; Sassen 1998; Sennett 1998) and the concomitant psychological effects of deregulated employment practices on unprotected workers: uncertainty, enhanced sense of risk, and perpetual anxiety, sometimes bordering on neurosis (Isin 2004; Mole 2010). Increasingly, however, a broad range of concerns from insecure work conditions to environmental hazards to our very frailty as human beings is subsumed either under the term "precarity" or its derivative, "the precarious," in fields including political science, geography, sociology, and cultural theory. Anthropology, in particular, has been quick to jump on this bandwagon. As the terms "precarity" and "the precarious" continue to expand, additional groups of people are hailed as the emerging precariat—most relevantly, undocumented migrants and refugees.

"Precarious" is also the adjective widely used to describe the experience of undocumented migrants in Turkey. In a 2017 review of the scholarship on Syrian refugees in Turkey, Eder and Özkul provide an excellent analysis of the extremes of racism, legal arbitrariness, and economic exploitation to which the refugees are exposed in Turkey. The authors resort to an enhanced version of the concept of precarity: "hyper-precarity" (Eder and Özkul 2017, 3). I find their term apt in that it distinguishes the predicaments of Syrian refugees from those of other precarious migrants in Turkey. I also wonder, however, whether the need for such a booster signals analytic trouble with the concept itself.

That trouble may have begun as early as when the original distinction between precarity and the precarious was blurred in favor of an all-inclusive "precariousness." In the earlier distinction, "precarity" was treated as a specific, historically inflected condition, while "the precarious" was posited as a predicament that could be universalized. The latter definition signals a more general concern about the fragility of the individual vis-à-vis life itself, while the former implies a comparison between individuals' current condition and a prior or future state of greater certainty and security. In Anne Allison's (2016) succinct description of Judith Butler's *Precarious Life*, which was influential in spreading the term to American academia, precarity is "the differential distribution of precariousness by such factors as class, citizenship, and race."

But that crucial distinction between precariousness as an existential condition and precarity as the differentially distributed forms of precariousness that characterize the lives of certain individuals, such as underemployed workers, suffering bodies, or radicalized citizens, is becoming increasingly indistinct. Anna Lowenhaupt Tsing's formulation exemplifies the move to universalize: "Once the fate of the less fortunate, now everyone's life is precarious" (2015, 2). In gesturing toward the universal, Tsing seeks to capture something shared about our global, late-capitalist predicament. But as compelling as the reference to a common predicament might be in fostering solidarity, it jeopardizes precisely what was most valuable in the original distinction between precarity and precariousness—namely, the recognition of the latter's differential distribution.

In this book, I work with the concepts of precarity and the precarious by pursuing instead the path of terminological delimitation. First, I want to retain the distinction between, on the one hand, precarity as contextually specific and structurally contingent, and on the other hand, vulnerability as a universal ontological condition.[44] To do so, I heed Didier Fassin's semantic reminder. Fassin recalls the word's original Latin etymology: precariousness involves lives that are "defined not in the absolute of a condition, but in the relation to those who have power over them" (2012, 4). The hopes of Bulgaristanlı migrants are precarious in that they are dependent on the words, acts, and whims of more-powerful individuals, including border police, officials at police stations, police on the street, employers, and representatives of migrant associations. Locating precariousness in the realm of interpersonal and institutional hierarchies enables finer distinctions along a continuum of fragilities that migrants face rather than subsuming disparate experiences under overly broad designations.

Second, I further delimit the notion of the precarious as being distinct not only from ontological vulnerability but from other kinds of structural vulnerability as well. With this second move, I follow Andrea Muehlebach's (2013) excellent intervention to attend to the temporality of the concept: a current state is precarious only in relation to an experienced or imagined prior state of greater security. The emphasis on temporality acknowledges the affective component as well: precariousness goes hand in hand with and acquires meaning only through a sense of entitlement, a sense that one once was, and still is, entitled to greater security and predictability.[45]

Attending to the tight relationship between the structural and affective aspects of precarity sheds light on how Bulgaristanlı migrants can manipulate relations of dependence to a greater degree than can other undocumented migrants in Turkey whose dependence on those with power over them is less mitigated. Many of the Bulgaristanlı migrants had options other than Turkey, including job opportunities in Belgium, Holland, or Spain. Because they are citizens of Bulgaria, they have an unrestricted ability to travel in Europe, but their rights to work and claim benefits in various EU countries were limited for the first seven years of Bulgaria's EU membership. In Turkey, the claim to *soydaş* status has provided them access to periodic amnesties that are unavailable to other groups. While women from Africa and the Former Soviet Union countries (FSU) frequently experience sexual harassment from employers, police, and other members of the public, Bulgaristanlı women have managed to hold at bay the perception of migrant women as sex workers. Bulgaristanlı women can even hope for a certain leverage in their encounters with officials by appealing to racial kinship, an appeal that often takes on gendered inflections. They are appropriated into the idiom of kinship through such terms as *bacım* (my sister), *ablam* (my elder sister), or *teyzem* (my aunt). Often addressed by such terms used by state officials, the Bulgaristanlı in turn take care to strategically cultivate this kinship terminology, especially in their bureaucratic interactions or brushes with the police. This is a cultural and linguistic resource unavailable to other, non-kin migrants, who are not viewed as being absorbable within the national family.

None of this is to suggest, however, that the post-1990 Bulgaristanlı labor migrants have an untroubled experience. To the contrary. Despite passages into Turkey that were generally less harrowing than those of other migrants, they too undertook clandestine border crossings and sometimes entrusted their children to smugglers.[46] Once they arrived in Turkey, the promise of legalization was constantly intimated through the status of racial kin, but it was not guaranteed. Each application for citizenship, even by *soydaş*, must be reviewed to determine whether the criteria of kinship and residence are met, criteria that have shifted over the course of decades as well as during the course of my fieldwork. Although their chances of legalization are better than those of other migrants, the Bulgaristanlı migrants work in the informal labor market and often continue to do so even after they have attained legal status. While they can generally avoid the most dangerous jobs undertaken by other undocumented workers, they still labor under precarious conditions. They are exposed to the whims of employers and usually work without contracts or social security. Indeed, even if they later obtain citizenship, their previous years of work do not count toward retirement benefits. Finally, while ethnic affinity provides some protection from the sexual harassment routinely faced by migrant women, especially those from the former Soviet Union and from Africa, the morality of Bulgaristanlı women, too, can quickly become suspect if they deviate from expected gendered norms of dress, demeanor, or work habits. There is a fine line between being tolerated as ethnic kin who can potentially be absorbed into the national family and being judged as former communist citizens from the other side of the border who have strayed too far in cultural terms.

This circumscribing approach to precarity allows me to bring into sharper view what is distinctive about the Bulgaristanlı migrants in terms of the legal possibilities they can anticipate and the cultural entitlements they rely on. In the broader global context, in which securitization of borders goes hand in hand with the exploitation of undocumented migrant labor, and humanitarian policy coexists with the criminalization of migration, undocumented Bulgaristanlı migrants in Turkey are neither criminalized economic migrants nor sanctified refugees. They are neither the most downtrodden of migrants nor are they joining the transnational mobile elite.

Attending to the relatively privileged means not relying on the moral certainties that characterize writing about the most downtrodden or the most dispossessed. Didier Fassin (2014) has asked that we consider "what we gain and what we lose, from the point of view of critical thinking . . . when we pay more attention to wounded subjectivities, when we represent, in both senses of the word, the wretched of the earth, and when we simultaneously make the anthropologist into a sort of moral hero" (9). Focusing on relatively privileged subjects entails relinquishing the more secure moral vantage point from which the ethnographer (or for that matter, the activist) may piggyback— even if unwittingly— on interlocutors' deprivations in order to claim moral authority. The challenge, then, is this: How does one properly acknowledge relative privilege without depicting Bulgaristanlı migrants—or other similarly positioned groups—as more powerful than they actually are? This book tells the story of the coexistence of privilege and precarity and invites the reader to reckon with how degrees of privilege factor into and play out within predicaments of precarity.

1 THE HISTORICAL PRODUCTION OF HOPE

"LET'S NOT ALLOW any Turk to remain illegal in Turkey!" read the slogan featured on the website of the Balkan Turks Culture and Solidarity Association (Balkan Türkleri Kültür ve Dayanışma Derneği, hereafter BTSA). During the time in which I was conducting my fieldwork, the BTSA was one of the most active migrant associations in Istanbul advocating for the legalization of post-1990 Turkish migrants from Bulgaria.[1] Unlike the hundreds of other Balkan migrant associations that exist mostly in name—known as *tabela dernekleri* (signboard associations)—and that lack knowledgeable staff who can address legal matters, the BTSA could boast that its president, a former migrant from Bulgaria who had arrived in 1989 and had acquired citizenship, was a lawyer. His activities focused primarily on the pursuit of property claims for migrants with citizenship who had come before or in 1989. However, and more pertinently for post-1990 migrants without citizenship, he also wrote petitions for resident permit renewals in return for fees categorized in the association's parlance as "donations." The fees, while seemingly minor at 100TL per petition (the equivalent of about $85 at the time), were not insignificant. For most migrants, the trip to the association and back plus the petition fee was equivalent to half a week's salary. Moreover, the president would also press them to apply for citizenship. He would couch his insistence in legal *and* nationalist terms: renewal of permits, he emphasized, was only a temporary solution and as *soydaş*, who were "of the same race and blood," they were entitled to seek citizenship in Turkey. If they decided to embark on this legal path of filing a lawsuit against the state and applying for citizenship, he offered his services for 4000TL (at the time the equivalent of $3,500, about five months' salary for a domestic worker in the informal labor market).

Despite my aversion to the president's thinly veiled sympathies with the ultra-nationalist right-wing Nationalist Movement Party (Milliyetçi Hareket Partisi, hereafter MHP), for lack of a better alternative, I would reluctantly mention the association to the people I met in the field when they asked for specific advice on legal matters. Indeed, the BTSA president mostly inspired mistrust among my migrant friends when they met him. Although no one that I knew considered pursuing the expensive citizenship lawsuit, many of them did end up resorting to his services for filing petitions for residence renewals, given the dearth of other governmental and nongovernmental bodies providing legal advice.

Given the president's busy schedule, the best time to catch him was to go to the association on its *halk günü*, literally translated as "people's day," denoting its open-house legal clinic. At these events, held every Saturday, individuals could speak with the president and ask specific questions about the status of their petition for a residence permit or their prospects for obtaining an amnesty for temporary legalization. The association at the time was pretty much a one-man show, with the vice president occasionally filling in, but with virtually no other staff to serve clients except for an administrative assistant whose dismissive attitude over the phone was a great source of frustration for those who tried to obtain information or to follow up on petitions. On one such visit in June 2009, several people were particularly concerned about the recent passage in May of the new Law No. 5901/2009 on Citizenship. According to the previous Law No. 403/1964 on Citizenship, individuals who could prove Turkish origin had the advantage of applying for citizenship after two years of residence rather than after the standard five. The new Citizenship Law of 2009 eliminated such obvious preferential treatment for co-ethnics by removing the advantage of shortened duration of residency and instead establishing a single rule for all "foreigners."[2]

I had already witnessed how the withdrawal of the reduced residency requirement had caused consternation among many of my interlocutors. Their dismay was accompanied by a certain degree of confusion and disbelief. In the first few months after the change, people would invariably broach the subject when we met in one bureaucratic line or another. "Why would they do something like that? Why are they doing this to *us*?" Selime, who was from

Razgrad and had migrated five years earlier at the age of forty-five, asked, her agitation stirred right after a woman she identified as Moldovan had tried to cut in front of us in the queue to inquire about the two-year grace period that the new Citizenship Law afforded. "This place is full of Moldavians. They are not Muslims! They are not Turks! Where is the advantage of the Bulgaristanlı Turks?!" she protested. Necmiye, also from the Razgrad region and a friend of Selime's, had been extremely scrupulous about keeping her residence status regular by exiting and reentering every three months since 2001. But she began to agonize about having overstayed her visa after the change in 2007 that allowed a maximum of ninety days of stay in Turkey for every one hundred and eighty calendar days. In an expression of discontent similar to Selime's, she asked, "I mean, the three-month rule was already disastrous for us, the feeling that I had to be on my toes all the time, and now this?! Are they completely giving up on us?"

At the association's open-house legal clinic, someone in the audience raised the same concern: "Will the right given by the previous Citizenship Law that allowed those of Turkish descent to apply for citizenship after two years of residence really be taken away by the new law?" The president, who rarely missed an opportunity to provoke anxiety and resentment against the present government, replied with rehearsed bitterness. "That is correct," he said emphatically. "If you were from Uganda, you could obtain a residence permit saying you own property here. But despite being of Turkish descent, you unfortunately cannot get such a permit. This is how much *hatır* [worth, weight] you have in the eyes of the state."

That day, I had come to the association to accompany Sevginas, on whose behalf the president had written a petition during a previous visit. Sevginas was seeking to renew her six-month permit. Sixty days had passed since she had filed the petition through the association and she had received no reply. We had been instructed by the president to return later because the lack of response would allow him to proceed with the lawsuit for citizenship, if Sevginas would agree to it. The original petition for renewal had been addressed to the Turkish Ministry of the Interior along with a request for "individual migrant" (*münferit göçmen*) status as stipulated by the Settlement Law. In order to qualify for this status, which does not place a demand for property upon settlement as the *iskanlı göçmen* status would, one must "be of Turkish descent, not demand property or land from the state, and have a first-degree relative who is a Turkish citizen." The president was secretive about exactly how he would argue his case if Sevginas decided to pay for the lawsuit. "Pay the price for the legal fees and you can see the full content," he finally retorted, annoyed with our repeated questions. But he did allude to the fact that in addition to grounding his claim in the Settlement Law, he would frame his appeal within the nationalist discourse that posits Balkan migrants as bearers of the Ottoman legacy and as desirable subjects of the nation-state whose unparalleled allegiance is to Turkey.

During another visit, Halil Bey, the association's newspaper editor and the vice president of the BTSA explained their political and legal stance. "Our association," the vice president said, "takes a radical stance on behalf of all these people." By deploying the phrase "all these people," he emphasized the association's distinctiveness—namely, that it worked not just on behalf of the 1989 immigrants with citizenship, but for all Bulgaristanlı migrants, including the undocumented ones who had migrated after the 1990s, a group both neglected and shunned by other Balkan associations. He continued:

> We demand citizenship for all of them. We lost all that land in the Balkans. Fine. But now we are losing these people as well. The state is losing its image as a brother state, as a father state. The tragedy of the Balkans is most significant. The Balkans have paid the price for the Ottoman Empire's not being able to renew itself after the French Revolution. But despite it all, these people have held on to their national and religious identities, and for that reason, the Turkish Republic owes the people of the Balkans a historical debt. Atatürk once said, "These people were placed in the Balkans to Turkify those regions." They may have mixed a bit, but the ones here did as well. So, in fact, they are just as pure as the Turks here.

At this point, the vice president turned to the crowd, who were waiting for the president to arrive at the open house and, pointing his finger at them, addressed me as if I were the only person present and the rest of them could not hear or see:

> Now look. These people carry historical melancholy in their eyes, not individual melancholy. You will not hear a love story from these people. They may be EU citizens, but their faces are still turned toward Turkey. The Balkans are Turkey's insurance policy. They say the foundations of the republic are being shaken. The guarantee of Atatürk's republic are the migrants. If there is any foundation for such fear, you will not see it in the regions where mi-

grants live. All of them have a house, a modern lifestyle. They are disciplined, hardworking.

In one breath, the vice president connected the current mission of the association—filing for citizenship for all migrants from Bulgaria—to its vision of history and historical territory. He pointedly referred to the loss of territory in the Balkans, a loss that looms as one of the greatest traumas in the transition from the Ottoman Empire to the Republic of Turkey, as it signals the demise of Ottoman ambitions for western expansion and sustainable statehood. His reference to the lost Balkan lands was coupled with an urge to substitute nostalgic yearning with proper pragmatism: "all these people" are desirable subjects to be incorporated into the national body because of their lineage and culture. Concluding his speech, the vice president again underscored the timeless allegiance of Bulgarian Turks to their symbolic homeland: "Now look, if you were to ask these people of ours, 'Would you prefer to go to Mecca or to Turkey?' they would instantly tell you, 'Turkey.'"

Among those in the audience was another Bulgaristanlı whom I knew well: Nefiye's sister Gülbiye, whose eyes expressed anything but historical melancholy. I returned her wry smile and asked her quietly, "If someone were to ask you, 'Would you prefer to go to Mecca or Turkey?' would you really say Turkey?" Gülbiye began to laugh. Covering her mouth, she said, "No, I wouldn't. I mean I'd be curious, yes, but that's it. Anyway, there are not many Turks in Bulgaria who go to Mecca in the first place." She added, "It's not like we are transfixed on Turkey. And I would never give up my Bulgarian passport."

While the BTSA may be unique in terms of its confrontational attitude (Özgür Baklacıoğlu 2006), the instrumentalization of ethnonational belonging is a discourse widely subscribed to by other associations as well.[3] The president of the local İzmir branch of the other most visible migrant association, BAL-GÖÇ, a composite acronym combining the shortened form of Balkan (BAL) with that of *göçmen* (GÖÇ), is also a lawyer. Instead of taking legal action, İzmir BAL-GÖÇ had prepared a detailed report outlining the problems faced by migrants from Bulgaria (Özgür and Çavuş 2011). The report struck a far more conciliatory note than BTSA. Instead of making demands, it appealed to the state to assist the Bulgaristanlı. But the reasoning and vision were remarkably similar to what BTSA representatives promoted.

The preface to the report recounts the history of the migrations from the

Balkans to Turkey: the Muslim Turks who had settled in the Balkan territories conquered by the Ottoman Empire were warriors of the *akıncı ocağı*
(raiders forces), having given their all to defend the state against attacks and
to conquer new territory. As a result, they were respected as the *evlad-ı fati-
han* (children of the conquerors). It is noted that these people also spread Islam and expanded the Turks' influence throughout the region. The report
then gives an overview of forced migration from the demise of the Ottoman
Empire to the present. In addition to highlighting the major exodus of 1989,
when around 300,000 people emigrated to Turkey as the result of ethnic repression in Bulgaria, the report states that despite Bulgaria's alleged cessa-
tion of assimilative measures following the demise of the Communist regime
in late 1989, only 1.5 percent of the children among the Turkish minority who
stayed in Bulgaria acquired Turkish language skills. Furthermore, despite
formal equality under Bulgarian law, Turks are still discriminated against,
leading "our people" to continue to migrate to Turkey. While highlighting social and political discrimination against the Turkish population in Bulgaria,
the report carefully elides any mention of economic motives that may have
played a role in migration, often articulated as the primary motive of post-
1990 immigrants, as we shall shortly see. The report also disavows any continuing attachments to the other side of the border. Instead, it locates the migrants strictly in the Turkish homeland, which they are professed to have
longed for throughout their exiled residence in Bulgaria: "By settling in our
country, they have ended this yearning . . . They do not have many ties left
with Bulgaria." The concluding assertion as to why these people ought to be
given citizenship rests on that potent mixture of purity of motives and purity of origin: "The people discussed above are the grandchildren of those
who originate from Anatolia and have settled in the Balkans. They are Turks
through and through (*öz be öz Türk*). Unlike immigrants of other nationalities, they have not come to Turkey merely for economic reasons" (49).

Regardless of what they actually knew or thought about the post-1990 migratory flows from Bulgaria to Turkey, this is what the association leaders believed to be the most effective emotional and ideological register as they appealed to the Turkish state. In this chapter I make sense of why the two major
migrant associations, which differed from each other in terms of their posi-
tioning vis-à-vis the state and in their legal strategies, nonetheless couched
their demands and pleas in almost exactly the same terms, and why Gülbiye

felt the need to hide her continued attachment to Bulgaria. Historicizing the Bulgaristanlı migrants' eclectic but enduring movements across the Bulgarian-Turkish border since the turn of the twentieth century, I situate these lingering desires for ethnic purity and privilege within the broader logic of contemporary migration governance in Turkey.

TURNING THE MIGRANTS OF THE OTTOMAN EMPIRE INTO *SOYDAŞ* OF THE REPUBLIC

Critical scholarship of the late Ottoman and early republican period has persuasively argued that there are more continuities between empire and nation-state than have heretofore been acknowledged in mainstream historiography, which posits an absolute rupture.[4] In the context of this new scholarship that brings to light such continuities primarily by giving due centrality to the Armenian Genocide as foundational violence, I first present a brief account of how Bulgaristanlı migrants figured in the tangled history of exclusions and inclusions and how the exile, genocide, and dispossession of some groups went hand in hand with the recalling, reclamation, and resettlement of others.

The turn of the twentieth century, in particular the Balkan Wars of 1912–13, was a time of mass migration from the Balkans to an Ottoman Empire on the brink of collapse. Muslim populations that had been settled at strategic boundary points during the expansionist phases of the empire fled as the territories were lost to various emerging nation-states in the Balkans (Altuğ 1991; Kasaba 1998; Tekeli 1990). The following figures give an indication of the scope of these forced migrations from the nineteenth century onward: the Crimean migrations after the Ottoman-Russian War of 1828–29, and later 1860–64, involved 1.8 million returning Tatar migrants starting at the end of the eighteenth century (Karpat 1985); the Caucasian migrations between 1859 and 1879 affected approximately 1.5 million people; and more than 2 million people fled from the Balkans to Anatolia after the Ottoman-Russian War of 1877–78 and then the Balkan War of 1912–13 (Eren 1993; Tekeli 1990). The waves of return migration from Crimea, the Caucasus, and the Balkans triggered by the rapid shrinking of the empire's borders, therefore, reshaped population policies (Kasaba 1998). The shift in policy can be described as a move from the Ottomanist ideology that saw strength in numbers to a position that was more ethnicist (Dündar 2001). As Nergis Canefe puts it, the policies of the Committee of Union and Progress, in power during the time of transition from empire to republic, were aimed at "the gathering together of Ottoman Muslims at the expense of ethno-religious minorities" (Canefe 2002, 138).

After the Armenian Genocide in 1915, the expulsion of the majority of the remaining Greek minority occurred through forced population exchanges between Greece and Turkey in 1923 (Iğsız 2018 ; Keyder 2005). Furthermore, laws would be made so as to justify the transfer of property from those who were eliminated to those ethnic and religious kin who were considered to be more desirable subjects of the emerging nation (Üngör and Polatel 2011).[5] In the words of Raymond Kévorkian (2011), the "displacement of the [Armenian] deportees, albeit 'temporary,' was to make room for the *muhacir*" (204). Mehmet Polatel (2009) cites a number of articles in decrees at the time that allocated "abandoned" Armenian properties to Muslim immigrants (*muhacir*) from various parts of the empire soon after the property rights of Armenians had been "secured." He also notes that legal terms and definitions such as "temporary" were employed to hide the fact that the law was aimed at ensuring the erasure of the Armenian population and signs of its existence in what was newly deemed to be Turkish territory.

A special status granted by the law to migrants reveals the legal codification of the material incorporation of the preferred subjects into the new nation-state. The Turkish Muslim immigrant communities arriving from the lost territories of the empire were designated as *iskanlı göçmen*: that is to say, migrants (of Turkish origin) who were to receive property upon settlement. The property on which they ended up being settled was, in turn, the property of the displaced and destroyed non-Muslim communities. Neither was this allocation of property to immigrants based purely on "need." Kurds who were equally in need of accommodation after they were forced to leave their villages following the Şeyh Said Rebellion of 1925 were not allowed to receive Armenian properties: "If the Armenian-abandoned lands in which the Turkish immigrants were settled were occupied by Kurdish people, these lands would be evacuated and Kurds would be sent to their former places" (Polatel 2009, 153–54). The new policy of the Muslimization and Turkification of Anatolia called for using the villages evacuated by Armenians to settle not only Russian and Balkan *muhacir*, but Arabs as well (Dündar 2001). Still, the migrants from the Balkans were strongly preferred by both the late Ottoman government and the founders of the early Republic of Turkey (Çağaptay 2014; Canefe 2002). Archives of an investigation by the government into a complaint re-

garding the mistreatment of a migrant from Bulgaria by the Yalova municipality reflect the spirit of the times: "While a population increase is being
planned for your province with migrants of clean Turkish blood coming from
Bulgaria, his excellency would certainly not condone the loss of such Turkish
immigrants who are already settled there."[6]

This volatile period of border crossings and the preference for migrants
from the Balkans would have an enduring legacy for the establishment of
the Turkish state on the ideal of an almost exclusively Sunni Muslim nation.
While most scholars of Turkey concur that there is a certain shift away from
an emphasis on religion toward an emphasis on ethnicity in the early years of
the new republic, the degree of this shift is a point of contention. Some posit
a clear break that occurs with the rise of Kemalism: on this account, the religious community of Islam as the primary index of belonging was replaced
with secular ethnonational belonging to the Turkish state. Others, however,
caution against overstating the religion/ethnicity dyad, suggesting that it is
a forced opposition.[7] Instead, they posit a constant interplay or even a steady
marriage between Sunni Islam and secular Turkishness. In Cihan Tuğal's formulation: "The young republic's identity was far from being based on an ideal
typical ethnic or racial nationalism . . . The Turkish nation was ambiguously
defined against non-Muslims. This implicit Islamic definition of Turkishness
enabled the state to assimilate several ethnic groups of various sizes" (Tuğal
2009, 39).[8] During the foundational years, Muslim Bosnians, Albanians, Cir-
cassians, and Tatars were accepted as migrants, but the settlement of Christian Orthodox Gagauz Turks and Shi'a Azeris was rejected (Kirişçi 2000),
suggesting that religious difference might override ethnic similarity or that
sectarian difference might override faith in Islam. But the combination of
Sunni Islam and a claim to Turkishness seems to have trumped all other con-
figurations as the most secure, desirable formulation for consistently qualifying for immigrant status.

While the identification of an ethnocultural core was already in the making before the establishment of the republican regime (Deringil 1998), the val-
orization of Turkishness defined as an ethnic/racial identity peaked during
the early republican period. One group of laws and regulations of the period
simply privileged citizens deemed to be of Turkish ethnicity over those identified otherwise, such as the 1924 law exempting "ethnic Turks" from customs
fees for imported ships. Others stipulated Turkish ethnicity as a prerequisite for certain occupations, such as government employees, doctors, dentists,

midwives, and nurses.[9] Aihwa Ong (2006) has singled out Malaysia as "the world's first affirmative action system tied exclusively to ethnicity" (80), given the existence of special government contracts, business licenses, civil employment, and the like in that particular national context. Ong's depiction of Malaysia's affirmative action system ironically describes the key mode of governance used by the Turkish state since its founding. In Turkey, too, governmentally and legally codified action grounded in ethnicity and ethnoreligious identity granted legal privileges to those considered to be Turkish, and especially to those who were Sunni Turkish. Concomitantly, this mode of governance generated legal impediments for members of other ethnoreligious groups— especially Armenians and Jews—including prohibiting them from holding certain government offices. It should be underlined that this was not a case of affirmative action in the conventional sense but rather a codification of the already existing privilege of Sunni Muslim Turks.[10]

The wording in most of the regulations under Law No. 1312/1928 on Citizenship explicitly stated that "ethnic Turks" were favored over other ethnically non-Turkish citizens (see Çağaptay 2003). The term "Turkish citizen" as a generic category was also occasionally used, which has led some of the more generous analyses of Turkish nation-state formation to locate an egalitarian politics of citizenship at this formative period (İçduygu et al. 1999). However, others point out that in practice "citizens" included only those of Turkish ethnicity (Kirişçi 2000). In a frequently cited parliamentary discussion in 1924 about the law regarding the customs exemption, a Member of Parliament (MP) felt the need for clarification and asked: "Are we calling the Armenians and the Greeks Turkish?" One of his colleagues replied, "They have never been Turkish" (quoted in Kirişçi 2000, 8).

The rejoinder of the MP in the exchange cited above exudes confidence. But the answer to the question of who possessed "pure Turkish ethnicity" was not so obvious. It seemed effortless to mark "the others," but who exactly constituted "us"? Or, who could *become* one of "us"? Was identity ultimately a matter of genes or was it the ability to assimilate? In a speech delivered in 1933 during a heated parliamentary discussion of the drafting of Law No. 2510/1934 on Settlement, another Member of Parliament, Ruşeni Bey, declared, "The stomach sustains itself by eating things that are alive; it lives by devouring the living. Just as individuals have stomachs, so do nations. And nations, too, can only survive by eating groups."[11]

This culinary brand of nationalism, bolstered by concern over population decline in the aftermath of the Armenian Genocide and the losses of World War I, sought to fulfill its vision in part by encouraging the migration of those deemed most likely to be able to assimilate into the new nation-state. And the statistics on those granted citizenship provide the most substantial clue to the question of who exactly were the desirable populations to be "devoured" by the emerging nation. It was the tens of thousands of Muslims coming from the Balkans. They were naturalized in accordance with Law No. 1312/1928 on Citizenship, making them the foremost recipients of Turkish citizenship in the formative years of the republic (Kadirbeyoğlu 2007). Furthermore, "those belonging to the Turkish race" could obtain an immigrant visa right away without the approval of the Ministry of the Interior as long as they did not ask for financial support. By contrast, "those not of the Turkish race but tied to Turkish culture, even if able to prove self-support" would need the approval of the Ministry of the Interior for a visa.[12]

Since the founding of the Turkish Republic in 1923, the main legislation to regulate migration in Turkey has been the various Settlement Laws, as I have already discussed in the introduction. Let me elaborate here on the restrictive definition of the term "migrant"—in Turkish *göçmen*—and its deleterious effects on the inclusiveness of Turkey's migration and citizenship regime. The Settlement Law of 1926 already reflected a preoccupation with policies that would ensure the ethnonationalist vision of the new nation-state. The Settlement Law that came into effect in 1934 consolidated this concern by limiting the definition of "immigrants" (*göçmenler*) to "those who are of Turkish descent and/or those with affinity to Turkish culture." The most recent Settlement Law (2006) has maintained the same racially restrictive definition. All other migrants are legally referred to as "foreigners" (*yabancılar*).[13] Article 4 of the Settlement Law of 2006 (No. 5543) also stipulates that "those who are not of the Turkish race and do not have ties to Turkish culture, or, those who are of the Turkish race and who have ties to Turkish culture but have been deported, and those who are seen as a national security threat, will not be accepted as immigrants."[14]

A definition of the term "migrant" that limits the scope to racial and cultural affinity is an exceptionally restrictive definition. It is not in and of itself unusual for the law in modern nation-states to enable preferential treatment of those deemed more similar or more assimilable. Indeed, special terminology exists in other national contexts for those groups considered to be ethnically closer to the dominant majority—*Aussiedler* (individuals of German descent) in Germany and *palinnostoundes* (repatriates) in Greece are two obvious examples. But the added peculiarity in the Turkish case resides in this: in addition to having a special word—*soydaş* (racial kin)—for those deemed to be ethnically and racially closer, the blanket term for "migrant"—*göçmen*—is not neutral. According to the legal terminology in Turkey, therefore, a migrant cannot but be of Turkish origin and descent.[15]

One might wonder whether the exceptionally restrictive definition of *göçmen* in Turkish is merely a technical glitch. The word *göçmen*, after all, is increasingly used in the press and in non-legal contexts in the broader sense of referring to all people who enter inside national borders. However, the more inclusive connotation of "migrant" in the public sphere is a rather recent phenomenon, one that has emerged in tandem with Turkey's rapid transformation into a destination for immigrants. Until 1990, when Turkey was still primarily a country of emigration, the use of the word *göçmen* (migrant) only for people associated with Turkishness was commonplace. And the older generation often used the Arabic word *muhacir*. *Muhacir*, the term historically used to designate the Muslim Turkish refugees fleeing back to receding Ottoman territory, has a more pronounced religious reference to Islam and carries a strong geographic reference to the Balkans as the place of origin. Whether the term used was *göçmen* or *muhacir*, until the nineties, there was a taken-for-granted and naturalized link between the cultural definition of "migrant" and the legal one. The corollary of either *göçmen* or *muhacir* in the public imaginary was someone who was ethnically Turkish, who was Muslim, and who came from the Balkans.

Both key terms, *göçmen* and *soydaş*, still legally refer to migrants of Turkish origin. While technically all migrants deemed to be of Turkish origin, regardless of geographical location, come under the definition of *göçmen*, the implementation of the rule has had its own internal hierarchy. Migrants from the Balkans, including Macedonian Turks, Albanian Turks, and primarily the Bulgaristanlı, have historically outperformed other groups identified as *soydaş*, such as İraqı Turkmen or the Uyghurs, or other Turkic-identified groups from Afghanistan. The latter have occasionally been granted citizenship through reference to *soydaş* status; however, these have been singular instances rather than systematic. In January 2009 an amendment was made to the 1992 law, which regulated the settlement of Ahıska Turks from the Meshketi region of Georgia in Turkey. It granted citizenship to Ahıska Turks who applied within three months and who held a residence permit issued before

January 2009. More recently, in 2017, the Uyghur Turks from China and Central Asia benefited from a special regulation that enabled legalization. Overall, the statistics provided by the General Directorate of Population and Citizenship Affairs show that Bulgaristanlı Turks, followed by Iraqi Turks, hold the competitive edge in the acquisition of citizenship not just historically but in the last decade of the twentieth and the first decade of the twenty-first centuries as well (Kadirbeyoğlu 2010). The reasons for the preference for immigrants from the Balkans are manifold, and a detailed historical account of how this favoritism played out in the top echelons of the bureaucracy would require further study. For my purposes here, suffice it to say that the positive bias toward Balkan immigrants had to do with the Balkans being viewed as at the "heart of the empire" and its identification with the West. The fact that many of the top members of the Republic of Turkey's founding party, the Committee of Union and Progress, traced their roots back to the Balkans also played a key role (Baer 2004; Bora and Şen 2009). It was this deeply entrenched legacy of favoritism for the Balkan migrants that led historian İlhan Tekeli to describe the migrations at the end of the nineteenth and beginning of the twentieth centuries as migrations of Balkanization (Tekeli 2002).

COMRADE CITIZENS OR ASSIMILATED MINORITY?

Following the surge in migrations during the founding years of the republic, migrations of this most desirable category of migrants, the "racial kin" from Bulgaria, continued apace. Often they were undertaken by individuals and families but there were also mass migrations. The first mass migration after 1925 occurred in 1950–51, soon after the advent of communism and the collectivization of land in Bulgaria. It was followed by another quantitatively significant wave after the signing in 1968 of the International Treaty between Bulgaria and Turkey regarding the emigration of close relatives to unite separated families.[16] The incentives driving these migrations hinged upon the political makeup of the regimes in Bulgaria and their diverse policies toward the Turkish minority *and* on the political and economic climate in Turkey. If Bulgarian communism fostered the ideology of ethnonational unity based on proletariat brotherhood, Turkish nationalism portrayed Bulgaristanlı Turks as racial kin who retained their distinct Turkish ethnic and cultural essence at all costs.

The actual degree of the Turkish minority's interaction with the larger

Bulgarian society varied greatly by generation and geographical location. In particular, Communist Party initiatives starting in the late 1940s aimed at spreading education, ensuring health care, and encouraging cultural activities and publications in Turkish were successful to varying degrees in integrating the Turkish minority and installing a socialist consciousness that sought to override ethnic isolationism. Diana Mishkova (1994) cites only a 4 percent literacy rate for the Turkish population in Bulgaria at the turn of the twentieth century.[17] After the nationalization of community-controlled Turkish schools in 1946 and their integration into the public school system, which also included the conversion of some religious schools to secular schools, the renovation of old schools, and the rebuilding of new ones, the enrollment numbers of Turkish children shot up dramatically. Within a few years, literacy rates among young Turks rose, approaching the national average. Compulsory study of Bulgarian in Turkish schools led to high rates of bilingualism among the young. Various Turkish pedagogical institutes, the Department of Turkish Philology at Sofia University, and the arts encouraged the development of a native Turkish intelligentsia (Eminov 2000). In addition to compulsory Bulgarian, Turkish-language education also thrived, a right granted to the Turkish minority by the 1947 Bulgarian Constitution. There was a concomitant surge in Turkish-language publications, Turkish- language radio broadcasts, and professional and amateur Turkish theater. This lively period of cultural production in the Turkish language as well as access to standardized education was a facet of communism deeply cherished and proudly remembered by my interlocutors across the political spectrum and generations.

If the nationalization and secularization of Turkish educational institutions sought to increase the integration of a minority population that had until the advent of communism remained rather insular, scholars of recent Bulgarian history point out that the Communist government also envisioned a two-staged development: first the creation of a secular Turkish- speaking intelligentsia that would enact a shift from a primarily Muslim identity among the Turkish-speaking minority to an ethnic Turkish identity, followed by a final shift from that ethnic identity to a socialist identity that minimized ethnic and cultural difference. But the eventual replacement of the initial encouragement of cultural production in Turkish by more aggressive assimilation programs that slowly eliminated Turkish newspapers and journals is seen by some of my interlocutors who migrated to Turkey in 1989 as a deviation from early Communist principles of respecting the constitutional right to native language. Others see it as the logical conclusion of the intended program of communism all along.[18]

The 1970s and the 1980s in Bulgaria saw gradual but steadily increasing attempts of the government to erase what it considered parochial ethnic identities and divisive cultural practices. Some Turks resisted the drive toward a common socialist Bulgarian identity, though others seemed to have met it with indifference. Ali Eminov (1997) argues that the attempt to impose a Bulgarian identity on Turkish speakers was strongly resisted across the board. However, I have also repeatedly heard the following utterance from Bulgaristanlı whom I met on either side of the border: "We were becoming Bulgarized and we did not care that much. Until, that is, they forced us to give up our names and take Bulgarian names instead."

The common breaking point for the Turks in Bulgaria seems to have been the year 1984, when the hitherto gradual policies of assimilation swung into higher and more violent gear. Under the leadership of Todor Zhivkov, the Bulgarian government launched what was infamously labeled the "rebirth campaign"—*yeniden doğuş süreci*, as it was called in Turkish, and *vızroditelniyat protses* in Bulgarian. During December 1984 and January 1985, the names of Turkish citizens were changed to Bulgarian/Slavic names, sometimes with coaxing, other times at gunpoint. Those who refused to comply were imprisoned. The forced name-changing was followed by bans on speaking Turkish in public spaces and on various cultural practices including circumcision and certain types of dress, such as *shalvar* (long, loose pants with a bell-bottom cut), which were viewed as (too) traditional. According to the 1982 census, the People's Republic of Bulgaria had a total population of 8,917,457, with ethnic Turks accounting for approximately 900,000, or roughly 10 percent of the whole, making them the most numerous minority. But the official claim used to justify the campaign was that the ethnic Turks were actually descendants of Bulgarians who had been forced to convert to Islam by the Ottoman authorities and that the name changes were simply a means of restoring these people to their real Bulgarian roots. In March 1985, the government issued a proclamation that thus denied the existence of Turks in Bulgaria: "There are no Turks in Bulgaria! Bulgaria is a single-nation state."[19]

In the face of the significant opposition on the part of the Turkish community to these violent measures and a growing underground resistance that was garnering international support, the Bulgarian government decided that the solution was mass expulsion. In an often recalled and cited TV speech on

May 29, 1989, President Zhivkov declared: "Those Turks who prefer capital-ist Turkey to socialist Bulgaria are free to leave," and asked Turkey to open its borders. Ahmet, İsmigül's husband, who was usually reticent in the company of his chatty wife, always chuckled when he alluded to that speech: "Zhivkov had kept saying there are no Turks in Bulgaria, and here he was admitting our reality in the moment he was trying to get rid of us," he would say with a cer-tain relish.

After the first, smaller groups of people who were given passports and de-ported, often through a detour from Vienna, Turkey's prime minister, Turgut Özal, met Zhivkov's challenge and declared that Turkey was ready to open its borders to its racial kin and welcome everyone regardless of numbers. The summer months of 1989 witnessed the last big exodus from Bulgaria to Tur-key—until the abrupt closure of the border on August 21, 1989. During these months, convoys of cars and trucks would line up at the two major border entry points, in Kapıkule and Dereköy, where people would wait for days to pass through. For Emine, who a decade later, in the comfort of her apartment in Istanbul, told me the story of their three-day wait at the border, the domi-nant image that impressed itself on her memory—to the exclusion of all else, she emphasized—was the mosquito bites on her two-year-old daughter's legs, arms, belly, and face. "Because it was so hot, we left her in only her diaper and by morning you could hardly see skin."

Prime Minister Özal's bravado-laden announcement to open the bor-der was partly a response to the protests in Bulgaria, some of which resulted in the deaths of demonstrators and to the growing international visibility of minority rights violations under Zhivkov's regime. But it was also expedi-ent publicity for internal politics. The migration was officially hailed as the great homecoming of *soydaş*, who, having ensured the survival of Turkish existence in the Balkans for centuries, were finally returning to their home-land. In his speeches, Prime Minister Özal repeatedly underscored the ways his own government embraced the racial kin from Bulgaria, unlike previous governments, which had abandoned them to their fate (Konukman 1990). He also highlighted their flight from Communist persecution.[20] For days on end in the months of June and July 1989, the news was replete with images of im-migrants kissing the earth and being given a helping hand by government representatives, particularly those immigrants who had not been allowed to take their cars or any possessions and arrived at the Kapıkule border on the "train of shame," a local branding that referenced the misdeeds of the Bulgarian officials. A government publication titled *The Great Migration and the Motherland* (Konukman and Doğan 1990) showcased photographs of arriving immigrants with dramatic captions. The caption for an image of the prime minister shaking the hand of an elderly woman immigrant with a traditional headscarf read, "A symbol of the power and compassion of the Turkish Government" (32). Another depicted the minister of state bottle-feeding an infant. The caption for a photo of an immigrant kissing the Turkish flag reads, "Under its shadow, there is room for you and you and you" (34). Other photographs aimed to document the provision of free transportation, tents for use during the migrants' transition, and a makeshift primary school. The actual experiences of the 1989 migrants and their feelings about their symbolic homeland are far more complex and ambivalent than the official depiction portrays (Parla 2006; Zhelyazkova 1998). In less than a year and following the collapse of the Eastern Bloc and the ousting of Zhivkov by his politburo, a significant number of immigrants—according to some figures as many as one-third—went back to Bulgaria, disillusioned in one way or another with what they had thought was their homeland (Vasileva 1992).

THE POST-1990 PERIOD AND THE INCREASING PROMINENCE OF INFORMAL LABOR

Though it was publicized as a seamless story about the homecoming of a people, the official discourse on the 1989 migration was also an effort to incite ethnic and nationalist zeal. By contrast, the post-1990 labor migration of the same "ethnic kin" from Bulgaria to Turkey has been publicly ignored. No official fanfare has accompanied the routine border crossings of the labor migrants, nor have they been extended an invitation to come and work in the homeland, as has been the case, for example, with ethnic Hungarian labor migration from Romania to Hungary (Fox 2003). There are no longer official proclamations welcoming the return of *soydaş*. Most significantly from a legal perspective, the post-1990 migrants, unlike the 1989 immigrants who were granted citizenship, have found that formerly porous borders have become more formidable. Between 1991 and 1997, the state only reluctantly allowed Bulgaristanlı immigrants to enter Turkey on visas, and even then only one member per family could obtain a visa. This was an unofficial but systematically implemented policy. It is a fact entirely overlooked in the macro accounts in the migration literature on that period, but emerged in the testimonies of numerous interlocutors during my fieldwork. Single men were denied visas altogether, and they accounted for more clandestine border crossings than any other group during this period. Children, also denied visas, crossed the border by traveling for many days with smugglers who would pick them up from their relatives on the Bulgarian side and deliver them to their parents on the Turkish side, as Rembiye's story in chapter 3 will illustrate.

Such clandestine border crossings came to an end in 2001, when Turkey switched to a flexible visa regime with Bulgaria in response to Bulgaria's removal from the "negative" Schengen list.[21] From 2001 to May 2007, Bulgarian nationals could thus enter Turkey as tourists, on visa waivers that were valid for three months. In May 2007, yet another new visa agreement went into effect. The procedure that had allowed Bulgarian nationals to stay as tourists on visa waivers for three months was replaced by permission to stay for a maximum of ninety days in a six-month period. The new visa regime was the result of a bilateral agreement signed between Bulgaria and Turkey following alignment with the Schengen visa regime. In the wider context of the European Union, the new procedure aligned the conditions for migration from Bulgaria to EU countries and from Bulgaria to Turkey by granting the right to free movement to Bulgarian passport holders within the entire Schengen area and in Turkey for a maximum of ninety days within a six-month period. However, for those labor migrants who come to work in Turkey—mostly in the domestic sector—the ninety-day limit has meant that they have to choose between losing their jobs and lapsing into illegality. This was the regulation that Necmiye was protesting earlier at the association meeting as having been "bad enough" before the change in the Citizenship Law that increased the residence requirement for citizenship applications from two to five years.

The post-1990 period has thus been a time of restrictions on the movement of *soydaş* with instances of temporary legalization through amnesties that kindled the hope of permanent legalization. The question that Bulgaristanlı migrants would often ask in exasperation was why Turkey seemed to be letting go of its policy of favoritism toward them. The ostensible explanation from a legal perspective is that the 1989 and post-1990 Bulgarian migrants are different sorts of migrants. The conventional distinction that is made between the two groups in terms of both the official line and societal perception is that the approximately 350,000 migrants who arrived in convoys throughout the summer of 1989 were political migrants, while the migrants who have been arriving intermittently but steadily since 1990 are economic migrants. According to this dominant narrative, the 1989 migrants fled solely to preserve their identity, language, and culture and not for economic reasons. Those who did not emigrate in 1989 are viewed as having chosen to migrate only after the collapse of communism in Bulgaria merely because they were seeking better economic opportunities in Turkey. The notion of coming "only for the money" carries the assumption that the immigrant ought to have a higher purpose than simple economic drive.

This alleged difference between the two cohorts of migrants is the legal justification for not granting citizenship to post-1990 migrants even though they assert the same claim of being of Turkish origin, the grounds on which the 1989 migrants were granted citizenship. The same legal precept gets interpreted and implemented differently at two different historical moments in accordance with the politics of the time, for which the economic/political migrant distinction serves as a convenient foil. Belying official contention and public perception, however, economic motives were not entirely absent from the politically purified accounts of the 1989 migration (Parla 2007, 2009). On the contrary, more than half of the migrants I met over the course of my fieldwork who were subsumed under the category of post-1990 labor migrants had in fact migrated or *tried* to migrate in 1989. Some migrated only to then return to Bulgaria, disillusioned with conditions in the symbolic homeland that they had glorified from a distance. Others tried to migrate in 1989, but despite the official policy of open borders to *soydaş*, were turned back at the border.

From the perspective of the local population in Turkey, the "ethnic kin" whose plight the locals were invited by media and political rhetoric to commiserate with have now been demoted to serving as "Bulgarian" nannies for their children. They are still more desirable than other "foreigners" because "they are closer to our Turkish traditions. In fact, they are seen as immigrants of Turkish roots" (Çakir 2004).[22] To a certain extent, the distinction between political and economic migrants, one based on a moral hierarchy of migrant legitimacy, is even reproduced by the 1989 migrants from Bulgaria who settled in Turkey. Emine, a thirty-two-year-old migrant who came from Kırcali in 1989 and was pursuing a doctorate in Istanbul, gently warned me more than once not to conflate the various migrations of Turks from Bulgaria to Turkey, saying that the 1989 immigrants were distinctive because they were political migrants. Similarly, Osman, a 1989 immigrant in his forties from Starazagora whose reputation as a massage therapist was soaring among his upper-class clientele, was proud of the general occupational success of the 1989 immigrants in Turkey. He expressed concern, however, that the post-1990 immigrants, who were "less educated" and had "fewer skills" and who came to Turkey "only for the money," were giving better-educated, highly skilled 1989 immigrants like him a bad name. It was as though those who had not joined the 1989 migration wave had lost their entitlement to the experience of persecution and marginalization.

Those who arrived post-1990 were well aware that they were often frowned upon by those Bulgaristanlı who came earlier and settled in Turkey. The latter were, in Elmas's words, *tepkili* (reactive) toward them. "They keep nagging us now: 'Why did you come then only to return?' 'Why is it your business?' I say. 'We came because we needed to. And now we come because again we need to.'" İsmigül, who had arrived in Turkey with her family in 1998 and was among those most staunchly committed to legalization, said in exasperation, "'Why did you not come in 1989?' I get asked. We get taken to task like this all the time." *Soydaş*, then, did internal boundary work even among Bulgaristanlı across different migratory cohorts. One had to prove purity of motive, and the motive of economic consideration was viewed as a blemish on the claim to *soydaş* status.

The demarcation between economic and political migrants has already been amply critiqued in the migration scholarship on both empirical and normative grounds.[23] The line between poverty and persecution, it turns out, is often not as well defined as the distinction implies. On a normative plane, why should political persecution be seen as more deserving of escape than economic poverty? And on the descriptive level, economic versus political is not a clear-cut dichotomy: even economic migrations are to some extent political when considered as a part of broader geopolitical forces, and even politically induced migrations might be entwined with deteriorating economic conditions.

Rather than revisit these well-established critiques in more detail, I present two narrative accounts of migration undertaken in 1989. Neither of these accounts was offered in response to a question about the political/economic distinction. Instead, both were spontaneous accounts that emerged over multiple interactions stretching across five years. Both accounts defy any strict formula for the decision to migrate. Instead, they are replete with the hesitations and ambivalences that go into such a decision. They also confound the assumed legitimacy of migration as only a last resort, whether the unrelenting impetus in question is the hope of escape from political persecution or economic poverty. Furthermore, these personal accounts belie the strict demarcation between the 1989 political wave and the post-1990 migrants, as well as the moral imputations that rest on that distinction. In that, they also grant due complexity to my own designation of the Bulgaristanlı migrants as "post-1990 labor migrants," even if the designation does usefully serve to identify a particular cohort in terms of its legal and cultural reception. In laying bare the difficulty of maintaining sharp distinctions between the 1989 migrants and the post-1990 migrants, these stories of border crossing defy the contortions that the nationalist narrative of ethnic homecoming requires in order to appear seamless. Finally, I intend them to serve as prehistories to the labor migration that this book traces, setting the stage for the hopeful quest for legalization that the same Bulgaristanlı migrants were to embark upon in Turkey in the 1990s and 2000s, some time after their first attempt at migration in 1989.

RED CHEEKS AND THE
DISAVOWAL OF POLITICS

Gülbiye and her husband, who lived in the city of Ruse in Bulgaria, began their preparations for migrating to Turkey at the end of May 1989, four years after the Bulgarian government led by Todor Zhivkov had launched its violent assimilation campaign and the prime minister of Turkey at the time, Turgut Özal, opened the borders. Gülbiye recalled:

> Now what month was it? It was tomato season, so it must have been August or September. Our furniture remained piled up for days, just like that. We had already prepared all of our documents. And of course, as we waited, we had been trying to collect as much cash as possible. We sold all of the big pieces, the couch, the TV. And then they closed the border. We could not leave. When we realized that the border was not going to be reopened, we moved to the village near my mother-in-law.

The inability to migrate resulted in a further displacement for Gülbiye, her husband, and their three-year-old son. They could not cross the border or go back to the house in the city that they had already abandoned. "The order [of our lives] was disrupted," Gülbiye said. They moved to the village where her husband used to live. Gülbiye said that what subsequently clinched their decision to give migration to Turkey a second try was the prospect of economic opportunities. She had worked in a textile factory in Ruse, which was where she met her husband. When they were considering leaving for Turkey,

Gülbiye was still on maternity leave, which at the time included two years of paid leave and one year of unpaid leave, an exceptionally generous provision in comparison to the rest of the Western world (and one that I return to in chapter 4 to describe the pervasive Communist nostalgia nursed especially by migrant women).

"We were even able to save [about one hundred dollars] per month then," Gülbiye recalled. "And then communism came to an end. Things started to get difficult. The textile factory shrank in size and many people lost their jobs." The village the family ended up settling in was a "mixed" village populated by Bulgarians, Turks, and Roma. They sold tomatoes, but the prices plummeted when too many people turned to similar work.

> Where we lived, there was no coercion or anything. You know, they just changed our names, just like that. They simply told us that this was how it was going to be. "Your names will be changed." We didn't care. And anyway, what would have happened if we had resisted? I mean, how could we have resisted? In Razgrad, and further down south, people were more attached to Turkey, to Turkishness. With us, it was not like that. I don't know. We had become quite Bulgarized anyway. As if we were ready for this. And in the end, it is just a name, so what? But then they started to say other things would also be banned, like wearing our *shalvar*,[24] or speaking Turkish, even our traditional weddings.

Gülbiye met her husband in 1985, just as the bans were getting under way and repression against the Turkish minority was spreading across the country. She told the story accompanied by her infectious giggles. "My fiancé said, joking with me, 'Let's speed up this marriage. In fact, let's do it in forty-eight hours so that we can guarantee a Turkish wedding!' Eh, I was already smitten the moment I saw him, he was so handsome."

"How did the name change happen in the end?" I asked.

Still giggling, she went on.

> The officer who came to my workplace looked at me—you know my cheeks were always red then, and my husband, he always says, "It was your apple-red cheeks that I first fell in love with"—so anyway the officer looked at me and said, "The name Svetlana would fit you well." And I said fine. Indeed, Svetlana is a very pretty name. Then Zhivkov got arrested, we got our names back, things like that. You know, I don't know much about politics.

But on another occasion, Gülbiye talked extensively about her father's take on migration and politics.

> My father repeats all the time now, "You should have gone when you had the chance, instead of having to deal with these difficulties now [of illegality]." He also says, "Those days are sure to return when migration will no longer be an option but a necessity."

At that point, Gülbiye's words merged into her father's and it was no longer entirely clear who the author of the utterance was.

> What can you do? After all, this is the country of the Bulgarians, you never know what can happen. Because they will always have this against the Turks, all this memory of Ottoman oppression and so on. But *we* never felt this hostility in the village we lived in.

The romance, the red cheeks, and the nonchalant disavowal of interest in politics during a period that others describe as the worst humiliation they have ever had to endure as their names were changed are all undercut in Gülbiye's own narrative by the interjections she makes in the voice of her father, who becomes the voice of caution and bleak outlook. Gülbiye's overall more cheerful tenor when depicting the chronology of events that led to her migration contrasts as well with the attitude of her older sister, Asaniye, who always had some of the most pungent opinions on matters of politics, law, and culture. In some ways Asaniye was even more integrated into the Bulgarian community—because she had married a Christian—a rather rare occurrence in the Turkish community. But she hardly held back her sharp commentaries on the injustices that had taken place during the assimilation campaign. She was also considering filing a lawsuit against the Bulgarian government for what she said was the confiscation of property that belonged to her parents. At the same time, she had accepted a few appearances on radio and TV in Turkey, hosted by activist platforms, to testify to the exploitative conditions faced by women working in domestic service. Asaniye was adamant about her pursuit of citizenship in Turkey, while Gülbiye would shrug off the idea of the "pink card" without a moment's hesitation. "I just don't like the clandestine status, otherwise I don't care about the citizenship," she said on several occasions. Her husband and son were back in Bulgaria, and she had just welcomed a granddaughter whom she could not wait to spend more time with back in Ruse, once she increased the family savings by working for a couple more years. Despite the differences between the two sisters with regard to political engagement and outlook on the past and the assimilation campaign, motivations for migration to Turkey and intentions to stay or leave, they were extremely close, sharing boundless affection and secrets, and both could readily name a member of their extended family from each migration wave. Their maternal uncle had come to Turkey before 1989, and her paternal uncles in 1989; all of them had immediately received citizenship on the basis of their Turkish origin.

IF YOU HAVE FUN,
THEY CANNOT GET TO YOU

Elmas worked in a preschool in a village near Razgrad teaching Bulgarian to three-year-old Turkish children. She had a second job at the municipality as secretary to the chief. She was a well-known figure in the community because she was a state employee. Her popularity was probably enhanced by her warm, extroverted, and contagiously jovial personality.

> One day, they brought the elderly in cars to the chief's office [*muhtarlık*]. The officials had rounded them up and brought them in to change their names. I said to one of the police, "Hey, *abi* [brother], what is going on here?" He said, "What are you doing here? Go back to your work in the preschool. Don't stay here." He was trying to tip me off to spare me. "I work here, too, you know," I said to him. And I stayed, of course.
>
> There was this old aunt among the ones they brought in. They said to her, "OK, now choose a name for yourself." She said, "What will I do with a name? I already have a name." "No, no," they repeated. "Pick one from this list, and from now on, that will be your name." She said, "My grandfather is long dead. What will I do with a new name?" They said, "Well, we'll change his name, too." You know, they also did that back then; they changed the names on the gravestones. The idea was that there are no Turks in Bulgaria. But that old aunt, you should have seen her, she just started talking back at them, shouting, sobbing. Her obstinacy and the fight she put up. I nearly fainted watching her. This other police officer, he must have seen me turn all pale. He rushed to me, he said, "Let me take you to your office." "Get her some water," he shouted. My vision went all blurry. I was really, really sad. I think only in that moment did I actually come to see what it all meant. Because until then, we were just hearing this and that, talking about what was rumored to have happened in so

and so's village. But when it takes place right in front of your eyes . . . and you fail to see any logic to it all. Why are you called Adem one day, and something else the next?

The chief I worked as a secretary for, he was a young guy, barely twenty-five years old, Bulgarian. But he was from the same village as my husband, the village where I got married. And because that is a village with a Turkish majority, the chief spoke very clean Turkish. I speak fluent Bulgarian. We worked very well together. Now when they began to change our names, what they did was to reassign these chiefs to a different location: for example, those from Razgrad got assigned to Targovic and vice versa. So that the officials would not be doing this violence to people they personally knew.

During that time, I would check on my mother every night. Her village was invaded by tanks, military tanks, you know, those armored and all. My mother left for work at 3:00 a.m. for the night shift. I was sick with worry for her making the journey to work at that hour with military tanks all around, but then if she did not go, they would accuse her of sabotage. So she had to go. And I was on the phone every single night, checking in before she left, checking back to see if she had returned.

Then they took my father away and he was gone for days. Meanwhile, my grandfather got sick and had a stroke. I am almost certain it was from stress. I got too worried about them and took the bus to their village. When I arrived, they said my grandmother had been called up and had gone to the municipality. I called on the phone and because I work at the office in my own village, they let me speak to her. I said "Grandma, what are you doing?" She said on the phone, "What do you think I am doing? Your father has disappeared, and they called me to change my name. I am not giving any name or anything until your father comes back here, until I see him alive and well." Then I heard her shouting, "Why are you speaking to me in Turkish, if you are trying to make me Bulgarian? Speak to me in Bulgarian, I speak Bulgarian." So I rushed to the municipality. What do I see, our very own chief had come to my grandmother's village to enforce the name change.

I said to the chief, "What did you do, why are you doing this?" He replied, "What can I do? It is my duty. But you know, that grandmother of yours, she wreaked havoc here. She destroyed us. I speak Turkish, she starts in Bulgarian; I start in Bulgarian, she switches to Turkish. She devastated us. And she is old, so we cannot order her about."

People were constantly changing places those days to avoid being rounded up. Of course, they would eventually catch up with you. . . . The chief in our village—and this was, like I told you, a primarily Bulgarian village—told the officials there were no Turks in the village when they called him from the municipality to ask for a report on how the campaign was going and how many names they had changed. Then he came to us and pleaded with us. He said, "You are registered in Serinköy anyway. Now please take the ambulance, I will put it at your disposal, you will be warm"—it was in the middle of a freezing winter—"Go to Serinköy and give your signature and get this thing over with. Whatever will be will be." So he tried to save us the humiliation at least. And then we had another friend, who said, "Go take the keys for your place in the village of D., and hide out there as long as you want. If there is any way you see that you can wiggle out of this mess, stay there." This guy was Bulgarian, a history teacher, and he was completely opposed to what was going on. We did not take him up on the offer of course, when we had no idea how long it would last. But we will always be grateful to him.

So in the end we went to my husband's village, which was much bigger than ours and primarily a Turkish village. They had dressed the kids in military school in uniform and let them out on the streets. The soldiers in uniform were marching all over the streets. Already psychologically they wore you down. We went to the preschool for the name change. But really funny things went on. For example, my grandfather's name is Müstecep, and he took the name Maxim. My dad's name is Mustafa, and he loved my grandad, may he rest in peace, and he said, "I will be Maxim too. Let us all be Maxims in this family." Then all the women in my family whose names start with an N, and there were many—Nefise, Nebiye, Necmiye—they said, "Then let us all be Nedejde." So we started to poke fun. In the face of tragedy one escapes to comedy. Because when you cry, you give the other side pleasure. But if you have fun, then they cannot get to you.

My dad, he took the name Stefan. Then two days later, he went again, and he told them, "I changed my mind, I really like the name Alexander, it fits me very well. Alexander, please allow me to be Alexander." Then a couple of days later he would go again. He would call to the official, "Sssshhh, could you see here for a minute? Here." The official would say, "What's up?" and my dad would say, "You know I am rather bored with this name, Alexander. I don't think it suits me after all. Can we change it to Dimitri, please?" As long as it was a Bulgarian name, they did not know what to say. If they hesitated, he would keep at it: "Look now I will be really offended if you won't let me take the name Dimitri. Such a great name, Dmitri." My dad, may he rest in peace, he was such a smart man.

But then, there were others, among the Turks. So in Serinköy, the Turks working in the chief's office all resigned, saying, "We will not carry out something like this." And guess who replaced them? Those wannabes, Turkish people who had not achieved anything in life and then seized the opportunity to get an iota of power. When we went, my husband Mecit and I, to change our names, it was a woman we knew who was going to do our paperwork. Mecit says, "Who on earth put her here? She hardly knows how to read and write, she barely made it through elementary school." He turned to her. "I will not have you write my name. How can I trust you to spell it correctly?" He kept poking fun at her like that, he was relentless. He said, "All the villagers have resigned, and you come sit here to do the job they refuse to do?" Of course, the officials intervened and threatened him.

They also beat Mecit up afterward, really badly, but I learned about that after the fact. That day, I had worked late and when I came home, he was sleeping with his face down. I nudged him, he would not turn, he said, "I am too tired, leave me be." We had a Lada, and you know in those days not many people had a car. Ours was orange, very conspicuous. Mecit had lent his car to a friend, a teacher, who attended a founding meeting of the Movement for Rights and Freedoms political party, which was underground then, of course. Mecit also attended some of its meetings, but this time he had not gone himself; he had just lent his car. Apparently they came for him and showed him pictures of his car. When he told them he was at work, they took him. I would later learn that for three days in a row they would come to work in the morning, take him away for questioning all day, beat him up, and then let him go at the end of the workday.

I only learned about this on the third day because I finally forced him to turn around and he started to moan. I saw bruises all the way from his chest down to his knees. He was still joking about it. "They beat me up a little," he said. I joked, too. I said, "They did quite a beautiful job on you, Mecit. But why?" I asked, and he would not tell me. So I went to the police chief in Oda-köy, who was our neighbor. I said, "This and this happened to Mecit. What is going on?" The police chief scolded me, "Why did he not come to me right away?" he said. "I will look into this," he said, and then what do you know, the guy who detained and beat him paid us a visit. "Why did you not tell me that you were the close neighbor of my chief? I am very sorry I did wrong by you, but I was just carrying out orders you know. I am really sorry, but you won't say a word to anyone [about] this." Mecit teased him, saying, "You really lost the fine-tuning there. Why did you have to beat me this badly?" I don't know, so some of these people, some did it out of ambition, for their careers. Others really believe in that stuff about the Ottomans, I suppose, how they oppressed Bulgarians, cut off their heads and so on. Some Bulgarians have deeply ingrained prejudice against the Turks. There would always be such stuff to feed that on TV. You know, actually even I was somewhat brainwashed by them. When we came in 1989, I was expecting men in fezzes, the Ottoman hats. I was really surprised. "These men look normal," I thought.

We came to Turkey in 1989 and returned to Bulgaria in 1990. We returned in March. My father had had an accident right after we arrived [in Turkey], and although he had found a job, he had to quit and lie in a cast for a month. And then, my husband . . . he was expecting something different from Turkey. Actually, I don't know what we were expecting. My younger son, he was just four months old when we waited for five days at the border. The roads were all blocked with all those cars in endless rows, waiting to pass the border. Everyone was leaving. We had no luxury to decide any other way. Everyone was leaving.

We stayed here in Turkey for less than a year. I worked in a textile factory. When we went back, we found our house just as we had left it. Our neighbors, our Bulgarian neighbors, had cleaned our house for us. We entered a spick-and-span house. And then in one week, I went back to work. Not to the kindergarten of course; they had fired me. The reason they gave was because my parents had put in an application in 1983 to migrate to Turkey. They said, "You cannot be a teacher. Is this how you are going to educate our children?" They referred to an article in the constitution, something about betraying the state. First, I went to my husband's workplace and worked as a welder. It was all men and they did not think I could pull it off. But I was relentless, I would say, just try me. Then my parents-in-law started to bake bread and asked me to join them. But because the bakery belonged to the state, it was against the law to have three people from the same family be employed. So I said to our local official [muhtar], "Then apply the same standard to your own family, you are the neighborhood chief, your wife is the accountant, your family runs the whole village!" "Okay," he said. "You can work there." And I worked there for seven years. But then, with so many people out of jobs after the fall of communism, people started bad-mouthing. "There are so many unemployed Bulgarians and you are running this place," they said. "So what makes us different?"

I replied, "And we bake such good bread." People really liked our bread, because it was all warm, freshly baked, not like the bread that would come from elsewhere and get cold. So people in other villages would say, "We will go out all the way to Elmas Abla's bakery and get the bread before going home." So then they started to say, "You are selling bread to the Turks. You are giving away our share of the rationed flour to the Turks."

In the end, the bakery was privatized. So what to do, we opened a little restaurant on the first floor of our house. At first it seemed to go well, but people just did not have money to eat out. No one came. This helplessness, lack of money, lack of a job, it really messes with your psychology. You might be a really great person, but when you come home and you no longer have anything to put on the table, then you start to fall apart. And so, we've migrated to Turkey once again. And this time, we are here to stay. We will eventually sort out the papers.

THE DECLINING VALUE OF SOYDAŞ

Like Gülbiye and Elmas, many of the post-1990 labor migrants, who are relegated to the less worthy status of economic migrants, did also attempt to migrate in 1989 as part of the political wave of migration. If the separation between these cohorts of migrants is not that clear-cut in reality, why the decline in state favoritism toward the Bulgaristanlı? Why the move toward a policy that, even as it preserves a certain leverage for soydaş, has become more checkered and unreliable in its granting of privilege?

One explanation concerns the changes in ideological alignments after the Cold War. There has been a shift in the symbolic utility of the migrants from Bulgaria. At the end of the 1980s, being a political migrant accrued even more value for the 1989 immigrants who were represented as fleeing the persecution enacted by a falling Communist regime. The post-1990 labor migrants lacked this symbolic validity.

But there is also an economic explanation. Immigration policies in Turkey—as elsewhere—are shaped by the demands of the neoliberal labor market for cheap and vulnerable labor. Bulgaristanlı women, because they are regarded as culturally closer and because they speak Turkish, are particularly desirable in the booming market of domestic workers and nannies. The migration of Bulgaristanlı women to become part of the informal labor force was thus tolerated, even encouraged, but without any commitment to their legalization on the part of the state.

In addition to the economic argument about market demand and the political argument about symbolic utility, my fieldwork has revealed other, less visible layers that articulate with these macro analyses. Most importantly, while not advertised publicly as such, the Bulgaristanlı migrants have increasingly come to be valued by the Turkish government as a transnational resource. More specifically, they are viewed as a handy reservoir of potential voters for the Movement for Rights and Freedoms Party (hereafter the MRF Party, or the MRF) (Hak ve Özgürlükler Hareketi in Turkish), the party that for the most part represents the Turkish minority in Bulgaria and the party that the Turkish government invests in with the aim of developing a stronger footing in Balkan and wider European politics.[25]

This is why the timing of almost every single amnesty granted by the government to regularize the status of illegal Bulgaristanlı migrants in Turkey coincided with local or national elections in Bulgaria. In 2001, 2005, 2007, 2009, and 2011, these amnesties were implemented through circulars rather than laws subject to a vote in parliament and were only sometimes made available on the Turkish Foreigners' Department website. Mostly, the news spread among the Bulgaristanlı through the Balkan migrant associations, with association workers notifying the migrants registered on their lists via text messages. These messages would cause a ripple effect, with people starting to line up at the designated police stations at midnight for the next day's queue. As the queues spread across police stations in Istanbul, officials would "whisper in people's ears" that those who failed to vote and show proof of having voted in the Bulgarian elections through a stamped passport would lose their chance to obtain the amnesty permit.

This was, in fact, not true: legally, no direct proof of voting was required to gain the permit. Anyone who lined up before the deadline received the amnesty regardless of whether they voted or not, and no one's permit subsequently got annulled if they did not vote. Nonetheless, such rumors were deliberately spun to encourage travel to Bulgaria to vote. Although some of my interlocutors were intimidated the first couple of times around with the alleged requirement that came with the permit, over time everyone grew incredulous of these warnings and would eventually wave them off with a smirk. Nonetheless, the most common course of action was to go and vote anyway. Just in case.

The figures provided by a post-1990 migrant who has volunteered for the Movement for Rights and Freedoms Party and spoke on condition of anonymity give a striking indication of the success with which the government instrumentalized migrants' illegal status for the benefit of the transnational political interests of the state. Before the Bulgarian elections in May 2001, the maximum number of votes cast by eligible Bulgaristanlı voters residing in Turkey was 3,000 to 5,000. In the 2001 elections, which coincided with the first Turkish amnesty providing three-month permits to those who were in illegal status, the number spiked to 41,000 votes. And with that spike in voter participation, the MRF secured a place for the first time in the ruling coalition led by the former tsar and later prime minister of Bulgaria, Simeon Sakskoburggotski, also the once-exiled son of the old tsar, Boris III. My informant said that this made members of the MRF Party realize that you had to promise something in order to motivate people to go to the ballot box. He also said that the Ministry of Internal Affairs in Turkey was explicitly instructed to undertake these amnesties for renewals.

He also described in detail the participation of migrant associations in this transnational political design. Even the typically passive associations would become active during the elections. "For a ballot box to be installed in a particular location, a petition with one hundred signatures must be filed," he explained. A second ballot box requires 1,001 signatures. This is where the associations worked hard to gather enough signatures, enter them into the system, and provide as many locations for voting as possible. The ballot boxes in Turkey served voters who already had citizenship in Turkey. For migrants without permits, associations arranged free buses to take them to Bulgaria and back.

The orchestrated effort that began at the top governmental level in Turkey and was disseminated through associations acting as intermediaries between migrants and state actors on both sides of the border brings to mind Nina Glick Schiller and Georges Fouron's diagnosis of the deterritorialization of the nation-state. Glick Schiller and Fouron (1998) deploy the term "deterritorialized nation-state" to refer to a state of affairs that embodies not a dissolution of the sovereignty of the nation-state, but rather a re-envisioning of the state as expanding beyond its national borders to appropriate and vie for the loyalty of its nationals abroad.

The Bulgaristanlı migrants, whose loyalty was being sought, were themselves deterritorialized. This made them even more vulnerable to the instrumentalizing whims of the state. As I will explore further in chapter 3, it also made them wary about the intentions of the states on both sides of the border. But that skepticism also opened up room for maneuvering and manipulation.

"Who cares about the elections in Bulgaria anymore?" asked Sebatiye, who was in her forties, worked as a live-in nanny, and was finding it hard to keep her status legal after the imposition of the ninety-days rule. She was relieved at the prospect of legalizing her status again through the amnesty of 2007, but was cynical about the elections. "They think they are playing with us, eh?" she said. "Well, from my end, no worries. I take my free bus ride, take five days off from work, party with my friends back in town, and maybe I will cast a vote, maybe not. Either way, I look at it as a free vacation." Zöhre, a woman in her thirties who was pursuing a certificate in computer programming and taking language classes in Istanbul and who had overstayed her visa for more than a year, was incensed when she found out that the amnesty promised during the 2009 elections was not for the renewable six months but just for the nonrenewable three. "This is it," she said. "Do they think we are stupid? This time I will not vote. Or maybe I will vote for any party *but* the Movement for Rights and Freedoms." Others were less defiant. Even if they were not enthusiastic about the MRF, they would shrug with a certain indifference and say, "It is after all the party for the Turks in Bulgaria. One should still vote for them, even if they, too, are not corrupt."

A board member from one of the migrant associations cautiously admitted: "It would not be wrong to say that a certain political inclination in Turkey is against accepting these Bulgaristanlı migrants into citizenship." He elaborated:

> Some of the politicians we [as association board members] are in contact with say as much. "Let them go back to Bulgaria and settle there," they say. There is no official announcement to this effect, but we hear it from politicians all the time. They do not want the Turkish population in the Balkans to diminish. They want a strong presence for the party that represents the Turks in Bulgaria. Turkey has a strong investment in the Balkans. The well-being of such a party is dependent on the Turkish population [there]. It is part of Turkey's transnational politics, to have a stake in the strength of the Turkish party there. For example, it is thanks to Bulgaria that five or six [ethnically] Turkish MPs are now representatives in the European Union. There they can raise their voices on behalf of Turkey and act in Turkey's favor.

According to the association representative's assessment, then, there was an unpublicized but significant change in state policy after 1990: The permanent settlement of Bulgaristanlı was to be discreetly but systematically discouraged. Instead, they were viewed as a minority in Bulgaria that could advocate, through the MRF, for Turkey's interests in the EU. This assessment was corroborated by a volunteer who had worked with the MRF: "When Bulgaria started negotiations with the EU, an informal deal was reached between MRF and the Turkish government to stop giving citizenship to Turkish migrants from Bulgaria. To have them return to Bulgaria, to have a strong Turkish contingency in Bulgaria, is to our advantage. The way the government looks at it: these migrants should stay a little longer [in Turkey], make some more money, but then in the long-term, they should go back [to Bulgaria]."

SOYDAŞ AS A DOUBLE-EDGED SWORD

The constellation of ethnonational appropriation, political instrumentalization, and labor market exploitation that constitutes the migration governance of the Bulgaristanlı migrants may be seen as what Aihwa Ong (2000) has called *graduated sovereignty*. Ong highlights the transnational dimension of the relationship between the state and its citizens, one that can no longer be contained solely within the terms of political power over legal subjects. Instead, rationalities of government that variously regulate forms of belonging involve the "differential state treatment of segments of the population in relation to market calculations" (57). These, in turn, get transposed into already existing "distinctions of race, ethnicity, gender, class and region" (57).[26] But Ong's emphasis on "considerations of profitability" (62) as the key underlying logic for the differential modes of treatment of various populations within a polity perhaps takes the economic emphasis too far for the case at hand. In regulating the legalization of the Bulgaristanlı, market calculations continue to be modified by the already existing "'pastoral' logic" (58; Foucault 1981) that treats certain populations in special ways because of their race and ethnicity.

There is another way in which the governance of differentially valued populations defies a single explanation and seamless implementation. For one thing, the production of hope of legalization is intimately related to practices of graduated sovereignty that exploit the migrants' vulnerable legal status in order to maximize transnational interest and market profitability. And no doubt such a mode of migration governance has been quite successful: the temporariness and arbitrariness of the amnesties, the constant promise of citizenship, and the lack of certainty make for a superbly efficient mechanism of governing through hope. If this is one side of the story I tell, however, I also

show that there are ways in which actual experiences may escape this particular logic of governance. The legal production of hope and the state's instrumental deployment of Bulgaristanlı migrants' illegal status give rise to its
own dynamic of perseverance and renewed hope, one that poses a counter-
vailing force even as it does not entirely annul the logic of migration governance dictated by graduated sovereignty. The state has been finding itself
making more concessions to the Bulgaristanlı migrants than the plans made
behind closed doors of politicians have envisioned. These concessions are the
result of both the deeply ingrained legacy of the privilege of racial kinship
and the migrants' own resourcefulness, perseverance, and persistence. These,
in turn, are the result of hope produced and cultivated as a collective structure of feeling.

In these entangled processes in which hope can become both an instrument of governance and exceed its scope, the term *soydaş*, as a legal and cultural designation, performs crucial work for the Turkish migrants from Bulgaria. But it is a double-edged sword. On the one hand, the status of *soydaş*
provides the only leverage through which ethnically Turkish migrants from
Bulgaria can make legal claims for inclusion and distance themselves from
the rest of the undocumented migrants in Turkey in the process. On the other
hand, the prestige of *soydaş* connotes second-class status for my interlocutors, one with which they voice chronic dissatisfaction. "Why am I *soydaş*?"
İsmigül would protest, when we met for coffee during one of my return visits
to the field and three years after acquiring the citizenship she had coveted and
pursued for more than a decade. "Why are we still called *soydaş*? I just want
to be a citizen—period."

By placing the focus on those who have more-privileged access to belonging, I have sought to demonstrate that even at the top echelons of the hierarchy of otherness, a distinction from unmarked belonging cannot be entirely
avoided. The status of *soydaş* thus embodies the paradoxes of hope: for the
relatively privileged Bulgaristanlı, it contains both the promises of legalization and the boundaries of belonging. While *soydaş* status incites hope for inclusion, it nonetheless retains a residual distinction from the norm and exposes the limits of the notion of putative sameness.

The term *soydaş* carries far more inclusive political and symbolic power
in Turkey than the term "minority"—a term that justifiably induces misgiv-
ing and fear among Turkey's dispossessed citizens. But in a national context
where, as Kabir Tambar (2016) has pithily put it, the designation of minority

"functions more often as an accusation hurled at socially vulnerable populations than as a strictly legal-bureaucratic category for allocating resources or
ensuring communal rights" (36), even the category of *soydaş* subtly reinstates
a distance from unmarked belonging.

Soydaş, therefore, is a legal and cultural term that the Bulgaristanlı migrants only reluctantly appropriate. Such strategic but uneasy appropriations
reveal the hegemonic grammar of racialized citizenship in Turkey. They attest
to the poverty of multicultural rights even from the point of view of the relatively privileged as well as to the lethal pervasiveness of an ethnoreligious nationalism that aspires to the myth of a unified, homogeneous body of people.

2   ENTITLED HOPE

WHEN HIS FRIEND AND BIOGRAPHER Max Brod asked Franz Kafka whether Kafka still thought that the universe allows for the possibility of hope, a question that Brod posed in response to Kafka's request to have all of his writings destroyed upon his death, Kafka is said to have replied, "Oh no, there is indeed hope, endless hope, just not for us" (Benjamin 1968, 118). When I asked Nebaniye Hanım, a Bulgaristanlı migrant in her fifties who was trying to legalize her status after having left Shumen, Bulgaria, and worked undocumented as a domestic for ten years in Turkey, whether she thought there was any hope, she replied, "People from Georgia, or Uzbekistan, or Africa have no hope of a *kimlik* card, but, well, we do."

Kafka seems to have taunted his biographer's queries by surrendering hope to a realm that may possibly rest beyond the worldly but lies emphatically outside the prevailing human condition. Nebaniye Hanım wanted to challenge any insinuation of a lack of hope in my question by reclaiming hope with a less lofty and far more mundane and pragmatic orientation, one in which hope was linked to a specific object, the identity card. It was her firm hope of its possibility and her prerogative in pursuing it that kept her going in her struggle. *Kimlik*, translated literally as "identity," is the main identity document in Turkey. It serves as proof of citizenship, and everyone is expected to carry it at all times.

When I posed the question to Nebaniye, we were in line at the Foreigners' Branch to have her "days counted"—that is, to find out if her days in residence in Turkey would add up to two uninterrupted years. Under the grace period provided by Citizenship Law No. 5901/2009, "those of Turkish descent" could still apply for citizenship after two years of continuous residence instead of the five required for all other migrants.[1] Although Nebaniye, like Kafka, distinguished an "us" from a presumed "rest" in assessing the distribution of hope, she claimed her place as being squarely among the recipients of hope, contrasting her position to those of other undocumented migrants who are marked by the absence of the hook that Nebaniye had on citizenship through her claim to racial kinship.

Unlike the hope abandoned by Kafka—a Calvinist strand of theological hope vigilantly safeguarded in order to cope with the eschatological uncertainty of redemption—the hope that permeates this book is very much grounded in the worldly, the material, and, even more narrowly, the legal. Nebaniye's stipulation of her position in the distribution of hope assumes a degree of privilege that gives rise to what I call *entitled hope*, which validates the quest of Nebaniye and other Bulgaristanlı migrants for legal inclusion. While chapter 1 accounted for the historical and legal conditions of possibility on which the relative privilege of the Bulgaristanlı migrants rests, this chapter describes the kind of entitled hope that such relative privilege produces.

IN OR OUT OF THE NETWORK OF HOPE?

In an interview with Dimitris Papadopoulos, Ghassan Hage (Hage and Papadopoulos 2004) powerfully argued that when it was still more or less confined to the nation-state, capitalism monopolized the ideological content of social hope in such a way that hope became synonymous with "dreams of upward social mobility, higher purchasing power" (109). While nation-state capitalism thus delimited the range of hope, it was still comprehensive in its scope: virtually everyone was included in its distributive network. Hage, of course, does not claim that people had equal access to upward mobility; he instead suggests that they had relatively equal access to the *hope* of upward mobility. But the new, transnational stage of capitalism is differentiated by a "shrinkage of the distributional network of hope" (107). More people are excluded from the network and perceive themselves as such.

The legalization quest of ethnically Turkish labor migrants from Bulgaria may be told from this compelling perspective as the story of a particular group of transnational migrants—without papers yet with a claim to belonging through their racial kinship—who are trying to convince a particular nation-state that they are still entitled to their place in its distributional network of hope. They are unlike "people from Georgia, or Uzbekistan, or Africa," as Nebaniye lists those "other migrants." They are unlike, one might add, the nearly five million other undocumented migrants in Turkey hailing from countries such as Afghanistan, Iraq, and most recently Syria. The Bulgaristanlı migrants have a structurally more privileged position, given the historical and cultural legacy of their *soydaş* status and its abiding reach in contemporary law.

Nebaniye was able to consider applying for citizenship in the first place by claiming Turkish origins. One of the key documents for the application is a *soy belgesi* (document of origins), which is similar to a birth certificate. Usually obtained from the official representative in one's village in Bulgaria or from municipal records, this document specifies the person's birthplace and parental names. The lineage/race, or *soy*, is proven simply by having parents who have Turkish Muslim names. This specific instrument of proof gains a certain complexity if the applicant has a Bulgarian-Slavic name and did not change it back to the original after the assimilation campaign in Bulgaria. In some cases, the person may have reclaimed the Turkish name, but switched back yet again to the imposed Bulgarian name if using a Turkish name continued to elicit discrimination. Still, Turkish officials will usually consider parents or grandparents with Turkish Muslim names to be adequate proof of the applicant's claim to racial kinship.

I have already shown that while the Turkish nation-state no longer embraces these migrants from the Balkans as unconditionally as it did up until 1990, the law still retains the possibility of citizenship for the Bulgaristanlı. This is because the definition of a migrant as someone who is of Turkish origin is kept intact in Settlement Law No. 5543/2006. Furthermore, despite the dwindling of the effusive welcome that migrants from the Balkans were historically privy to, a significant way in which being of Turkish origin has continued to translate into legal advantage for the ethnically Turkish migrants from Bulgaria has been through routine amnesties that waive their months of overstay and temporarily legalize their status. Although there have been occasional cases of such amnesties for other groups—one for the Ahıska Turks of the Republic of Georgia in 2009 and for the Uyghur Turks from China and Central Asia in 2017—Bulgaristanlı migrants are the only undocumented migrant group in Turkey to have been systematically granted amnesties since 2000.

In addition to these formal mechanisms through which being of Turkish origin provides legal leverage, there are informal ways in which claiming Turkishness eases the anxieties of undocumented status. Migrants from Africa or women from the former Soviet Union countries, including Moldova and Ukraine, whose inhabitants "look Russian," are far more likely to be selected for inspection and detained, for reasons of racial and gendered profiling, including the suspicion of sex work. But migrants who can present themselves as *soydaş* are able to get away if accosted by police for an identity check even if their residence papers have expired, though sometimes they must pay a bribe. As we shall shortly see, though most other undocumented migrants in Turkey avoid police stations at all costs because of (justified) fear of deportation and physical abuse, Bulgaristanlı migrants with undocumented status are allowed to walk away even after voluntarily entering a police station to plead for legalization.

This chapter considers how the predicament of being neither firmly in nor decisively out of the network of hope in belonging to a nation-state results in ways of hoping not against the odds but with them. Instead of viewing hope as an overarching category of analysis or experience, I seek to lend specificity to hope by demonstrating how it is inflected through degrees of privilege. I ask in this chapter and the next how the hope of belonging for ethnically Turkish migrants can be distinguished from the hope (or hopelessness) that may be nourished by other undocumented migrants in Turkey who lack the advantage of a claim to racial kinship.[2] I have challenged a monolithic understanding of hope by historicizing in chapter 1 how migration bureaucracies and laws variegate and structure experiences of hope with criteria of differentiation that withhold access to some and promise it to others. This chapter, in turn, delves into the affective aspects of the distribution of hope. Digging deeper into what Hage has captured so well in terms of the more quantitative aspect of hope and its differential distribution, I probe here the qualitative grammar of hope. I base my analysis not only on utterances such as Nebaniye's, which explicitly demarcate those who can invest in hope of legalization and those who cannot, but also on embodied acts as they are performed during legal and bureaucratic encounters. Thus I develop the notion of "entitled hope." On its affective spectrum, entitled hope oscillates between confidence and anxiety, between expectation and doubt. In its institutional underpinnings, entitled hope is firmly rooted in and relies on legal and historical structures of relative privilege.

HOPE, EXPECTATION, AND ENTITLEMENT

According to the famous formulation by the philosopher Isabelle Stengers (2002), hope is "the difference between possibility and probability" (245). In other words, if we hope for what is probable, it ceases to be hope and turns into expectation. For other philosophers, too, hope seems to have been tied up with probability assessments; but unlike Stengers's dyadic formulation, it is usually placed on a spectrum of probability, with no lower boundary specified as a requirement for hoping.[3] I explore the implications of this investment in the possibility/probability distinction for the politics of hope and hope as political category in the conclusion, "Troubling Hope." Here I stay at the more elemental level of definitional clarity. I am particularly interested in the upper bound of probability: (How) can we determine exactly when hope ceases to be hope and turns into expectation or confidence? What qualifies as (too) probable to then disqualify that feeling or affect from being hope? And more broadly, what is the analytic investment in enforcing a strict boundary between the possible and the probable?

The emphasis on the possibility/probability distinction when it comes to migrant hope seems to derive in part from the twenty-first-century predicament of the intensified global movement of people. News articles, human rights reports, and popular discourse abound on the miserable conditions of migrants around the world, documenting the journeys of people who risk perilous, often fatal border crossings in flimsy and overcrowded inflatable boats or airless truck containers. The dominant trope to depict the plight of these migrants is one of hope against hope. And it is certainly the case that migration, that very basic right to freedom of movement, has become, in a world designated as global and connected, a major cause of death, irreparable physical and psychological wounds, and struggle for survival in undignified conditions.

My contention is with this dominant trope that frames hope exclusively as hope against hope. Such a framing leaves little room to the predicament of those migrants whose hopes are distinguished by the likelihood, but not the certainty, of attaining legalization. Tracking the hope of Bulgaristanlı migrants as it is expressed and performed in migrants' encounters with the law and bureaucracy renders less clear the distinction between hope and expectation[4] as well as the strict assignment, à la Stengers, of possibility to the former and probability to the latter. Though they live or work without the required papers sometimes for years on end, the post-1990 Bulgaristanlı migrants are not the most vulnerable group within the broader migrant landscape in Turkey. Instead, they have a reasonable expectation that they will fare better than other migrants. The hope entertained by Bulgaristanlı migrants is therefore not the miraculous hope based on patient waiting that Simon Turner (2014) finds to be characteristic of clandestine Burundian refugees in Nairobi. Nor does the hope I describe lead to the "paralyzing hope" that Vincent Crapanzano (2003, 18) diagnoses among white South Africans during the last years of apartheid: "One hopes—one waits—passively for hope's object to occur, knowing realistically that its occurrence is unlikely, even more so because one does nothing to bring it about" (18).

Instead, the hope entertained by the Bulgaristanlı migrants echoes a different lineage of thinking about hope that locates its kernel in rationality and attainability. Indeed, not all considerations of hope draw the line in exclusive terms between possibility and probability or between hope and expectation. The Oxford dictionary definition calls hope "a feeling of expectation and desire for a particular thing to happen."[5] And for an earlier host of thinkers, from Aristotle to Hobbes, the emphasis on the rational aspect of hope and on the attainability of hope's object was accentuated too strongly to sustain such a clear gap between possibility and probability. The rational emphasis in the philosophy of hope may be traced to René Descartes ([1649] 1985), who saw hope as a form of confidence, even if a weak form of confidence that involved a belief in the likelihood even if not the certainty of a hoped-for outcome (389). While Thomas Hobbes ([1651] 1998) identified hope as an appetite, he also qualified that designation by calling it a complex passion, one dominated not just by sensation but also by thinking. In Hobbes's own evocative phrasing, which juxtaposes passion with thought, hope is an "appetite with an opinion of obtaining" (36, I.VI.14). In fact, in contradistinction to the recent turn that distinguishes between hope and expectation, Hobbes seems to have used the terms interchangeably.

And while theological hope is often relegated to the realm of the nonrational, certain strands of the theological tradition are not necessarily at odds with the rationalist thinking on hope.[6] Most notably, the thirteenth-century Dominican priest and theologian Thomas Aquinas defined hope as "a movement of appetite aroused by the perception of what is agreeable, future, arduous, and possible of attainment" (cited in Day 1991, 27). According to Romanus Cessario's elaboration of Thomas Aquinas, even as one can classify something as within the realm of hope only if the future object involves some difficulty, it is also the case that "only something that is attainable elicits hope; a person must judge that the hoped-for reality lies within the realm of possible options" (Cessario 2002, 232–33). In his *Summa Theologica*, in reply to a hypothetical objection that hope is not a theological virtue, Aquinas writes: "Hope has no mean or extremes, as regards its principal objects, since it is impossible to trust too much in the Divine assistance; yet it may have a mean and extremes, as regards those things a man trusts to obtain, in so far as he either presumes above his capability, or despairs of things of which he is capable" (quoted in Kaczor 2008, 92–93). The first would be the vice of presumption; the second would be the vice of despair. Aquinas also states his agreement with his contemporary Peter Lombard that "hope is the certain *expectation* of future happiness" (emphasis mine). Aquinas's focus on attainability and expectation would thus seem to diminish the gap between possibility and probability.

Several centuries later, this time from a secular perspective, Durkheim, too, would explain hope in empirical and rational terms, namely, as evidence of the "relative bounty of life" ([1893] 1960, 267). With a similar proclivity for foregrounding probability and likelihood as being constitutive of hope, in *The Division of Labor* [1893] (2014) Durkheim brings into critical conversation the optimistic and pessimistic perspectives. His rendition of the pessimist position is that the latter views hope to be an illusion: "If, in spite of the disappointments of experience, we still cling to life, it is because we hope vainly that the future will redeem the past" (192). According to the pessimist, hope charms to intoxicate so that we are barred from seeing the bare reality of suffering that pervades experience; instead we delude ourselves with hope's empty promise of compensation for past disappointment with some future well-being. But Durkheim contests the very empirical grounds of the pessimist's charge that hope is merely a rosy distortion of facts. For him, hope exists not because it is cultivated in the absence of fortune or as a shield against misfortune. It is not merely the optimist's lack of courage and acumen to confront the brute reality of misfortune. Rather, hope exists because we have enough recollections of well-being and moments of fortune based on our past experience to cultivate hope as a collective sentiment. It flourishes in the human species because of the experience and persistence of life's "relative bounty":

[Hope] has not miraculously fallen from heaven into our hearts, but must have, like all the sentiments, been formed under the influence of the facts. Thus if men have learnt to hope, if under blows of misfortune, they have grown accustomed to turn their gaze toward the future and to expect compensation for their present suffering, it is because they have perceived that such compensation occurred frequently, that the human organism was both too flexible and too resisting to be easily brought down, that the moments when misfortune gained the day were exceptional and that generally the balance ended up by being re-established. (192)

As resonant as Durkheim's depiction of hope as a sentiment learned over time and through experience is with viewing hope as a collective structure of feeling, his generalization of the existence of relative bounty to the entire human condition is premised upon his ultimately conservative vision of society. Except for those extraordinary periods of unusual suffering or misfortune, which in turn cause anomie and, Durkheim ([1897] 1966) posits, a spike in suicides, he views such moments of crisis as exceptional experiences that can be corrected by restoring the ideal division of labor based on organic solidarity that befits stratified societies. Ultimately, however, the fact that he can assume the existence of relative bounty attests to Durkheim's lack of critical concern for the existence of (class) inequality that routinely hampers the experience of relative bounty for all.

While Durkheim's attempt to salvage hope from the pessimist's accusation of being merely chimerical inspires my attempt to examine the hope cultivated by Bulgaristanlı migrants, I part ways with Durkheim in his key assumption that such hope based on relative bounty is available to everyone. Following Hage's attention to the differential distribution of hope instead, I would suggest that what Durkheim generalizes as a blanket category of experience is in fact only one form of hope. I call this *entitled hope*, a hope that is available to those who already have a certain access to "relative bounty" and, more specifically to my case at hand, those who have ethnic privilege.

A collective structure of feeling, as Raymond Williams mapped it out (1977), probes the "complex relation of differentiated structures of feeling to differentiated classes" (134). Williams's Marxist focus on the complex relation between feelings and class difference sheds light also on how hope as a collective structure of feeling varies in relation to legally and culturally differentiated migrant groups. My aim, then, is not to establish the truer meaning and experience of hope, but to bring into view (also) the hope that is intimately related to expectations that arise from relatively privileged positions for hoping.

A KILLING AND AN ADMONITION

Two migrants move through the same legal space—an Istanbul police station—on different days, at different paces, and with different expectations. In 2007, an undocumented migrant was taken to the police station in the central district of Beyoğlu and later died. An aspiring footballer from Nigeria, known as Festus Okey, was taken into custody after arousing suspicion for walking in his neighborhood after midnight. During his interrogation, Festus was killed by a bullet fired from the gun of the officer interrogating him.[7] Along with two hundred other activists gathered under the rubric of the Migrant Solidarity Network who followed the hearing, I had access to what transpired during that murderous encounter only through court records.

In 2011, another undocumented migrant entered another central police station, this time in Beşiktaş, and received only a paternalistic warning. Nurcan, an undocumented Turkish woman from Bulgaria, insisted on meeting with a police officer because she hoped that he would legalize her status. Once her status of having overstayed her visa was ascertained by the officer, he paternalistically scolded her and advised her to leave the country after paying her fines. I had access to the details of this second case as part of my ethnographic fieldwork.

How is it that one undocumented migrant is arrested for arousing suspicion by walking at night and later killed during his interrogation while another undocumented migrant is given the benefit of the doubt and can walk out of the police station unscathed? In addressing this seeming conundrum, it is necessary to note that in the absence of ethnographic access to the murder scene, my "thin" interpretation of the murder of Festus Okey is primarily based on a reading of the court records and my attendance at trial hearings as a member of the Migrant Solidarity Network, an activist group that revived what had become a stalled case. The absent, murdered body of Festus Okey haunts and informs the encounter that took place at a different police station to which I had ethnographic access and which, in turn, constitutes a "thick" description of anxiety, expectation, and risk-taking.

There is another potential methodological quandary: Festus's own grammar of hope is beyond reach. I thus make no claim to characterizing the kind of hope held by Festus or the other undocumented migrants I came to know through my activism with the Migrant Solidarity Network.[8] However, the way in which I frame the distinctiveness of hope as a collective feeling among the Bulgaristanlı migrants is facilitated by encounters with other undocumented migrants in Turkey and the systematic police violence perpetrated against them. Without laying the same claim to ethnographic intimacy and thick description, therefore, my analysis of the structural vulnerability of Festus Okey and other undocumented migrants who do not have the relative privilege of racial kinship aims to make explicit the comparative frame in which I situate Bulgaristanlı migrants' hope.[9]

ENTITLED HOPE AT THE POLICE STATION

In December 2011, I met Nurcan and two of her friends in front of the Beşiktaş police station in Istanbul. Nurcan had arrived from Bulgaria's Silistra region four years before and had been employed as a domestic worker ever since. At the time we met, her visa had been expired since the previous year. However, her hope for an amnesty that would legalize her status had not faltered. Such temporary amnesties have been granted to Bulgarian Turkish migrants every other year since 2001, and Nurcan had already taken advantage of the 2009 amnesty that had annulled her previous overstay and provided her with a three-month temporary residence permit.

Nurcan was particularly excited that day. She had heard that an amnesty for Bulgaristanlı Turks was once again in the works. I, on the other hand, was incredulous; no such news had traveled through the migrant grapevine, as news usually did. To add to my misgivings, Nurcan's source was the employer of one of the two friends present, Hoşgül, who had also migrated from Silistra. My understanding of Hoşgül's account was that her employer had come across a notification regarding a procedural change on the Foreigners' Branch section of the Istanbul Police Department website: from that date on, one would be able to apply for a residence permit at the local police station instead of having to make the trip to the central Foreigners' Branch. But Nurcan and her two friends believed that this announcement was the harbinger of another amnesty specifically for the Bulgaristanlı.

When I could not convince them of my own interpretation, I began to plead that the police station was a dangerous place for an undocumented migrant. The memory of the unresolved lawsuit against the police officer who had shot Festus Okey was still all too vivid. I repeatedly explained that my presence would be no help if something went wrong. But Nurcan was adamant about keeping the appointment. And Hoşgül simply said, "Oh, come on, just relax!" Only the third friend present, Emine, was cautious: she said there was no way she was going in and risking it today. The police had come to her home just one week earlier, and she had imprudently opened the door. When the authorities discovered that she had overstayed her visa, she had been told to leave the country immediately, but was not taken into custody, as might easily have been the case.[10] That day, as reluctant as Emine herself was to go in, she kept encouraging her friends and prodding them toward the entrance of the police station. She almost seemed disappointed that she would have to remain behind. When Hoşgül insisted once again that Emine join us, she hesitated, and then said no. At the time, I thought that Emine's was the only levelheaded response and that Hoşgül and Nurcan were throwing caution to the wind.

The three of us—Hoşgül, Nurcan, and I—walked through security and approached the head officer. Nurcan demurely showed him the appointment slip. I was nervous as I introduced myself as a friend of Nurcan's and a professor researching the legalization difficulties faced by Bulgarian Turkish migrants. Hoşgül, meanwhile, appeared as carefree as a guest at a tea party. When asked for her slip, she executed a flirtatiously indifferent shrug. "Oh, I don't have one. I am simply taking advantage of her appointment." "And what is your situation?" the officer asked. "Exactly the same as hers," Hoşgül replied. "But first I want to see what will happen to her. If all seems to be going well, I will explain my case."

The officer responded to her irreverent style with a joke veiled as a threat—or perhaps the other way around, given the ambiguity that police officers seem to be so skilled at manipulating: "So, then, who knows? Perhaps we will arrest you in the end." As Hoşgül replied with a giggle and went on to make herself comfortable in a chair, crossing one leg over the other, Nurcan handed over her paper with what I could see was a shaky hand. "Wrong appointment slip," the officer said. "This states that you are working as a domestic." In fact, the online interview form did not offer a category that Nurcan could have checked off, given her illegal status. The officer did not dwell on this. Turning to his computer monitor, he proceeded to review every statement issued over the past decade that might pertain to Nurcan's situation. After nearly ten drawn-out minutes of silence interrupted only by the officer's monosyllabic responses of surprise at what he was viewing on his screen, he sighed and reached the conclusion that we all knew too well: Nurcan had been staying illegally in Turkey for nearly a year now.

"But isn't there anything, anything we can do?" asked Nurcan, her voice tremulous yet insistent. The police officer reached for the phone and dialed. "Chief, I have a Bulgarian national here. Her most recent entry is 29/12/2009. She has overstayed by twelve months. What shall we do? Hmm, yes. Yes, of course, of course. Transient stay conditional on exit, right . . . And is she going to pay fines at the airport then?" Hoşgül, who had managed to keep quiet during that brief interval, pounced on his ignorance: "What airport are you talking about, officer? We travel by bus!" Meanwhile, Nurcan's trembling had extended to the rest of her body. We kept exchanging glances, and I tried to cast my most reassuring look her way, although I too was becoming fearful. Despite this so far hospitable reception, she was, after all, subject to detention and deportation.

The officer hung up and addressed Nurcan firmly: "Get your exit card immediately and pay your fees so that you won't have a headache. Otherwise you will be banned indefinitely. But if you do what I say, you will only be blocked temporarily. Now, you have come today accompanied by"—and nodding to me, he used the customary deferential word for teacher—"*hocam*, and I will not arrest you in front of her." His voice then softened: "I know that you are victims, too. Just this once, I'll set aside my identity as a police officer." His tone became firm again. "But, if you do not take the proper steps, the next time I see you on the street, I'll take you into custody, understand?" Hoşgül let out an exaggerated, playful "Aaaaggh," drawing the officer's attention to her. "Hey, listen to me, the same holds true for you, so watch it," he told her. Nurcan, who had not yet uttered a word, shakily approached his desk and started to plead: "I just had an operation. I have no one here. I am *soydaş*. I have a daughter in Bulgaria." The police officer was gentle again: "I know, I know. I am not saying this to you personally. But this is my job. Go to your village, go to your daughter. Otherwise, you will be sitting on a thorn. Make your exit, then come back. And then apply for citizenship here."

THE REALM OF ATTAINABILITY

My futile attempt to advise Nurcan and Hoşgül against walking into the police station given their legal status was driven by my mistrust of the police and the workings of the law in Turkey. This incredulousness was reinforced by four years of activist work with the Migrant Solidarity Network, during which I witnessed how a small group of extremely dedicated refugee advocates in Turkey carried out their work in the near absence of any coherent body of legislation on migrants and in the face of the systematic human rights violations that never made it to the news.[11] I learned of routine detentions with no trial, explanation of procedure, or access to a lawyer,[12] as well as less frequent but more dramatic violations. In one particularly chilling incident, asylum seekers in an eastern border city in Turkey were told to gather in the main public school courtyard to be given supplies but were then forced onto buses that headed for the nearest border to "dump" them on the other side.[13]

Exposure to systematic bias and arbitrary police violence results in most undocumented migrants' diligently avoiding law enforcement, even when they have been the victims of assault or abuse. For example, a group of young men from Congo who got in touch with the Migrant Solidarity Network were bullied, insulted, and threatened by other residents who wanted them out of the neighborhood because they were black. These young men, each of whom was just over eighteen, had aged out of the state orphanage that was required to provide shelter to them as unaccompanied minors but had no obligation to them once they turned eighteen. There are no provisions for unaccompanied minors to ease the transition into an independent life outside of the state orphanages. Each of the young men had standing applications for refugee status with the UNHCR, and yet they still refused to call the police for fear of endangering those applications or being exposed to further mistreatment. In another instance, a group of Ugandan women had to explain several times in a solidarity meeting attended by feminist groups why they could not file complaints with the police even in cases of harassment or rape by their employers—regular occurrences for African women working in textile ateliers in Istanbul—for fear of deportation or sexual abuse at the hands of the police. Solidarity and advocacy alone could not overcome justified fear. In yet another instance of police abuse, we watched helplessly as an undocumented domestic worker from Turkmenistan withdrew the complaint that she had prepared with the assistance of feminist lawyers against the police officer who had stopped her to ask for documents and then had taken her to a private residence and raped her. She "chose" deportation instead.[14]

My familiarity with the daily violence and danger that undocumented migrants face as they navigate their lives in Turkey, a familiarity gleaned from activist work, influenced my reaction as an ethnographer to Nurcan's insistence that we walk into that police station. Having spent a decade of activism and scholarly research on exposure of women from various backgrounds to new reproductive technologies, Rayna Rapp (2000) describes "how methodology bleeds into daily life" (1) in ways that made it hard to separate her sometimes disparate, sometimes congruent commitments as feminist activist, anthropologist, and friend. I find Rapp's metaphor especially apt because it captures the inevitable connectedness and lack of control over such multiple commitments that the intimacy of the ethnographic encounter both benefits from and puts to the test.

When the ethnographic encounter I describe here took place, the bleeding of activist experience into ethnographic participant observation obscured rather than illuminated. I hastily assumed that Nurcan was acting on false hope without distinguishing between the structural predicaments of migrants positioned differently along the spectrum of formal and informal privilege. I perceived Nurcan and Hoşgül as being unable to recognize the limits of legal possibility because they obstinately refused to see that the realm of the possible was incompatible with their own hope. However, my understanding and appreciation of Nurcan's venture was radically reconfigured over the course of fieldwork and the retrospective space provided by the gap between the experience and the time of inscription.[15] I came to understand that by walking into that police station undocumented and taking a shot at legalization, Nurcan had a far more sophisticated assessment of risk and hope than I did at the time.

"I am *soydaş*." This plea, which I heard from so many of my interlocutors and to which Nurcan resorted in addressing the police officer at a critical moment when things appeared to veer in a more dangerous direction with the vague threat of arrest, exemplifies the structural conditions of possibility on which the rest of Nurcan's performance rests. The appeal may be laden less with ethnonationalist sentiment and more with legal pragmatism. However, the status of *soydaş*, that is, being of Turkish culture and descent, has historically qualified migrants for inclusion in the Turkish nation. This history of relative privilege resonated in Nurcan's immediate lifeworld. One of her great-aunts left Bulgaria in 1950 after the collectivization of land under communism and gained citizenship upon arrival in Turkey in addition to receiving property under the legal category of *iskanlı göçmen* (migrant to be settled with property). Nurcan also had a distant cousin who left Bulgaria in 1989 following Todor Zhivkov's infamous assimilation campaign against the

Turkish minority. She, too, was granted citizenship along with the more than 300,000 migrants who constituted the last big exodus from Bulgaria. Nurcan often evoked this distant cousin and her great-aunt in our conversations as proof of the likelihood of attaining citizenship.

Nurcan was also well aware that as a post-1990 labor migrant, she did not carry the same political cachet of earlier migrants, such as her cousin, whose migration was hailed by Turkey's anti-Communist, NATO-allied state tradition as an honorable flight from Communist persecution. Nor did being a post-1990 migrant have the same prestige as her great-aunt who had migrated in the fifties, when *soydaş* were still considered the most desirable prospective citizens of the Turkish nation.

Yet, even as the historically privileged reception of Turkish immigrants from Bulgaria has somewhat declined, and even as Nurcan and the other post-1990 migrants from Bulgaria are increasingly viewed as labor migrants, Nurcan has been privy to glimpses of remaining privilege. She knew from her migrant friends that periodic amnesties in the form of three-month or six-month temporary, nonrenewable residency permits had been granted in 2001, 2005, and 2007. And Nurcan herself took advantage of the three-month amnesty offered in February 2009 and in July of the same year, receiving yet another three-month permit.[16] These amnesties allowed her to keep her residency status even as she worked without a permit. She also knew of a friend of a friend who had "won the lottery," as she liked to joke: her friend was among the nine hundred people who found themselves on a mysterious one-year renewable residence permit list. There was no official explanation as to who had made it to this list of nine hundred, but the Balkan Turks Solidarity Association victoriously claimed the list as the outcome of its hard advocacy work on behalf of Bulgaristanlı who had placed petitions through the association.[17]

From the great-aunt to the distant cousin to the friend of a friend, Nurcan's repertoire thus included stories of privileged access to citizenship or, short of citizenship, exceptional access to legalization, however temporary or tenuous the latter may have been. Even as Nurcan's circumstances differed from those of the previous waves of migrants from Bulgaria, she could still claim the overarching and still legally privileged *soydaş* distinction. She shared the collective sensibility that assures of the benevolence of the Turkish state toward the Bulgaristanlı, even though the benevolence has been more erratic since 1990. If amnesties are made routine and exceptions legalized, and if there are exceptions even to the exceptions for the Bulgaristanlı—

such as the list of nine hundred people to be granted renewable residence permits—it does indeed seem reasonable to ask a police officer whether the vague announcement on the police department's website might be a promise of legalization and to assume that one has a certain bargaining power with the police.

In fact, reason is precisely what Terry Eagleton (2015) finds to be constitutive of *authentic hope*. In contrast to optimism, which is based on self-delusional or false hope, authentic hope "needs to be underpinned by reasons" (3). While steering clear of the designation "authentic," with its attendant assumption that there is a universal, contextual, and timeless structure of hope that one could somehow pin down, I follow Eagleton's positing of the presence of reason as a prerequisite for hope to capture the sense of hope that Nurcan acted on that day. Far from a false hope that courted her own deportation, or what Erik Erikson has called "maladaptive optimism"[18] that failed to discern the limits of state benevolence, the hope that propelled Nurcan and Hoşgül to walk into that police station despite my pleas hinged on a hope based on a rational calculation of risk. It was the kind of hope, to recall the Hobbesian genealogy of hope again, marked by "an appetite with the opinion of attaining."

Such hope based on reasonable expectation stands in stark contrast to the hope described by Simon Turner (2014) as characteristic of clandestine Burundian refugees in Nairobi. Distinguishing open-ended hope from goal-oriented hope, Turner argues that the very uncertainty and indeterminacy that saturate the lives of these city refugees make room for open-ended hope that is not directed at a specific object but is instead a matter of being patient, waiting—even "waiting for miracles" (181)—and "accept[ing] one's life en route" (176). According to Turner, this does not necessarily involve placing one's trust in God but certainly requires trusting in someone else's agency.

Instead of such agency-deferring waiting, Sevcihan, who was originally from Razgrad and had been working in Istanbul as a nanny for three years, actively pursued amnesties in the hope of permanent legalization. She had kept her status as regular as possible by exiting and re-entering Turkey in accordance with her visa expiration dates as well as by taking advantage of the amnesties offered since her arrival. In 2009, she had just missed the application deadline for an amnesty for a three-month residency permit. As she shuttled back and forth between the migrant association and the police station on her day off and tried to make sense of the vague explanations she was given as to whether she was eligible for this particular amnesty, she ended up misplacing the petition the migrant association had written on her behalf. She knew she would not be able to get permission from her employer for another trip to the police station because it would mean yet another day off from work. She was frustrated but not devastated. "Oh, well," she told me, "we will just wait for the next amnesty." Bulgaristanlı migrants did not have to wait for miracles. They waited for the next amnesty, because they could. Similarly, Nurcan's friend Hoşgül, who took matters into her own hands by walking into the police station that day, told me with obvious pride on another occasion, "I have been undocumented on and off for eleven years now. I have never paid fines [for overstaying]! I simply wait for my amnesty."

Even the willingness of the officer at the police station to take the time to judiciously go through each decree passed since 2000 rests on the possibility that there will be some attenuating regulation that applies to Nurcan and Hoşgül as undocumented migrants who are *soydaş*. When he failed to find anything that might be applicable, he told them to pay their fines, exit, and return to apply for citizenship, relying on a similar sense of possibility. When he made that recommendation, there was no path to citizenship beyond the exceptional acquisition clause. However, within a year, a new decree would indeed make it possible for all Bulgaristanlı migrants with undocumented status to apply for citizenship under a temporary amnesty. I doubt the officer had any concrete information about the forthcoming decree, but he would not have presumed its likelihood for a person from "Georgia, or Uzbekistan, or Africa."

As different as their behavior was—Nurcan cautiously timid, Hoşgül hyperbolically outgoing—they were feeding off of each other's hope that there would be a new development that might help them normalize their status. Nurcan could not help shuddering as she walked into the police station. But she also held on to hope cultivated on the basis of the collective historical knowledge of a legal system that delivers to *soydaş* certain privileges and hope sustained by the shorter-term memory of amnesties. And if they walked out without the exact gain hoped for, it was also without much damage done.

DAMAGE

Just one month after my visit to the police station with Nurcan, I found myself in court attending the ninth hearing of the police officer charged with the murder of Festus Okey. The trial had been outrageously mismanaged: The officer charged with the murder remained on duty. Key missing evidence was not pursued. The cameras in the interrogation room at the time of the shooting were said to have been broken. The bloodstained shirt, a critical piece of evidence that would have allowed an expert to determine the distance and direction of the bullet, was "lost" at the hospital. The hearing concluded with yet another postponement: the jury had decided to keep waiting for documents from Nigeria that would certify the victim's identity. The only novelty was that close to two hundred activists, lawyers, and academics were now charged with libel and attempting to influence the due course of justice because of the petitions we submitted to become a party to the case.[19]

An earlier testimony of the officer charged with murder, which I was able to view thanks to one of the lawyers from the Contemporary Lawyers Association[20] who had obtained transcripts of the previous sessions of the trial, read:

> I was the team captain and we were conducting an investigation on drug trafficking. Black persons and citizens who come from the east attract more attention when it comes to drugs. We headed toward Tarlabaşı with this goal in mind and spotted two black persons ahead of us as we approached the [Sakız Ağacı] street traffic lights. I stared into the face of the two black citizens as we were cruising. The one walking in front, the one who died, put his hand in his pocket, acting in an uneasy manner. I said, "Okay, guys. Let's check this out."

"The one walking in front, the one who died." Walking one minute, dead the next. The haste in the discursive transition in the officer's testimony relies on the absent subject (the victim) to race past the killing and the killer. It also betrays something of the experiential speed with which the walking body can become the dead body. Unlike any of my undocumented but ethnically Turkish interlocutors, Festus Okey could not have counted on preferential treatment. Though he had registered with the UNHCR as an asylum applicant, the court refused to acknowledge that document as proof of his identity. This refusal was also the key justification for stalling the case for three years. "Documents can never stand completely alone. They always refer back to an 'originary person,'" Tobias Kelly writes (2006, 92); despite their veneer of officialness, documents are never entirely trusted. The Turkish court conveniently resorted to this mistrust in denying recognition of a UNHCR document. But documents refer back to an original person in another, more corporeal sense, according to Kelly: "Legal and physical aspects of personhood are brought back together as the indeterminacies of legal documents penetrate into the private lives of the people who hold them. People wear their documents on their bodies, due to the apprehensions they produce" (92).

"He acted in an uneasy manner," the officer had testified. What gesture communicated that apprehension? Was it an evasive backward glance at the police car as Festus started walking faster? Was it a sudden hunching of the shoulders to defend himself at the prospect of an unwanted encounter with the law? What could have transmitted an affect strong enough to attract unwanted attention, an investigation, and, subsequently, a killing? Given the lack of access to the scene and given that the testimony was tenuous evidence at best, should we disregard entirely the legal document as an unreliable source?

There are multiple layers of ambiguity with regard to the affect that has been coded as "unease" in a legal document. If ethnographic knowledge relies foremost on observations of bodily enactments and expressions articulated by one's interlocutors, how can we assume the existence of unease without having been present at the scene? But the methodological problem does not end here. Even if one were a participant observer at the scene of arrest, how would one have corroborated "unease"? Does the other encounter with a police officer that I depict, one that benefits from ethnographic presence, rely on more solid ground in terms of my ability to claim anxiety-ridden hope on the part of Nurcan? How can the ethnographer claim to understand the affect experienced or exuded by others even if she is present at the scene of action? These questions go to the heart of the epistemological difficulties of discerning emotion or affect in the ethnographic encounter.

A heated recent controversy swirls around whether there is a difference between emotion and affect, and if so, what asserting a distinction between the two would entail in terms of methodology and epistemological pathways for further inquiry and, some would suggest, even radically different normative orientations to the world. And within this broader questioning around how to define and discern emotions, what are the definitional criteria and the theoretical implications for thinking about hope as an emotion versus considering it as an affect?[21]

THE AFFECT-EMOTION GAP, OR, A MEASURED CRITIQUE OF AFFECT THEORY

There has been significant contention around parsing the distinction between emotion and affect, with one voluble camp insisting on the need for a strict terminological separation, given what they view as fundamental and irreconcilable distinctions between the two.[22] On this account, emotion is radically different from affect because emotion is sociolinguistically fixed, narrativized, and claimed as personal experience. Affect, on the other hand, is before and even beyond language. It is unnarrativizable and thus beyond individual consciousness to be claimed as one's own experience. To highlight some of the terms ubiquitously used by affect theorists: affect has to do with "intensities," "energies," and "resonances" that "circulate" in collective space and float around bodies, not possessed by any single individual but with an impact on each through creating an interdependent circuit and a particular, palpable "atmosphere."[23] While a few theorists of affect further delimit what they mean by these intensities and energies strictly to neurological responses, such as speeding heart rates, sweating glands, or increased blood flow (see, for example, Damasio 1994), the majority is more liberal in their usage to refer to a wide (and inevitably vague) range of unspoken and unspeakable, inchoate energies, auras, and even spirits. But all seem to concur on the prescient elaboration by Daniel Grossberg that affective states, unlike emotions, "are neither structured narratively nor organized in response to our interpretations of situations" (Grossberg 1992, 81) or Brian Massumi's pithy formulation (1995) that once something is categorized and fixed by language, it is no longer affect. Linda Zerilli (2015) describes the distinguishing characteristic of such insistence on the autonomy of affect as ontology itself, an ontology that claims to radically break with post-structuralism and other related predecessors: "Affect is seen as a distinct layer of experience that is both prior to and beneath the language and intentional consciousness, an irreducibly bodily and autonomic force that shapes, without the subject's awareness, conscious judgment" (286). For those who insist on the autonomy of affect, the analysis of emotion—already contaminated by the fall into language—will never be able to capture the excess layer of experience. Emotions stick, affects slip. Only affect theory, therefore, can strive to get at that pre-discursive layer, that which has not yet been put into language or that which is beyond language altogether (Thrift 2007).

Not all theorists of emotion, and certainly not all anthropologists of emotion, are convinced by this hard distinction between affect as pre-discursive, impersonal intensity versus emotion as subjectivitized feeling and narrativized experience. Their objections range from the definitional and methodological to the implications for the political. The definitional objection is that affect theorists overstate the distinction between emotion and affect. There need not be such absolute untranslatability between the registers of intensity and symbolic mediation. On this account, the term "affect" can be deployed by various analysts of emotion without dispensing with the discursive or the cognitive altogether.[24] This is done either by refusing any irreconcilability between them, such as in Yael Navaro-Yashin's sophisticated synthesis of affect theory with theories of subjectivity,[25] or by conceding, as Sianne Ngai does in her *Ugly Feelings* (2005), a degree in difference but not in kind.[26] Such refusals to make sharp distinctions between emotion and affect are also aptly expressed in William Mazzarella's insistence on addressing both the sensorial and the discursive: "Our use of affect draws on those who have argued for a closer attention to the dual registers through which all life unfolds—through sensuousness as well as discursive ordering, intensity as well as qualification" (2009, 299). These nuanced approaches that refuse to move beyond signification and instead mediate the ever-present tension between language and experience also avoid the irony that besets the radical version of affect theory when it is viewed from a historically contextualized perspective: by favoring a constructivist account in which language and cognition mediate emotion, scholarship in the anthropology of emotions rescues emotion from the monopoly of psychobiology, while affect theory, in its hard version, ends up reinstating the hegemony of the biological and the non-linguistic.

Indeed, I would suggest that Raymond Williams's formulation (1977), "structures of feeling," provided a prescient bridge between emotion and affect before the two would come to be viewed by some as starkly opposed. In his initial usage of the term, Williams refers to structures of feeling as the practical consciousness of lived experience in a particular time period, which the novelistic forms and conventions of the time reflect considerably but can never entirely capture. Williams wrote that a structure of feeling is "as firm and definite as 'structure' suggests, yet it operates in the most delicate and least tangible part of our activities" (64). It bears on those experiences that lie "at the edge of semantic availability" and "which do not have to await definition, classification or rationalization before they exert palpable pressures and set effective limits on action and experience" (134). For Williams, structures of feeling lie at the edge of semantic availability both because the literary form can never entirely capture lived experience as is and because life as lived will always exceed or elude the immediate interpretations of those who experience them: "The peculiar location of a structure of feeling is the endless comparison that must occur in the process of consciousness between the articulated and the lived" (1979, 168). However, the semantic tension that Williams identifies is different from the more radical claim of affect theory that certain experiences are beyond language altogether. Certain experiences may indeed elude established linguistic forms because they are still emergent—that is, they are in "an embryonic phase," having not yet become "fully articulate" (131). Hence, his wonderfully calibrated phrase that structures of feeling lie at the edge of semantic availability but not beyond discursive recuperation altogether. In her programmatic statement that outlines the premises and goals of the Public Feelings project, Ann Cvetkovich (2007), too, draws on this legacy and refers to the affective as "structures of feeling, sensibilities, everyday forms of cultural expression and affiliation that may not take the form of recognizable organizations of institutions" (461).

But even if we thus mitigate the terminological quandary, the methodological challenge of affect remains formidable. If emotion sticks and affect slips, this renders emotion more ready for capture in writing and analysis, while affect is by its nature elusive. How then does one talk through language about something whose very essence depends on eluding language? The quandary is exacerbated in the case of anthropology, a field that relies foremost on local categories of knowledge and on expressions articulated by one's interlocutors. How can the ethnographer claim to understand the affect experienced or exuded by others (let alone by objects) if that affect is supposed to come before language or ceases to be affect the moment it is articulated? After all, emic articulations constitute a substantial set of the data on which the ethnographer relies. Beyond this epistemological impediment, Allen (2017) points to another key implication of the elusiveness of affect: "[The hiddenness of affect] provides two forms of power: one is the freedom to interpret and assert, and the other is the claim to an extraordinary ability to read beneath the surface of things, which gives a privileged access to truth" (403).[27]

Finally and relatedly, there are concerns about the political implications of the insistence on the autonomy of affect. If affect lies beyond language, it is also outside the realm of the ideological: "Affects must be viewed as independent of, and prior to ideology—that is prior to intentions, meanings, reasons, and beliefs—because they are nonsignifying, autonomic processes that take place below the threshold of conscious awareness and meaning" (Leys 2011, 437). In two separate and equally scathing critiques, Ruth Leys (2011) and Emily Martin (2013) have objected on normative grounds to this preference on the part of affect theorists for the bodily subject with unregulated dispositions over the rational subject with formulated intentions. Furthermore, some affect theorists also promote the capacity of affect "to be affected and to affect" in the name of emancipatory projects. This position veers dangerously close to having one's cake—denying any conscious, articulated intention to affects—and eating it too—investing in the liberatory potential of affect. Even if one were to grant a certain potential to such unarticulated unconscious responses, Leys and Martin ask, and recognize the significance cherished by affect theory of the split-second gap before felt intensities become categorized as specific emotions, what is there to guarantee that the outcome of that potential will be a form of action we would desire and not, for example, one that is violent or harmful to others?

Taking these critiques of affect theory in its hard version to heart, I ask in turn: Would the officer who decided to stop Festus have been so attuned and attentive to what he coded as "unease" had he not had a preconceived notion of who was already suspect? Would he have decided to investigate a person walking on the street were it not the case that he believed that, as he alleges in his testimony, "migrants and black persons attract more attention when it comes to drugs?" Is the response to the transmission of unease unstructured, beyond cognition and intention? Pursuing a less prominent, historically inflected thread in Maurice Merleau-Ponty's otherwise predominantly presentist phenomenology, Didier Fassin writes: "The present of the world is informed by the past of previous states of the world: perception is always remembrance" (2011c, 428). For the police officer, the knowledge regarding the always already suspect status of migrants and black persons impacted his decision to interrogate; for Festus, the knowledge of what the police could do to a black man for simply walking on the street likely triggered the affect that got coded as unease.

Switching gears from authorized murder to authorized generosity and moving from one police station to another, we get an entirely different response to unease. Nurcan's anxiety elicits paternalistic benevolence and impunity. Her anxiety, as well as Hoşgül's exaggerated ease, play out against an already sustained conjecture that they are not likely to be hurt in that police station even though they have the same illegal status as Festus Okey.

Wholesale insistence on the "pre" of the discursive or the autonomy of affect traps us in the moment because it ends up neglecting the already existing structural violence and structural privilege that precede affect. Or, put most simply and somewhat provocatively, affect, in this hard version, claims to dispense with history. Attention to affect understood as nonnarrative, nondiscursive, beyond sequence and narration, gives short shrift, in Pierre Bourdieu's phrasing, to "systems of durable, transposable dispositions, structured structures predisposed to function as structuring structures" (1977, 72). The durable disposition in this instance is Nurcan's and Hoşgül's practical knowledge that the Turkish state has been paternalistically benevolent toward them. Nurcan's particular interpretation of the rumor about the amnesty as confirming her hope of legalization stems from her experientially informed sense that she has a certain bargaining power with the police. Similarly, while Hoşgül's nonchalance seems risky in the ethnographic moment, it is also a way of negotiating a situation in which one has a reasonable hope based on embodied, durable dispositions that are entrenched in and affirmed through formal and informal legal codes.

This is not to deny that there was room for a certain range of possibilities and different outcomes in the encounter at the police station. Nurcan's unease might have aroused suspicion instead of evoking compassion; Hoşgül's flirtatious giggle might have irritated instead of eased; the title of "professor" might have provoked instead of dissuaded. However, contrary to the insistence on "affect as wild card" (Connolly 2002, 90), the range of possibilities is not arbitrary or endless. There were differences in comportment among the three women that day from the very first moment I encountered them in the courtyard of the police station. The circulating affect of unease evinced itself as tremulous appeal, as flirtatious provocation, and in the instance of Emine, the third friend who decided against going in at all, as cautious participation without full involvement. And yet, despite these differences in comportment and action, a degree of underlying logic and limitation to the range was evident. Despite her trembling, Nurcan chose to move forward and approach the desk as she pleaded for a permit. As she flirted to exploit the gendered dynamic to her advantage, Hoşgül knew to heed the bounds of gendered propriety expected of "kin" in the way she was far more conservatively dressed that day in a longer skirt and full sleeves rather than the sleeveless shirts and tight pants she generally favored. Even Emine, who decided it was not wise to go in the police station, did not mind coming and hanging out in the courtyard, a week after she had been told to leave the country during a police check at the house where she worked. Despite the unease shared by all, each was willing to expose herself to a certain degree of vulnerability precisely because each relied on a shared sense of entitlement.

Surely something was going on at the neurological level of heart rates and pulses—I saw the visible tremor in Nurcan's hands as she approached the police officer's desk. And she would say to me later, "I could not stop shaking even after we walked out." But I am not convinced that we gain much analytic ground by asserting either an ontological gap between affect and emotion or an epistemological gap between how a body experiences sensation and how that body becomes aware of and makes sense of experience. More definitive, it seems to me, is the structural logic to how unease gets performed and received by migrants who are differently positioned on the spectrum of relative privilege. There is a structural logic and probability to why the unease of Festus Okey ends in murder and the unease of Nurcan culminates in paternalistic benevolence. That difference in privilege, a sociologically objective condition, results in the difference in the affective quality of hope that I describe as entitled hope for the Bulgaristanlı migrants.

My argument has been against universalistic conceptions of hope. I urge instead attention to how it is differentially distributed, which, in the lives of Bulgaristanlı migrants in Turkey, is correlated with their objective chances of legalization. My approach, however, still leaves intact the question of whether the actual distribution of hope can be completely explained by objective degrees of privilege. I do not assert the absolute determinacy of structural conditions over the idiosyncracies of individual trajectories. In fact, I have tried to capture the varieties of the hoping stance by attending to how hope is differently embodied and performed by different individuals even in the presence of identical degrees of objective privilege.

A more phenomenological account might, of course, place greater emphasis than I do on the contingencies in the relationship between the objective structure of privilege and the actual distribution of subjective hope. But I am interested in foregrounding the institutional and legal production of hope. My emphasis in this book thus veers toward an exploration of the structural conditions of possibility, even as I try to capture and depict the varieties in the individual, lived experiences of hope and hope-based action.

Insisting that anxiety, dread, unease—those affects deemed to be intricately related to and even constitutive of hope—are structurally shaped does not render them experientially less real or psychologically less intense at a personal level. Similarly, reclaiming those genealogies of hope that emphasize its rational, reasoned component does not mean that I am favoring the cognitive at the expense of the conative. Andrea Muehlebach and Nitzan Shoshan (2012) identity Antonio Gramsci as another precursor to thinking about the intricate relation between, on the one hand, affective capacities organized at the level of the nervous system, over which we do not have total sovereignty, and, on the other hand, our rationalizations of the way things are. On this account, ideology, in its promise of the good life, is as powerful as it is precisely because it works through both affective capacities and our rationalizations. Or, in William Mazzarella's masterful formulation, "any social project that is not imposed through force alone must be affective in order to be effective" (2009, 299).

The perspective on affect advanced by those who see it as critical to political governance resonates with earlier, classic work on the anthropology of emotions that views emotions not just as personal states but as indices of social relationships and assert a correlation between the distribution of power in society and the structuring of emotion (Abu-Lughod 1986; Lutz 1988; Myers 1986). If fear is the more visible emotion that is deployed as an efficacious tool to sway a national citizenry by evoking, for example, the fear of the foreigner or the stranger, hope perhaps works less visibly but just as effectively. Enforcers of the law in Turkey reiterate daily who can and who cannot hope to belong to the nation-state either by reference to explicit criteria as specified in legal norms or through the informal conduct they display at a police station or an ID check. And the hope expectantly avowed by Nebaniye in the opening of this chapter—that "we" have hope of belonging, but "they" don't—fosters emotional legitimacy for investing in norms for inclusion and exclusion by potential subjects of the nation-state.

But belonging is no simple matter, even for those with legal and cultural privilege. In perhaps the most influential critical take to date on hope/optimism as affect, Lauren Berlant (2011) writes that cruel optimism "names a relation of attachment to compromised conditions of possibility" (21). Berlant's brilliant treatment of cruel optimism is a political one—that is, she explores optimism as capitalist zeitgeist. But it is important to recall that she defines optimism itself—when stripped of the qualifier "cruel"—as the very stuff of life, irrespective of any particular epoch. Optimism is what makes it possible to live on, to hang on to a sense of continuity in the world. It also always harbors a potential for cruelty: the structural relation that optimism makes possible between the subject and a whole series of substitutive objects that promise wholeness is a relation that is bound to fall short. The promise of wholeness is an impossible one (a compromised condition of possibility in the first instance) because the promise is trying to compensate for the loss of something that never existed in the first place and gave rise to the desire through its very lack. At this point comes Berlant's crucial twist to this typically Lacanian narrative: not all optimisms are equally prone to cruelty. And the difference has to do with the realm of the political. Berlant thus pushes the psychoanalytic paradigm toward a new paradigm of subjectivity that takes seriously political economy, and more generally, the political: late capitalism is a particular breeder of optimism that is more intensely cruel.

Berlant brings together under the rubric of cruel optimism all sorts of states necessary to survival in what she calls "zones of compromised ordinariness" (35). These range from "the poor who work themselves to death" to "those who defer life because they do not have the skills to live any other way" to the rich suburbanites whose attachment to particular objects of desire falls short of the expected satisfaction (36). In qualifying different kinds of hope and in thinking about entitled hope, I seek to bring contextual specificity to the generalizing move that subsumes the poor and the rich under the same rubric of cruel optimism. Festus Okey, a black migrant from Nigeria, is detained because he draws attention by his mere presence on the street, is forced to the police station, and is carried out of it fatally wounded. Nurcan, an undocumented migrant from Bulgaria, voluntarily walks into the police station, all but declares illegal status, pleads for regularization, and is threatened with deportation but also encouraged to apply for citizenship. The notion of entitled hope I have developed in this chapter is thus inspired by but also departs from Berlant's depiction of cruel optimism in that it differentiates states of optimism according to degrees of relative privilege.

Chapter 3, which goes on to explore the precarious facet of migrant hope, is indebted to Berlant's other key insight: optimism has cruelty built into it because our very attachment to objects of desire that promise happiness might be obstacles to our flourishing. This is not (just) because these objects may be impossible to attain. More insidiously, even if the desired objects were to be attained, they do not necessarily prove conducive to our well-being in the ways hoped for.

* * *

The four of us—Nurcan, Hoşgül, Emine, and me—walked back from the Beşiktaş police station toward Ortaköy along the Bosphorus, with a glorious view of the sea brimming with winter light on an exceptionally bright, sunny day. But we walked hurriedly and out of breath, as though we needed to get away from the place as quickly as possible. Nurcan had clutched my arm the moment we exited security and had not let go since. She huddled even closer as we passed two policemen walking in the opposite direction and, once they were a safe distance away, she whispered, "For a moment I thought they had come to arrest me."

Once we reached Ortaköy and settled with our tea on the stools on the sidewalk of a coffee shop, any remaining sense of fear dissipated and jokes were being cracked about who had showed the most fear. Nurcan began to lament that she had wasted her weekly day off from work. She normally took Sundays off so that she could hang out with friends. It was already an unpleasant negotiation to get your employer to agree to substitute for a weekday, even if, Nurcan noted testily, her employer herself was on maternity leave, implying that Nurcan's absence from work could easily be covered without making such a fuss. She lamented the fact that she would have to cover the travel expenses to and from the police station for a trip that had garnered no result. Now, she supposed, she would have to wait for the next amnesty to legalize her residence. She did not for a moment give any consideration to the police officer's command to leave. "I wonder if the residence permit granted in the next amnesty will let me apply for citizenship," she said. "I hope it will."

Five years later, while finishing this manuscript, I received a message from Nurcan asking if I knew of anyone who was looking for a nanny. I told her I happened to be in the city and we met. As we caught up on the years we had not seen each other, Nurcan told me how she eventually got her citizenship as one of the highlights of an otherwise difficult five years.

> Remember Alara Hanım, the one I was still working for when you left for America? She kept telling me, "There is no way you can get that citizenship." Her mother, too, would say, "My dear, do you think it is that easy to get citizenship?" They never believed I would get it. But you know me, I have faith. Inside, deep inside me, there is always hope. So I did not listen to them and put in the application after that last amnesty was announced. There was no news for a year. Meanwhile I had to keep renewing the residence permit of course, otherwise I would lapse into clandestine status. You remember how I had stayed as clandestine for two and half years. I also needed to go to Bulgaria, to see my granddaughter. When I went to renew, they messed up with my documents and I created a scene. I shouted, I said, "It is your fault." I demanded to see their superior. I was so angry, my blood pressure must have gone through the roof. Finally, the superior came, and can you imagine, he

apologized! He said, "Nurcan Hanım, yes, it is our fault," and he approved the renewal. When I was crossing the border, the officer who looked over my documents, he said, "Hey you don't need to exit and enter anymore. Your citizenship card has been processed!" When I came back, I told Alara Hanım. She still did not believe it. "Oh, come on, she said, how is that possible?" When I insisted, she called the Ankara office, and there was my name on the list. I went to that same police station in Beşiktaş we had gone to together, remember? So that time, it did not work. But this time, I walked out with my citizenship card. I don't know if *walked* is the right word. I flew. I flew all the way from Beşiktaş back to the house.

After we admired the pink card she eagerly showed me, together with her EU citizenship ID, which she was equally proud of, Nurcan's effervescence gradually subsided.

Crossing the border is a breeze now. But in terms of the money, nothing has really changed. I can only find work as a nanny. And I am over fifty now, how many more years can I keep up with such demanding work? And there is this: now I work with social security, but all the years I worked before I got the citizenship, they don't count. Now that Alara Hanım's children are grown up and she has let me go, I need to find myself a new employer. I am currently "on trial" with this potential employer. If her children like me, she said she will keep me on. But there are things that already make me uneasy. The fish smells sour from the onset. She negotiated already for the 50 Lira pocket money I am used to taking on my days off. She told me to give a list of my expenses today for example, how much the bus ride cost, how much the snack, and this and that, and so she will calculate whether fifteen dollars for the day is an amount she is willing to pay. I am at the mercy of these kinds of calculations.

In chapter 3, I turn to what it means to be at the mercy of such calculations or, more broadly put, to the precarious facet of hope.

3 PRECARIOUS HOPE

MY FLIP PHONE, a source of amusement among my interlocutors, several of whom possessed far superior technology, started to flash at eight in the morning with a warning that the incoming-message box was full. I saw that the first and the last text messages were from Şefika, who had migrated from Shumen and worked in Istanbul as a nanny for two toddlers. Though she was in her late fifties, she possessed an apparently boundless supply of energy. She was also somehow always the first to pick up the scent of a potential amnesty. The last message from her that my inbox had been able to store was an impatiently terse "Just call me!" I suspected right away that another amnesty for legalization was in the works.

Before returning Şefika's call, I took a few minutes to glance at the websites of the major Balkan associations to see if they had already jumped on the wagon to kindle hope among the Bulgaristanlı. Sure enough, the BAL-GÖÇ (2009) website featured the news with this announcement: "Great news for Bulgaristanlı Turks! Under the purview of the regulation of amnesty for a residence permit, the decision to grant a one-year residence permit has been reached on condition that applications are made to the Foreigners Department of one's respective municipality before March 6, 2009." [1]

Such amnesties as these, which had been granted to Bulgaristanlı migrants also in 2001, 2005, and 2007, are called *af*, a term that carries even stronger connotations of forgiveness in Turkish than it does in English. Of the three previous amnesties, the 2001 and the 2007 offers had only temporarily legalized irregular status by granting three-month non-renewable residence permits. The one in 2005 included a six-month renewable permit, but only those who applied for citizenship during the first six-month window were able to obtain citizenship; others who renewed their permits and applied after fulfilling the two-year residence requirement were denied. None of these amnesties, therefore, offered a legally codified and consistent path to citizenship. Nevertheless, they constituted one of the key bureaucratic instruments of the legal production of hope for the Bulgaristanlı migrants.

The granting of yet another amnesty for the Bulgaristanlı was thus not atypical. But in this instance, in March 2009, three things appeared to deviate from the previous amnesties. The first had to do with the timing. All of the previous amnesties had coincided with elections in Bulgaria. The Turkish government made no effort to pretend that the timing was not contrived. Instead, as I have already elaborated in chapter 1, the government explicitly advertised these amnesties to Bulgaristanlı migrants as their unique chance to obtain legal status in exchange for casting a vote in the Bulgarian elections, the assumption being that the party they would cast a vote for would be the Movement for Rights and Freedoms, the party that represents the Turkish vote in Bulgaria and had a close working relationship with the Turkish government. But the March 2009 date was puzzling. No elections were scheduled to take place in Bulgaria at that time.

The second peculiarity was the rumor that this particular amnesty promised a one-year permit. Another running joke among my interlocutors was to try to guess whether the new amnesty was going to be "for three months" or "for six months." But the joke works only in Turkish: the phrases *üç aylık* and *altı aylık* exactly correspond to the way a pregnant woman would typically talk about the term of her pregnancy. When my interlocutors thus played around with the pregnancy metaphor to talk about the permits, they evoked the connotation of being pregnant with possibility and hope.

The difference between three months and six months was significant. The three-month non-renewable permits granted only the most transient form of legalization. They were still welcomed by the migrants because they provided exemption from fines accumulated for overstays. The six-month permits, on the other hand, had the possibility of being renewed. This in turn led to the likelihood of citizenship if one could maintain the renewals uninterruptedly for five years. But a one-year permit was simply unprecedented.

Third and finally, to add further mystery to the unfolding drama, another Balkan migrant association in Sefaköy, a residential neighborhood on the outskirts of the city that was predominantly populated by generations of Bulgaristanlı migrants, announced the news as "an application opportunity via migrant associations." Thus when news of an amnesty began to circulate through the migrant grapevine, the ad hoc norm—with all the implications that that paradox is intended to carry—was to rush to the closest police station to queue up in hopes of putting in an application in time.

So how was it that one could apply for the permit through the migrant associations this time around instead of at a legal institution? And which migrant associations? When I called Şefika back to report the information I had been able to glean, those were the questions she immediately posed. After a quick deliberation, she opted for the migrant association in Sefaköy simply because it charged less for petitions. And indeed, this time the representative at Sefaköy ended up writing the application free of charge as he took a few moments to bad-mouth the rival association in Çemberlitaş for ripping off our "soydaş in need" by charging 100 lira per petition. The Sefaköy association representative also tried to assuage a frustrated Şefika by telling her that the March 6 deadline, which Şefika protested was too soon, would be extended until the end of the month and that she did not have to worry about beating the crowds that day. The news circulating through the grapevine had warned of a notoriously long queue at the Foreigners' Department in Istanbul. But the prospects of a long line did not deter Şefika, and she was not convinced by the association representative's assurance of an extension. Association representatives were generally viewed as suspect by the post-1990 Bulgaristanlı migrants.[2]

We arrived at the Foreigners' Department branch that has its offices inside the Istanbul Police Headquarters on Vatan Street, one of the most spacious boulevards in the city and the location of several other major institutions of the state bureaucracy as well. In stark contrast to the atypically vast urban space of the street, the interior of the building was cluttered and hard to navigate. It was difficult to tell where one should start queuing amid the clusters of people. Şefika recognized a friend in the middle of a crowd that did not seem to be forming separate lines. The friend waved enthusiastically at us to join her, and we edged our way over to her with no visible outrage on the part of anyone we cut in front of. The friend, who was introduced to me as Hasine, told us that a police officer had collected passports earlier in exchange for queue numbers. The officer had also explained to the crowd that this particular amnesty application was *only* for those who were eligible. "If you are not eligible," he had reportedly said, "you need to wait for the next regular amnesty, although when the next one will be, we cannot say."

While I pondered the wonderful irony of the term "regular amnesty," Şefika and Hasine's immediate concern was different: What eligibility criteria could he have been referring to? Wasn't the amnesty for all the Bulgaristanlı Turks as usual? Hasine was also disgruntled. "These associations are messing things up for us," she griped. "In the old days, we would come, take our number for the queue, and submit our application. Now they are first sending us to the association for the initial paperwork."

Unable to get a number that day, since (as the queuing jargon went) "all the numbers had been used up," we went upstairs to try to find someone from whom to extract information about the particulars of the amnesty. It took almost an hour to locate the officer who was supposed to be standing behind the information desk. He said, "You have to put in an application for why you want to stay in Turkey permanently." "I don't understand," Şefika said to me afterward. "Why can I not simply say I want to take advantage of the amnesty? Why do I have to apply for permanent residency? How am I to know what I am supposed to say in the application?" Şefika had already used up her day off for the week. Employers of domestic workers rarely agreed to an extra day off, and even switching days could be a source of tension, although the possibility of legalization was a reason that usually trumped employer resistance.

So we lingered at the Foreigners' Department, talking to acquaintances and trying to figure out the parameters of the amnesty. It finally became clear at the end of three more hours that only those who were on a special list were eligible for this particular amnesty. We could not obtain any official information as to who was on the list and why. Back at the BTSA in Çemberlitaş the next day, the association president boasted that this one-year amnesty was entirely the result of his own efforts. According to him, all the names on what would quickly become branded in the migrant network as the "list of nine hundred" (900'lük liste) were people on whose behalf he himself had written petitions after the expiration of their six-month residence permits in April 2008. [3] The president's claim seemed to be corroborated by the cases of people like Nefiye, whose legalization quest I described in the introduction and who had filed the petition the president alluded to. [4] There were, however, other people who had sent similar petitions via other migrant associations and had not been included. The BTSA president's explanation for this was that the simultaneous lawsuits he had filed for citizenship on behalf of the undocumented Bulgaristanlı migrants who could afford to pay the 3000TL fee had been so persuasive that the state had offered this one-year permit as a midway solution to prevent a positive verdict for citizenship. A positive verdict granting citizenship would have established a precedent that would in turn have paved the way for en masse acquisitions of citizenship for all undocumented Bulgaristanlı migrants. The state was trying to circumvent such a precedent, since it would make citizenship almost automatic, rather than at the discretion of the Committee of Ministers, as was currently the case. Hence, the state had come up with the nine-hundred-person list as a compromise.

Meanwhile, Şefika, who discovered only after another trip to the Foreigners' Department that she was not on the list, was irritated that her extra day off had resulted in a cut in her monthly salary. But she had not given up her hope of temporary legalization: "Worst-case scenario," she said to me over the cup of bitter coffee that she said would "take the edge off the disappointment," "there are the elections in June in Bulgaria, and we will get our amnesty then."

And indeed, come June, right before the elections in Bulgaria, the migrant grapevine was once again abuzz with news of an amnesty. The phone traffic for the next several days was consumed with tips about which police station had smaller crowds, where one might have an acquaintance who could obtain a queue number on one's behalf, whether it made sense to start queuing the night before, or which police station's chief officer made a note of the people whose turn did not come that day in order to assign them priority for the next day's queue. During the disorderly but hopeful waiting, the rumor was that the residence permits that came with this amnesty would definitely be renewable. Another whisper that circulated was that these particular permits would count as work permits.

In the end, neither rumor was borne out. The amnesty granted only a three-month non-renewable permit that simply provided exemption from punitive fees that may have accumulated. But surely another amnesty "would soon come around," Şefika said, and she had hope that this time the path to citizenship would be straightforward.

CIRCUMSCRIBING MOVES ON THE EVER-EXPANDING CONCEPT OF PRECARITY

If chapter 2 covers terrain that is paved with expectation and that is productive of what I call "entitled hope," this chapter shifts the gaze to how that terrain is simultaneously checkered with uncertainty, unpredictability, and insecurity. These are the three key features of the increasingly widely used concept of *precarity*. The experiences of Bulgaristanlı migrant women in Turkey in their encounters with the law and in the labor market bear these features: from their legal status, which wavers between temporary permits and lapses into undocumented existence, to the kind of labor that Bulgaristanlı migrant women engage in as domestic workers and nannies without work contracts, to the everyday encounters with the law and bureaucracy that routinely offer the promise of security and stability without ever quite guaranteeing it.

I do not want to simply to demonstrate how the everyday lives of the Bulgaristanlı in Turkey provide (yet another) instance of precarity. Rather, I want to show what my ethnographic account of the Bulgaristanlı does to the concept of precarity, and more specifically, how it might help circumscribe a concept that risks losing its analytic edge through its ever-expanding deployment in the current scholarship. To briefly foreshadow my key argument: The circumscribing moves toward specificity that I make traverse the affective as well as the structural components of precarity. Together, they urge retention of the distinction between vulnerability and precarity, accompanied by a greater recognition of a sense of entitlement in the condition of precarity.

Precarité was once a rather provincial and very specific coinage, used primarily in France, Italy, and Spain in reference to contingent, irregular work conditions adopted by labor movements of the 1970s, again mostly in that part of the world. In an excellent review from 2009 that traces the primarily Western European genealogy of the term, Louise Waite notes, with a tinge of chagrin, the scarcity of its usage in the Anglo-Saxon world. Alas for that lament. Now everything, from insecure work conditions to environmental hazards to our very frailty as human beings, is increasingly subsumed under either precarity or its derivative "the precarious" in fields spanning political science, geography, sociology, and cultural theory.

Anthropology, in particular, has been quick to jump on the bandwagon. Following Judith Butler's *Precarious Life* (2006), highly influential for the spread of the term to American academia, engagement with precarity and the precarious is ubiquitous, prompting the excellent 2013 review in *American Anthropologist* by Andrea Muehlebach and, three years later, a curated issue on precarity in *Cultural Anthropology* (Shaw and Byler 2016). As the ground covered by precarity and the precarious keeps expanding, yet other groups of people are hailed as the emerging "precariat," including undocumented migrants and refugees. "Precarious" appears to be the most widely deployed adjective to describe the predicament of undocumented migrants in Turkey in recent scholarship spanning various disciplines. In fact, in a 2016 issue of *New Perspectives on Turkey* that focused on Syrian refugees (Eder and Özkul 2016), the editors resort to an enhanced version of the concept, "hyper-precarity" (3), to describe the vicissitudes faced by the three million Syrian refugees in Turkey.

I entirely agree with Eder and Özkul's move to differentiate the predicament of Syrians from that of various other migrant groups in Turkey: they provide a much needed corrective to the use of the term "precarity" as a blanket expression to describe various migrant groups without due attention to significant differences in terms of access to resources among them. But I find that the need for such boosters signals analytic trouble with the concept itself. In fact, I would contend that the analytic trouble began much earlier, when the original distinction that had been made between precarity and the precarious became increasingly blurred in favor of an overly inflated usage of "precariousness."

In the earlier distinction, "precarity" was acknowledged as something more specific and historically inflected, while "the precarious" was posited as a more general predicament that can be universalized. In Anne Allison's succinct formulation of Judith Butler, precarity was originally described as "the differential distribution of precariousness by such factors as class, citizenship, and race" (2016). But that crucial distinction between precarity as differentially distributed forms of precariousness that characterizes certain lives, whether those of underemployed workers, suffering bodies, or racialized citizens, and precariousness as an existential condition is increasingly blurred. Anna Lowenhaupt Tsing's formulation (2015) exemplifies the move to close the gap and to universalize: "Once the fate of the less fortunate, now everyone's life is precarious" (2). Anne Allison (2016) acknowledges the historicity of the term as it refers to European social labor movements of the 1970s, deployed specifically in reference to flexible, contingent, and irregular work conditions. She simultaneously suggests, however, that "a modality of being marked by indeterminacy for lives lived is less the exception and increasingly the very condition of our times."

This universalizing move has also had a particular politicized uptake, especially by those involved in collective organizing efforts. Bringing together differently positioned workers under the rubric of precarity aims to foster solidarity among migrant workers and disadvantaged citizens. The expansive usage of precarity insists on the occluded connections between workers who are positioned differently within neoliberal modes of exploitation. But as compelling as it might be in fostering a sense of solidarity through reference to a shared predicament, it jeopardizes precisely what was most valuable in the original distinction between precarity and precariousness—namely, the recognition of the latter's differential distribution.

I would suggest that before the distinction between precarity and the precarious began to be blurred, a fundamental terminological ambiguity was already smuggled in when the notion of "the precarious" was appropriated by the Anglo-Saxon world from its more limited designation in the European context of post-Fordist labor. In Butler's *Precarious Life* (2006), probably the book most responsible for the rapid uptake of the term by scholars in the United States, "precariousness" often serves as a substitute for "vulnerability." Vulnerability concerns the ever-present danger and possibility of being hurt in the act of living. But I think it is important not to conflate precariousness with vulnerability. One is vulnerable to death, for example, but not quite precarious in relation to death because there was never an assurance of "not dying" in the first place. Holding on to the difference between vulnerability and precariousness serves as an important reminder of the historical and structural specificities that the latter meant to index as well as its differential distribution.

Guided by these concerns, I pursue the path of terminological delimitation to highlight the precarious in relation to structures of privilege. I do not do so for the sake of terminological puritanism. These circumscribing moves allow me to bring into sharper view what is distinctive about the Bulgaristanlı migrants in relation to other undocumented migrants who struggle to survive in Turkey. How are the Bulgaristanlı differentiated from other undocumented migrants through the partial privileges they hold in terms of legal possibilities and cultural entitlements? The broader implication of my intervention is to show the coexistence of privilege and precarity and to reckon with the role of privilege *within* precarity.

ON ETYMOLOGY AND SEMANTIC DIFFUSION

A more precise definition of precarity might underscore its distinction from a sense of ontological vulnerability while at the same time acknowledging the uncertain and insecure dynamics within which precariousness positions subjects. I take my first cue from Didier Fassin's analysis of humanitarian government (2011a), in which he recalls the archaic definition of the term "precarious": "The concept of precarious lives needs to be taken in the strongest sense of its Latin etymology: lives that are not guaranteed but bestowed in answer to prayer, or in other words are defined not in the absolute of a condition, but in the relation to those who have power over them" (4). Following Fassin's semantic reminder and analytic perspective, I seek to show the ways in which precarity is enacted as the differential distribution of precariousness and as it plays out in the Bulgaristanlı migrants' dependence on the words, acts, and whims of structurally more powerful others, whether they be border police, officials at police stations, police on the street, employers, or migrant association representatives.

Etymology does not give us the absolute truth about the meaning of a term. Neither should it conclusively bind the ways in which a word is to be deployed. However, etymology can offer useful hints for clarification. While I thus acknowledge the many commonsense ways in which "precarity" and "the precarious" have come to permeate everyday language and bureaucratic jargon to refer to all sorts of uncertainties and vulnerabilities, I reappropriate the precarious as a concept and recall its etymology so as to clarify a term that has become too diffuse to sustain its analytic rigor. Specifically, I trace precarity in the hopes and lives of Bulgaristanlı migrants as the formal and informal codifications of the asking and bestowing of favors rather than rights. Concomitantly, I insist on precarity as a condition that is different from the "ontological vulnerability" (Lear 2006) on which all life is ultimately founded. This double analytic—differential precarity as it plays out in intersubjective domains of hierarchical relations—allows me to encapsulate how Bulgaristanlı migrant women manipulate relations of dependence both at the level of individual encounters and at the structural level of the law to greater degrees than do other undocumented migrants, especially when compared to those from Africa and the former Soviet Union.

PRECARIOUS ESCAPES

Rembiye, in her late twenties, had earned a bachelor's degree in economics in Bulgaria and was working in Istanbul as an accountant for a small company. She had managed to keep her residency regular as much as possible by taking advantage of each amnesty offered, but her last temporary residence permit, obtained via the June 2009 amnesty, had expired a few months ago.

She would have to wait for the next amnesty. Her boss did not have a problem with her checkered legal status, she said. Given the restructuring that the company was undergoing and the expertise that Rembiye had accumulated, she was quite certain she had become indispensable to her boss and was hoping for a promotion. Meanwhile, she had filed a petition on the basis of her *soydaş* status with the Ministry of Internal Affairs to renew her permit. Unlike most others, she had done so without seeking the help of the migrant associations. Instead, she had completed the paperwork through a self-declared "legal advisor": these intermediaries were often former police officers who did "advising" as a sideline in their retirement. Although the "legal advisor" had told Rembiye that she was non-deportable as long as she had a standing application with the ministry, she became more anxious, she told me, after recently enduring a police check.

Identity checks in public space during the flow of everyday life are legal and a routine occurrence across Turkey, a country with a record of multiple military interventions, including three full-fledged military coup d'états. [5] As a legacy of these routinized states of exception, residents are required to carry their national identity card on them at all times. This makes the situation of undocumented migrants, who can never fully escape regimes of deportability wherever they might be in the world, all the more susceptible to police scrutiny in Turkey.

Rembiye was with her boyfriend when they were stopped by a police officer who was conducting identity checks in front of the central mosque in Avcılar, a sprawling suburb of Istanbul that hosts a significant immigrant and student population. When Rembiye showed her passport, the police officer said, "Uh-oh, your ninety days have long expired." Rembiye told him that she had already requested a renewal and showed him the receipt. The officer said, "But how do I know you ever had a residence permit? Where is that?" Rembiye told him that she did not carry all of her documents with her for fear of theft. The officer insisted on seeing the permit and said he would accompany her to the police station while someone else went to her house to pick up the document. Rembiye did not trust that the officers at the station would understand either. She was not sure whether she herself could explain all the intricate details. She finally realized that the officer was after a bribe when he said, "Look here, isn't it a shame that you two will have to spend your romantic Sunday at the police station? What could we do about this?" Rembiye and her boyfriend gave him all the cash they had with them, a total of 280 lira, and he let them go.

Sıdıka, a friend of Rembiye's and also in her twenties, commented on the incident not without a hint of pride: "Even though we rarely get stopped, I actually get stopped all the time because of my looks." Distinguishing herself from the collective "we" of the Bulgaristanlı migrants in terms of outward appearance, Sıdıka went on to say, "They always mistake me for Eastern European or Russian." She paused and seductively batted the eyelashes that framed her wide green eyes. "I mean, with these eyes, of course they do! But once they realize I am Turkish, they let me go. "Bacım Türküm desene," they say. [Sister, why didn't you say "I am Turkish?"] Of course, sometimes they let me go only after a small 'gift,' twenty lira, thirty lira, whatever I may happen to have on me."

These escapes were mediated by states of precarity and privilege. Bulgaristanlı migrants tended not to get stopped because they passed as locals for the most part. Passing, however, was not guaranteed. The presence of a boyfriend or a pair of striking eyes deemed foreign might provoke surveillance. Ethnic kinship did not provide impunity from the widespread practice of bribes, but it did provide impunity from detention.

A meeting I attended in 2013 brought together various feminists, activists, and migrant women to forge a solidarity campaign against the systematic harassment of African women by their employers. These women testified to how employers in textiles reserved special rooms in the workplace for sex, which they demanded before paying the workers their weekly earned wages. An undocumented Senegalese woman offered an unflinching diagnosis: African women were perceived as always sexually available. This meant that not just the basements of textile shops were dangerous for the women, but the street itself in broad daylight was dangerous. "The moment I walk, I am game for anyone on the street. They assume I am out for sex, and they just act on that. This also goes for the police. So who can I turn to when the police [are] no different from these men?"

The common perception of migrant women as sex workers, or as sexually available, coincides with Turkey's speedy transformation into a migrant-receiving country beginning in 1990. With the collapse of the Communist bloc, there was an overwhelmingly feminized wave of migration to Turkey from the countries of the former Soviet Union. The name Natasha was appropriated into the local lexicon as the term that referred to women who arrived from the former Soviet Union and sold sex for money. Designations of these migrant women as "natashas" first emerged in the Black Sea region and spread quickly to urban areas like Istanbul.[6] According to a recent NGO report, the violence against these migrants includes encounters with police who "harass women, take them under custody, ask for bribes, or deport them" based simply on their looks (414). After extensive research among migrant women from various countries of origin, Erder (2011) notes that even high-class status did not override racialized and gendered bias when it came to the natasha stereotype: Russian housewives in upper-class neighborhoods reported that they avoided wandering the city alone, could not randomly take a cab, and sometimes even on evening outings with their husbands had been accosted and harassed by the police.

If women identified as Russian bore the brunt of sexual harassment and violence throughout the 1990s, women from Africa are fast becoming another extremely vulnerable target for abuse. In her research among Ugandan women, Emel Coşkun (2018) presents women's accounts of working in manufacturing and textiles. The foremen would repeat the n-word and a sexist swear word so often, Coşkun recounts, that the women employees got curious about what the words meant and sought out the answers. Women from sub-Saharan Africa also are subjected to racism on the street on a daily basis: In addition to complaining about people staring at them and avoiding seats next to them, Ugandan women living in the migrant hubs of Kumkapı and Aksaray complained the most about harassment from adolescents, who would swear and spit at them, and on occasion pull out knives. The rape and murder of two Ugandan women in 2014 and in 2016, both at the hands of acquaintances who were brought to trial only after feminist lawyers stepped in to take over cases that were being covered up,[7] was only one tragic manifestation of the violence to which African migrant women in Turkey are increasingly and systematically subjected.

Against the backdrop of this routinized and racialized sexual harassment, Bulgaristanlı women can hold at bay the pervasive perception of migrant women as sex workers and even hope for leverage in their encounters with officials through their putative kinship. Bulgaristanlı women are precarious: they are dependent upon the whims or the goodwill of officials in their encounters with police surveillance. They are not, however, structurally vulnerable or exposed in the same way as women from Africa and Russia, who are perceived and acted upon as literally being there for the taking by foremen or acquaintances or the police. The analytical distinction I make between states' precarity corresponds to the experiential difference between risk and danger, between everyday insecurity and everyday trouble, and occasionally between life and death.

ACKNOWLEDGING PRECARITY

Precariousness may not always be named as dependence on the will and whim of a more powerful other, especially when it occurs under the guise of benevolence. Vasfiye migrated at the age of fifty-five from the southern Kırdjali region of Bulgaria after working as a crane operator during communism. She told me that her daughter, who was in her early twenties, used to work in a small textile shop. She worked *kaçak* (clandestinely), Vasfiye said, and told me the following incident:

> The atelier was very close to where she lived. Someone must have reported them, because there was a raid. Everything about my daughter screams that she is not a local, from how she dresses to how she moves around. But the police, they were honest folks, and they turned out to be people with humanity. "Do you have an ID?" they asked her. She lied and said yes. They asked where, and she told them at home. "Call home," one of them said, "and have someone bring it while we wait here." She was terrified, but then the boss intervened. He said to my daughter, "Come on, go home, my girl, and come back here right away with your ID." And the police, they allowed her to leave. The moment she left, they said to the owner, "Look, of course we know she does not have ID." They could easily have detained her, or they could have accompanied her home if they'd really wanted to check. The police then told the owner, "At least tell her to get a residence permit, and then let her work. Now if there is another raid, we will be placed in a difficult position for having looked away."

In *Humanitarian Reason* (2011a) Didier Fassin insists on full recognition of the paradox that underlies the politics of compassion, which he argues has been given short shrift by philosophers who stress its egalitarian aspect. This egalitarian aspect of sympathy for the other, which results in the motivation to provide assistance, is often foregrounded at the expense of the hierarchical aspect of humanitarianism: the exercise of compassion in public space flows unidirectionally from a position of power toward a position of precarity. In bestowing upon the officer the virtue of someone "with humanity," Vasfiye personalizes or moralizes what Fassin calls a "strictly sociological" situation (Fassin 2011a, 3). This is a situation in which the hierarchical relationship between the officer and the undocumented migrant annuls the possibility of reciprocity and obscures the structural violence that occasions the precarious predicament in the first place. When confronted with those who are at the edges of legality, the police have room to act in ways that are "full of humanity," as Vasfiye described it, or in ways that are gratefully perceived as such by those who are made to feel that precarious escape is their best chance. Looking the other way approximates the humanitarian gesture. "This tension between inequality and solidarity, between a relation of domination and a relation of assistance, is constitutive of all humanitarian government," writes Fassin (2011a, 3).

Just like the police officer whom Vasfiye imbued "with humanity," another police officer obliged Atiye and me by looking the other way when we went to the Mecidiyeköy police station to inquire about the June 2009 amnesty. Atiye, who came from a village near Razgrad, Bulgaria, was in her late fifties and had been engaging in circular migration for five years, working on and off as a nanny. Because she had family in Bulgaria, including a newborn granddaughter that she doted on, she considered her work in Turkey temporary and took extreme care not to lapse into illegal status. But this became very hard after the regulation allowing only ninety days of stay for every three months went into effect.

Atiye had found a way despite the new regulation. Since 2007, she had been alternating with a co-villager. Each took a three-month turn to work for the same employer, who had agreed to the arrangement. On that day, we had gone to the police station to inquire whether Atiye, who was still within her ninety-day visa bracket, could take advantage of the amnesty to gain an extra three months of residency. I made the inquiries while Atiye stood without speaking, preserving her usual calm, graceful demeanor, which I had not ever seen shaken, not even while waiting in the most hectic of queues or in the midst of boisterous interactions with others. The police officer asked me, "Is she at the university, like you, *hocam*?" I was caught off guard, perhaps by his amicable manner, since I was used to being waved off by officials, especially on such crowded days. "No," I replied, regretting it the moment it came out of my mouth. He said matter-of-factly, "But you know, it is forbidden." "I know," I said, extremely uneasy, dreading the consequences of my foolish admission. He lowered his voice to a whisper. "So unfair that these folks do not get a work permit easily. If she were from the Philippines, she would probably have gotten it by now. So hard, their situation. There, they are persecuted because they are Turkish. Here, they are treated as Bulgarians. An old uncle [honorific for an older man couched in kinship terms] came here once. I told him, 'Sit down. Tell me.' He sat and cried and cried. All the things they had to endure just because they are Turkish, spoke Turkish, and they prayed according to Islamic precepts."

These two official gestures of looking the other way—the first in the actual scene of breach of the law and the second in my confession of a breach—present a further twist to the lack of reciprocity identified by Fassin in the logic of compassion at work in humanitarian attention. Compassion is triggered not because one's universal humanity is exposed in all its vulnerability, but because the subject in question exhibits the right traits of Turkishness and Islam. Compassion in this instance is based not on shared humanity, but on ethnic and religious kinship. Atiye becomes the object of compassion because she belongs to a group who "spoke Turkish, and they prayed according to Islamic precepts." The already hierarchical nature of the humanitarian gesture is thus further delimited in the Turkish legal and policing context by the circumscription of the object of empathy to ethnic and religious kin.

As a technical designation, the term *af*, amnesty, refers to exemption from the rule. But in colloquial usage, amnesty also means, as it does in English, forgiveness, mercy, and pardon. In fact, the most immediate connotations of the Turkish word are pardon and forgiveness. Waiting for a technical exemption is thus evoked in language as waiting for one's forgiveness by the state. "I have been clandestine for nine years now," Asaniye Hanım, with whom Atiye and I had struck up a conversation while at the Mediciköy police station, declared. Then she added, with unmistakable aplomb, "I have not once paid fines for overstay. I simply wait for my amnesty. We know anyhow that there will be an amnesty at some point." *My amnesty*, Asaniye had said, just like Şefika, who had shrugged off the disappointment of her absence from the list of nine hundred by reassuring herself that "we will get our amnesty in June." Among other Bulgaristanlı women, too, the proprietary deployment of the term as *my amnesty* was a recurrent figure of speech.

On the one hand, reclaiming the amnesty that instrumentalizes migrants and their votes is a means to use the system right back. The migrants were aware that the state grants them amnesty in exchange for political mobilization. But there were different interpretations of the government's strategic act. Some were outraged: "They are playing with us." Others were pragmatically indifferent: "So what? If it will give me temporary regularization, I will take it." Yet others were commiserative: "Well, it is natural for the state to want the Turkish party in Bulgaria to be strong." Notwithstanding the different opinions they held toward the amnesties, migrants had come to rely on and expect these exceptions as a convenient fix, even if temporary.

On the other hand, while savviness and strategic disaffection were at work in taking advantage of these state-sponsored amnesties, there is also a way in which the appropriation of the amnesty as *my amnesty* or *our amnesty* engaged in the interpellation work of the state. I never heard Bulgaristanlı migrants express guilt for lapsing into undocumented status. In that, they were immune to the criminalizing discourse of the state as it apportions legality and illegality. Nonetheless, the discursive circulation and enactment of these technical exemptions as pardons result in a certain subjectivization whereby waiting for one's amnesty restored the image of the state as the benevolent grantor of forgiveness. Though the Bulgaristanlı migrants had no illusions about the purity of the government's motives, they partially submitted to an acceptance of legality that was bestowed upon them in the form of a pardon.

But it is not only the ethnographer who should presume to discern the ideological stakes around this legal term. The hierarchical nature of the humanity that may be exercised by the official at the border, the police station, or the workplace was not lost on many of my interlocutors. For example, the issue came up one day when a group of us were waiting in line to inquire whether Bahriye Hanım's sister, who was within the time bracket of her current residence permit when the new amnesty was issued, could still benefit from the extra three months that it offered. During our heated discussion of various technicalities, Bahriye Hanım interjected, visibly exasperated, "Tell me this. We keep saying 'amnesty this,' 'amnesty that.' Why is this even called an amnesty/*af*? Isn't it something . . ." She paused, searching for the right words. "Isn't this something we should simply be demanding?"

Bahriye Hanım's call to replace the existing posture of seeking forgiveness with one of voicing demand goes to the heart of the paradox underlying a politics of compassion. In addition to constituting a convenient foil for thinly veiled transnational political interest, amnesty/*af* reinforces the general predicament of precarity in the sense of being at the mercy of another. Precarity is to wait for rather than to demand. It is to hope that the state will bestow a residence permit, or that the chief officer will pay attention to who is entitled to have the first spot in the queue the next day, or that one's employer will grant a day off for a trip to the Foreigners' Department. Amnesty/*af* reinforces the predicament of precarity by routinizing uncertainty to the point that the very logic of legalization-via-amnesty appears to be a predictable system, though it is in fact based on indeterminate premises.

There were those who also explicitly expressed their misgivings with how the production of hope was complicit in a system of governance based on favors and exceptions. Right after the 2011 announcement of the amnesty that also promised a path toward citizenship, I was leaving the Foreigners' Department after a long day, and I ran into Şemsiye, a Bulgaristanlı woman with whom I had cultivated a casual friendship while waiting in lines. Şemsiye appeared to be in her fifties and carried a big smile. "Of course there you are again," she teased me. But her face turned sour as she told me that her husband's last citizenship application had been rejected. He could demonstrate five years of residence in Turkey, but he had spent too many days in Bulgaria, which Şemsiye thought was the cause of the rejection. She then surveyed the crowd. "All these people think that just because they submit the application, they are going to get the citizenship. But they won't, will they? They just keep creating this gate of hope."

PRECARIOUS CROSSINGS

As I demonstrated in chapter 1, the historical norm for Turkish migration policy until 1990 was to ease the passage of *soydaş* from their country of residence, Bulgaria, into the imagined homeland, Turkey. In the aftermath of the largest migration from Bulgaria to Turkey in 1989, of more than 300,000 Bulgaristanlı, that norm was reversed. During the early 1990s, the border between Bulgaria and Turkey became impenetrable for the Turkish minority. Visas for Turkey became hard to obtain for Bulgarian citizens, *especially* for those who were identified as ethnically Turkish. Consulates in Bulgaria would deny a visa to an unmarried man or woman and grant only one visa per family. Nearly every person I met during the course of fieldwork either had a personal story to tell about being denied a visa in the 1990s or knew of a family who strategized accordingly in the face of the one-visa-per-family rule, a systematically enforced policy that was never officially put in writing.

"I spoke in Bulgarian throughout my visa interview. I was pretty sure I could fake it," recalled Atiye, who was from Ruse, Bulgaria, and worked as a nanny in Istanbul. She was still laughing at the memory of a performance that would, in the end, not hold up and at the irony of trying to pass as Bulgarian. Only a few years before she was denied a visa, many in the Turkish minority had put up a struggle in Bulgaria to assert their Turkishness against the assimilation campaign of the last Communist president, Todor Zhivkov, who had claimed that "there are no Turks in Bulgaria." Now in her fifties, Atiye was just as fluent in Bulgarian as in her native Turkish, as are most members of the Turkish minority educated in Communist Bulgaria under a system that ensured a minimum of eight years of standardized schooling for those residing even in the most remote villages. "And I did not take back my Turkish name [after the assimilation campaign]," Atiye went on to explain. Taking one's name back or not was a point of contention among the Turkish minority: for some, reclaiming one's original Turkish Muslim name after it had been forcibly Slavicized in 1984 was a non-negotiable act of principle and dignity; for others, not doing so was a reasonable act of survival in a country that continued to discriminate against its Turkish population even after the severe repression of minority rights ended in 1989. "So as far as they were concerned," Atiye said, "I was Lilya the Bulgarian during that interview. And I really thought I had managed to wing it, until the very end, when the officer asked me if I knew so and so from my father's village. Caught off guard, I exclaimed, 'Of course! She is my great-aunt!' 'Aha,' he said, 'you are Turkish!' And they [at the Turkish consulate] rejected my application."

This unwritten policy is also of particular importance because it resulted in a hitherto unprecedented pattern of illegal crossings of Bulgaristanlı children. Typically, one parent would obtain a visa and find work in Turkey. The other parent would then enter Turkey with the children via smugglers. The term used by Bulgaristanlı was usually not *kaçakçı*, which would be the direct equivalent of the English word "smuggler." Instead, my interlocutors used the term *kanalcı*, or "channelers." In some cases, when both parents somehow managed to enter Turkey via an unofficial route, the children would be entrusted to one or two channelers, who would take groups of twelve to fifteen people, primarily children, across the border.

Sevginar, now a scholarship student at a prestigious university in Istanbul who had not yet been granted citizenship even though she came to Turkey in 1998, attempted two clandestine border crossings. The first was with her sister and father, and the second just with her sister when they were seven and ten years old. Both her father and her mother migrated in 1996 through a trick her father pulled off with their documents. They left Sevginar in the care of her aunt and her sister in the care of their grandmother, who was too old to take care of both of them on her own. Sevginar's parents were employed by a wealthy family in Turkey and lived on the family's premises—the most coveted arrangement for migrant couples. Her mother worked as a domestic and her father as a mechanic, gardener, and handyman. They became indispensable to the family, and when they asked permission to bring their children to live with them, the family agreed to the plan, not wanting to lose the labor they had come to rely on. Initially, Sevginar's father tried every legal way to bring the children back to Turkey with him on one of the trips he took to Bulgaria, but to no avail. "In fact, practically all my friends from our village came as clandestines," she added, referring to her hometown, near Sliven. "This route through the channelers was really popular at the time. Actually, it had become a very feasible, very common solution for people back then, so routine that it had become completely normalized." Although I had been privy to pieces of her story earlier, when she talked about it with courage and grace in the classroom, I now learned more as we sat at a café and she recounted the full story of her crossing. In her characteristic vivacious style, she recalled:

The first time around, my father made a deal with some Bulgarian smugglers. We met them in Haskovo, a town in the southern part of Bulgaria, very close to the Turkish border. Although they had already agreed on the price, the men tried to bargain for more at the last minute. When my father told them, "I am not giving you a penny more, you take us or you leave us," they ended up adding three more people to our group: two girls, one younger than me and one slightly older, and an older man in his fifties. The families of the little girls had been told that they would not have to get out of the car for the duration of the journey, so they were dressed in these short, pretty skirts. It was hot—it was the month of August. And when we walked through all those bushes and the sunflower fields, their legs were terribly scratched. I can still visualize those legs all scraped, red, bleeding. We were not allowed to carry anything with us, no food, nothing, because if you drop anything, a napkin or a bottle, they can follow your trail. There are too many police near the border.

When we met with the smugglers, it was noon. First we just waited in a park until it got dark. Then we started walking. Not even with a flashlight; we walked under moonlight. Finally we reached the barbed wire. The guy who was leading us, he dug a hole beneath it, and we passed through one by one. We walked again for a little while and reached another line of barbed wire. If we passed through that second wire, we would be on the Turkish side. At that moment, three Bulgarian police with guns jumped on us, shouting, "Lie down on the ground." Of course my father had warned us at the outset. "If we get caught, no escaping," he had instructed several times. "We lie on the ground and surrender immediately." I was on my dad's shoulder; you see, I had had a hard time walking through those sunflower fields that were taller than me. We instantly ducked, my dad and I, and lay flat on the ground, but my dad kept shouting, "Sevginar." I said, "Dad, I am here on your shoulder.

Call out to my sister." He had meant to shout out to my sister, but he had gotten all confused from the panic. When the police pounced on us, the smuggler started to run away, and the fifty-year-old man tried to follow him. And my sister mistook him for my dad and dashed after him. So my dad started to shout, "Fatma, Fatma," and she heard him and came back and lay down with us.

The soldiers rounded us up and took us to the military barracks along with the other two girls. They eventually caught the old man, too. Only the smugglers somehow got away. They put us, the children, in a huge dorm in the military barracks, and they locked up my dad and the other guy in a cell. In the morning, they took us to a different room. This one had bunk beds with colorful sheets and all. It was a nursery of sorts. Because they were catching so many children at the border in those days, they had turned one of the rooms of the barracks into a nursery! They asked us if my dad was really our dad, and when we said yes, they allowed him to stay with us at night so we would not be scared. They would take him away for questioning for the entire day. This routine went on for four days. During questioning, they apparently threatened him and said that normally they would beat him but were refraining from doing so only on our account. They were trying to get him to testify that another man who had been caught that same night was the smuggler who had tried to take us across. But my dad refused, saying, "I cannot do wrong by God's creature."

During those four days, they brought two siblings to our room. They had been caught by the Turkish border police, and after staying at the barracks on the Turkish side, had been deported to the Bulgarian side. So we were six kids in that room. We could leave to go to the toilet, but that was it. We could not leave the building. And it was so hot, when we opened the windows for some air, all the mosquitoes at night flooded into our fully lit room. I got so many bites that my face grew twice its size and I could not feel my tongue. I could not eat anything. Meanwhile, the guards who caught us, they were in a splendid mood because at the time, for each person they caught crossing illegally, they were given time off to go visit their families. Finally, by the end of the fourth day, my uncle managed to track us down. He bargained with a lawyer who was there for someone else to also get my dad out. As he let us go, the chief said, "This time, we let you go. But if you get caught once more, forget it."

So the next time we tried to cross the border illegally, my dad could not come with us. But this time, he made a deal with channelers who were Turkish. And we ended up taking a different route, a much longer one. Another difference was that the channelers took us from our homes in the village. They said, "You will not have to walk at all, you will cross the border in a car." But of course we knew the deal from the first time, so my sister and I were like, "You can't fool us with that crap." We folded our sweatpants into our small nylon bags. But my second cousin, we could not convince her. She was thirty-five, single, so there was no way they were giving her a visa. So my dad told her that he would pay for her journey too if she kept us company. My cousin dressed up for the journey as if she were going into town, and you know how women in Bulgaria dress up when they go on an outing, like they are entering New York high society. She had a fancy dress, makeup, high heels, and all. By the sixth hour of our walk, she could barely limp along.

We changed cars several times, until finally around nine o'clock in the evening, they loaded about fifteen to twenty of us into the trunk and shut it. There was some air, but it was all dark. My sister and I, we looked at each other and said, "They are definitely making us walk." And we put on the sweatpants over our shorts. Half an hour later perhaps, we got off near an orchard and started to walk. We walked for at least six hours; it was almost dawn when we reached the Turkish border. I don't recall any fear from the first journey. But the closest I got to feeling fear was during this journey, when we would rest during the five to ten minutes they were giving us every hour or so. I was so exhausted that when I sat on the ground my head would fall onto my knees. And I was terrified as I dozed off—"What if I fall asleep and they leave, and they leave me here?"

At certain points along the way, we would hear the soldiers, and we tried to hold our breath. Finally, we reached the barbed wire which I think might have had detectors on [it] and which they wrapped with pieces of cloth. This time, we only passed one set of wires. I think the reason is that this was a much longer route that took us way away from the main border. After the barbed wire, we kept talking, through the forest, and when we reached an opening, three or four cars came to meet us. They loaded us into them. I think they might have put a couple of the smaller kids in the trunk. Then they took us to a barn—I still do not know why a barn first. There we were able to call our parents, and as we were calling, the smugglers warned us—they had not been paid yet— "Don't tell them you walked." And the first thing we said was, "They made us walk!" Then they put us in cars again and took us to their homes, where we slept for what I thought was a whole day. But it was only a few hours, and when I woke up, the women in the house had prepared a huge breakfast table. We all sat together, ate, spoke, and watched TV until my aunt came to fetch us. When we arrived in Istanbul, we switched yet again to another car my mother's employer had sent to take us to the house. By then it was midnight. They rubbed us in the tub for hours that night to scrape off the layers of dirt—grime, you call it.

For a long time afterwards, we had so much fun telling the story of our escape. The highlight of the reenactment was when my father would turn to me and make me repeat for everyone's benefit what I thought the soldiers who had caught us had said. You see, I was really young then and my Bulgarian was almost nonexistent because I had not yet gone to school. So every time the story of our crossing was told, my dad would turn to me and say, "So what did the soldiers say, my daughter?" And I would venture my best imitation of what I thought the soldiers said. Of course it was gibberish Bulgarian, nothing remotely close to the real words. And everyone in the room would just explode with laughter. And I don't think it is just us who find comedy in these stories of crossing the border. Other people whose stories I have listened to, they also laugh when talking about it. It is something so normalized for us, so ordinary. But when you think about it, of course, there is nothing ordinary about it: you are entering a country through illegal means, then you start attending school without being registered, your parents are working in the informal economy.

Separating from her parents, a nocturnal hike through sunflowers that towered above her, fear of being left behind if she fell asleep, being ordered to lie down at gunpoint—these are no doubt extraordinary events for a seven-year-old. Still, they are not quite the desperate journeys undertaken by migrants from Syria, Afghanistan, Eritrea, or Somalia to Europe, journeys that make the headlines only when corpses are discovered in the airless cargo containers of trucks on a Hungarian highway or washed up on the shores of the Aegean or the Mediterranean when overcrowded rubber dinghies sink after departing the coast of Libya for Italy or Turkey for Greece. In the 1990s, the Bulgaristanlı children, even though they were entrusted to smugglers, were not systematically exposed to injury, starvation, and death, like the unaccompanied minors who began journeys from Afghanistan and crossed deserts, forests, and continents on their own to reach Calais,[8] or the children whose deaths have become a common occurrence as they attempt to cross the border from Mexico into the United States through the Sonoran Desert of Arizona, described by Jason de Leon (2015) as the land of open graves. Narratives of precarious crossings recounted by Sevginar and others, often punctuated by moments of comic relief such as little Sevginar's garbled reenactment of the border official's command, are different from the potentially fatal border crossings that are the "last-ditch efforts for social, economic, and political survival" (Petryna and Follis 2015, 402).

These precarious crossings, contingent as they were on the grace of the employers who were willing to take the children in or the trustworthiness of the channelers, were nonetheless to a designated destination at which one could expect to be bathed after the arduous journey by a relieved and caring parent. Neither did the smugglers match the widespread image of the trafficker as heartless villain.[9] The channelers to whom the Bulgaristanlı entrusted their children were invariably acquaintances. Their whole families were involved in the transaction, with the women of the house preparing food for the children and spending time with them after the journey. Gürcan, who had crossed the border with his brother on the top ventilation section of a train, explained to me the intimate network through which one made arrangements with a smuggler: "Someone knows this or that person, or they have a family friend who crossed and they give you the contacts. This is always how one gets to the *kanalcı*. . . . And the other thing is that there were no bad stories circulating. I mean, we did not hear one story about a child dying or even about anything bad happening to a child on a journey. Nothing like that. That is also why people were able to entrust their children."

In distinguishing the crossings of the Bulgaristanlı children from migrant journeys marked by desperation, the imminent risk of death, or hope against hope, I tread a fine line. The danger is to dismiss the real risks of injury and trauma both to the children and to the parents who held their breath as they waited for them to cross over in safety. Nonetheless, I pursue this distinction precisely because the border crossings I was told about do not fit the tales of tragedy that make the headlines. But even those border crossings that are not escape as last resort are precarious. The fact that there is a degree of choice, room for maneuvering, and ample opportunity for comedy in the retelling does not render these acts any less dependent on the grace, will, and whim of structurally more powerful others. As Sevginar reported in her narrative, the normalization of the extraordinary is part and parcel of precarity.

PRECARIOUS FOOTINGS IN
THE COMPANY OF CHILDREN

After eight years of living and working in Turkey, Cemile was still waiting for a response to the citizenship applications submitted three years ago for herself, her husband, and their two children. But even before that, they had not resided illegally, she explained. "Not quite. We were so grateful that we got our boy and girl enrolled in the neighborhood school here. It is all thanks to the president of the school, who feels for the plight of *soydaş*. He also discerned right away what kind of people we are. So he accepted us. After the children started going to school, we were able to get the *refakatçi izni*."

The *refakatçi izni*, literally translated as "companion permit," is a special type of residence permit extended to adults who are accompanying minors. But access to this permit was not a straightforward matter in the 1990s. When increasing numbers of parents resorted to entrusting their children to smugglers, there suddenly emerged a sizable population of undocumented children from Bulgaria. Initially, the attitude of the state toward the growing numbers of undocumented school-aged children was one of sheer indifference. Although Turkey is a signatory to the Convention on the Rights of the Child, which stipulates that all children must be provided access to primary education regardless of their legal status, in practice, children's access to education in Turkey is barred through a Ministry of Education circular that requires an ID number upon registration.

Because of the impediments to educational access, Bulgaristanlı parents had to resort to informal means of enrolling their children in school, and they were successful virtually without exception. In several firsthand accounts I heard, any initial frustration was eventually overcome. The first school they approached might have turned the parents away, but the second or the third would invariably have a principal who was sympathetic to the "plight of *soydaş*" or, with a little nudge, was willing to be coaxed.

"So this is how we began school," explained Aylin, who had arrived in 2000 after being led across the border at dawn by channelers. "There was a school in the neighborhood where we lived and where my parents work. My father said, 'I want to register my daughter in second grade.' But the principal would not take me. 'You have no record,' he said. 'Your child is illegal. I will not accept her into my school.' So there was this other school, a twenty-minute walk away. My dad's cousin lived there, and because they came in

1989, they have citizenship and everything. Her children were about to graduate from the middle school there, and they were very well liked at the school.
So they became intermediaries for us. They talked to the principal, saying,
'You know, these are our relatives, we vouch for them, they will not cause you
any trouble,' and so on. And then on top of that, as usual, with a little bribe
that gets called a donation to the school, they took us in."

Access to education, a basic right for all children and a right to which Turkey is internationally committed on paper, was thus attainable only through
goodwill, sympathy, and favoritism. Bulgaristanlı migrants pleaded with a
principal, or got their relative or employer to testify on their behalf, or per-
suaded the neighborhood representative to act as an intermediary. These stories of happy endings, which allude to the support and solidarity of various
school principals, neighbors, or relatives, also reveal the power asymmetry
that marks the act of compassion. An already legally sanctioned right, the
right of access to education regardless of legal status, was rendered contingent
on the goodwill of those who hold the keys.

In narrating this act of compassion that set them apart from other undocumented migrants who have no such acts of compassion to rely on for securing a fundamental right for their children, Cemile, who migrated from
Zavet in 1993 with her two children, described such compassion on the part
of the school principal, who "discerned right away what kind of people we
were": people who were reliable, educated, and not strangers, characteristics
perceived by school officials to be common among those who could claim the
status of *soydaş*.

Executed in a depoliticized and depoliticizing field, acts of compassion
and solidarity are unevenly distributed across different groups of migrants.
While Bulgaristanlı children can count on becoming the recipients of compassion, the same does not hold true for undocumented children with no
claim to ethnic kinship. For example, another new and fast-growing population, children of migrants from Africa, have no access to primary education
in Turkey.[10] Even some of the more optimistic interpreters of the Law on Foreigners and International Protection No. 6458/2013, who view the law as offering significant improvements regarding the rights of foreigners, acknowledge that this new body of legislation entirely eschews the question of access
to compulsory education for undocumented children.[11]

The precarious school attendance among Bulgaristanlı children acquired
slightly more firm legal grounding in 2003. This was not the result of a pol-

icy commitment to uphold children's right to education but the by-product of an extraneous bureaucratic development: the Ministry of Education switched from old-fashioned handwritten records to a centralized, Web-based registration system called e-School (*e-Okul*). With e-School, it suddenly became apparent that there were many Bulgaristanlı *kaçak öğrenci* (clandestine students) attending primary and secondary schools, especially in Istanbul. For a while, there were rumors that the undocumented Bulgaristanlı children would be banned from school, which created worry about mass deportations. "But we were too many," said Aylin. "It would have been really hard to deport us."

In addition to Aylin's astute assessment of the government's feasibility considerations, the government would not have wanted to put itself in the position of undertaking mass deportation of its *soydaş*. The state solution to what threatened to become public controversy was a legal concession: all Bulgaristanlı children who were without papers and attending school in Turkey were registered and given residence permits based on school attendance and temporary citizenship ID numbers. Once the children were thus formally registered, parents could apply for the companion permit for accompanying a minor in Turkey. For a brief window of time, between 2005 and 2007, it seemed as if the companion permit might also lead to citizenship: some families who obtained companion permits through their children during this period and then renewed them for two years were able to submit citizenship applications.

However, this path to citizenship was short-lived. In 2009, without warning or explanation, the companion permit as a valid type of residency for citizenship application was annulled, disappointing many who had built their hopes on this type of permit and who had spent a great deal of time and money collecting the required documents. While registration in school was certainly a move forward for the children from the previous informal arrangement between parents and the school principal, it still did not guarantee a diploma. Until they acquired citizenship, migrant children attending school received an informal document that allowed them to continue on to the next grade with the provision that once they became citizens, they would be able to retroactively receive a proper diploma. Most families I knew took the chance. But at least one family I knew sent their eighth-grader back to Bulgaria after two years in Turkey, choosing the pain of separation rather than the perpetual anxiety of risking a wasted education.

PRECARIOUS LABOR

If one analytic track for giving the notion of the precarious more precision is through the etymological cue that the term provides, another track has been through delimiting the lifeworlds to which precarity pertains. Kathleen Millar (2015) chooses the latter path. Rather than equate precarity with a generalized condition of vulnerability, which, she point outs, "would likely turn up precarity everywhere we looked," she restricts her deployment of the term to conditions of work. I share with Millar the concern to differentiate precarity from vulnerability. And although I have also so far traced precarity as it manifests itself in multiple aspects of life as an intersubjective relation of domination, in this final section I home in on precarious labor.

As elsewhere, migrant work in Turkey is primarily off the record, labor-intensive, and underpaid. Construction is the only sector in which men outnumber women (Akpınar 2010). The food and tourism sector seems to have an equal gender distribution, while domestic and care work, the entertainment industry, sex work, and textile and manufacturing ateliers are entirely dependent on women's labor (Toksöz and Ünlütürk-Ulutaş 2011). On the whole, migrant women work without permits. All of these lines of work, therefore, render them unprotected to different degrees and are particularly open to abuse, exploitation, and gendered harassment. Nonetheless, there is an internal hierarchy of relative danger and protection within the informal migrant labor as well: women who do sex work and women who work in textile ateliers are far more vulnerable to sexual violence and to deportation if they file a complaint.

According to Emel Coşkun (2018), the routine sexual violence that these women encounter in the workplace includes being asked to do overtime alone, being forced to watch pornographic videos during overtime, and being forced to have sexual intercourse with the accompanying threat of being denied their weekly wages. The gendered violence that they are subjected to is exacerbated, Coşkun (2018) writes, by the color of their skin and the widespread assumption that they are "voluntary prostitutes." The women Coşkun interviewed attributed the prevalence of sexual abuse to the lack of legislative bodies that they could appeal to. Their employers, who knew this all too well, often threatened them by handing them over to the police.

Cutting across the gender divide, African migrants are on the whole relegated to menial and workshop jobs that have acquired a colloquialism of their own: *çabuk çabuk*. Literally translated as "quick quick," this original verb form signifies what the employer yells out to the laborer. But it has been reappropriated as a noun by African migrants to describe the kind of transient tasks to which they are invariably assigned, usually involving heavy lifting, moving, and cleaning, tasks that need to be done fast and are short-lived, with no prospect of longer-term employment.[12]

The internal hierarchy of risk and vulnerability is reflected in the distribution of migrants from different countries across these sectors: whereas African women (and increasingly Syrian youth) work in textiles and women from the former Soviet Union work in the entertainment sector and both groups of women can cross over into sex work, Bulgaristanlı women are virtually absent from these domains. Instead, post-1990 Bulgaristanlı women work in the domestic and care sector, and a few of my interlocutors were able to secure jobs as secretaries or personal assistants, even if this too meant a demotion from their previous positions in Bulgaria. Over the full course of more than a decade in the field, I was referred only once, with reluctance and in hushed tones, to a woman in her forties who lived in one of the migrant settlements. During my visit with her, she did not explicitly acknowledge but only insinuated her involvement in sex work. But the whole visit was marked by her own reiterations of her outcast status in the community.

I am not singling out domestic work as a realm of labor that is free from exploitation. To the contrary. Migrant domestic labor in Turkey is a domain of precarity par excellence. I do, however, want to delineate the contours of precarious labor that undergird the domestic labor market as precisely as possible so as to show what it shares with but also how it differs from other domains of labor, where migrant women are structurally more exposed to being denied payment and to violence and deportation. Domestic work has become the only sector in which work permits for migrants are legally codified: according to the revisions made in 2012 to the Law on the Residence and Travel of Foreigners in Turkey (Law No. 5683/1950), the procedures for work permits of those in domestic labor— and only in domestic labor—are subjected to a facilitated, fast-track legal procedure. This has meant the relative privileging of domestic work above work in other sectors such as construction, textiles, or sex work, which continue to be entirely unregulated and offer no prospects for migrants who work in these sectors to obtain legalization.

But once again, "relative" is the operative word here. Although the 2012 change to the Law on the Residence and Travel of Foreigners paved the way for work permits for foreigners in domestic labor, it came with the stipulation that one can apply for the work permit and subsequently for the residence permit only through one's employer. Furthermore, the work permit is valid only as long as one is employed by that particular employer. This stipulation renders migrant women entirely dependent on their employer to obtain and to sustain their legal status, leading one analyst of the new law to call it "a bail system that is organized by the state itself" (Demirdizen 2013).[13]

The Turkish domestic work sector was initially dominated by migrants from the Philippines, Moldova, and Bulgaria, and now includes women from Turkmenistan, Uzbekistan, Azerbaijan, Tajikistan, and Armenia. Bulgaristanlı Turks, who speak Turkish, are presumed to share cultural and religious values, and are not suspected of getting involved in sex work. They occupy a privileged niche in the hierarchy of the segmented labor market in domestic work, in terms of both pay and treatment (Toksöz and Ünlütürk-Ulutaş 2012). With a monthly salary ranging from $300 to $1,000, Bulgaristanlı get paid at the higher end, just behind nannies from the Philippines, who can claim the highest salaries due to their fluency in English, which is viewed by upper-class employers as a cultural asset for their children. Still, the 2005 data from the General Directorate of Security are indicative of the coexistence, once again, of privilege and precarity. According to the figures provided, those with Bulgarian citizenship had the overwhelming majority of residence permits, with 54,000, attesting to their advantage in comparison with other migrant groups.[14] Equally striking, however, is another statistic that these data provide: of these 54,000, only 450 had work permits. The Bulgaristanlı were able to access strikingly higher numbers of residence permits through their ethnic privilege; this, however, did not exempt them from being precarious in the labor market.

PRECARITY AND ENTITLEMENT

On the basis of their depiction of how people in post-Fordist contexts mourn the loss of the promise of security and the predictability of Fordism, Andrea Muehlebach and Nitzan Shoshan (2012) make the brilliant point that something is always precarious in comparison to a prior state of (more) security. This insight informs my final circumscribing move on the use of precarity.

Sevdiye, who had migrated from Silistra, called me to say that we were going to be neighbors. She had quit her job because she could no longer put up with the unending workday. Just when she thought she was done after putting the kids to sleep, cleaning up in the kitchen, and preparing the six-year-old's special lunch box because he was allergic to several foods, the "lady of the house" would call down the stairs, robbing Sevdiye of the few moments of peace and quiet alone in her room that she had anticipated all day, moments in which she would enjoy the most recent photos of her two-year-old grand-daughter in Bulgaria. "Please do not forget to iron my dress, the midnight blue one, and those new sheets that just got washed, too, while you are at it." It was not the work itself, but the never-ending nature of the work that bothered Sevdiye. It was not ever being able to say, "This is my free time now."

"I don't know what got into me," Sevdiye said, referring to the evening she quit. "Maybe it had accumulated and I exploded, or maybe I was just too tired that day." A day earlier, she had passed out in the queue at the police station where she and a few of her friends had been waiting since five in the morn-ing to submit their application for the amnesty for a three-month permit. She had called me, still shaky, from the police station. "The words just came out of my mouth somehow. I said, 'I thought I was done for the day.' There was a moment of silence and then she heard the ice-cold retort: 'Who do you think you are? You are done when I tell you you are done.' The thing that got to me is that I [had] soothed her so many times when she was secretly crying be-cause of trouble in the house with her husband. So that ice-cold voice really offended me. As if we had not been intimate during those four years I spent at that house, raising the kids with my own hands. I cried all night in my room, but I had made up my mind. I went down to the breakfast table slightly late the next morning, my stuff all packed up. I think she knew the moment she saw me. She said, extra sweetly, 'Good morning, dear Sevdiye, do you want some tea?' I said, 'No, Sevda Hanım. I am leaving.'"

Sevdiye had worked in a textile factory in Bulgaria until the fall of com-munism. At the time of our conversation, her daughter was pursuing a degree in criminology and had a two-year-old child. Making sure that her daughter earned her degree was one of the primary reasons for Sevdiye having come to Istanbul to work. "I worked under a boss in the factory, too," she reminisced more than once. "But when we talked to each other, when we addressed each other, when we sat down at the table, we were equal human beings. I respected him, he respected me. One could joke around." On another occasion, she had said, "Back in the days of *komünizma*, I knew there would always be bread to put on the table. I didn't worry about getting sick, losing my job, not receiv-ing my pay."

Sevdiye narrated these details of the upsetting exit at a Starbucks with a gorgeous view of the Bosphorus in Bebek, the fancy new neighborhood where she now worked. "Now we can meet for coffee all the time with a view of the sea instead of once every amnesty, standing in those queues," she said. She spoke highly of her current employer in Bebek. "The best part," she said, "is that the baby is my only job—there is another woman for the daily cleaning and cooking, and a third woman who comes in every other week for the heavy cleaning, windowsills, and all." Sevdiye added, "She treats me with real respect. Her husband, too. They said from day one: 'You are one of the family.' I sit with them at the table."

"There is one thing that upsets me, though," Sevdiye continued. "She took away my passport. It stays with her, and she gives it to me only on Sundays, on my off day, right before I leave the house. Every Sunday, I wait at the door for it, like a beggar. I mean, come on, if she were to work abroad herself, would she surrender her passport to someone? You know I have kept quiet these past two weeks, because I do not want to lose this job, and on the whole, the conditions are good. But I will talk to her soon. This is not the kind of document that you just hand over. If she wants, I could give her a duplicate of all my relevant information. I will not be begging for my own passport."

The confiscation of domestic workers' passports is widespread among employers in Turkey. In 2012, on one of the most popular websites for mothers, a post consisting of recommendations for "how to treat your child's foreign nanny" went viral. The fourth item on the list read: "Confiscate her passport immediately and lock it in a safe place." The ease with which such advice can be offered on one of the most popular mothering sites in Turkey is no less than the normalization of what Ong has called the "house-bound form of labor incarceration" (2006, 201), a normalization that is aided by the register of familial affect—"you are part of the family."

But in Sevdiye's disturbingly common story, what surprised me was to hear that she had handed over her passport in the first place. Several of the other Bulgaristanlı women told me similar stories of being asked to turn over their passports. Not only did they refuse, but they expressed outrage. When the same demand was made of Elmas, she told me that she had literally exploded with laughter right in her employer's face. "Come on, Zeynep Hanım. Do you not hear with your own ears how ridiculous you sound? That passport is my only identity here. If you traveled somewhere abroad and you stayed with some people there, and they asked to keep your passport, would you just hand it over to them? You can't really be asking what I think you are asking?" In Elmas's rendition of the incident, her sarcasm seemed to have put the employer to shame. Elmas said that Zeynep went on to mumble something to the effect of how it was just advice that she had received from a friend of hers, a friend who was doing this with each of her employees because it took care of certain worries. "But no, of course, it should not be necessary in this case," Zeynep Hanım had retreated, according to a victorious Elmas, who recounted the incident with pride and amusement.

The refusal to yield their passports was one among many acts through which Bulgaristanlı migrants asserted their entitlement. Indeed, they were often recognized by employers—sometimes with admiration, other times begrudgingly—for their wisdom and pedantry about a whole range of practices, from hygiene to correct mothering to equal gender relations, and for generally taking an assertive and confident stance vis-à-vis their employers. More importantly, even when expressing endearments to a particular employer, Bulgaristanlı migrants would often be vocal about the substandard conditions they routinely faced at work. Several of the migrants I got to know consistently nudged their employers to apply for work permits on their behalf. They were also usually more selective in choosing an employer, and once they did, were able to negotiate slightly better workloads and schedules.

REAPPRAISALS OF UNCERTAINTY AND PRECARITY?

In the more conventional usage and as it bears on the field of migration studies, uncertainty has been viewed mostly in terms of the constraints it imposes on possibilities for action, or what Nicholas de Genova has called "an enforced orientation to the present" (2002, 427). Uncertainty as experienced by migrants is a structurally produced condition by the constant threat of deportation.[15] The pervasive uncertainty that deportability creates for those who perpetually live under its threat results in "the revocability of the promise of the future" (Carter 1997, cited in de Genova 2002, 427) and, according to de Genova, keeps the undocumented in line as an exploitable workforce and prevents them from making many long-term plans (see also Coutin 1993).

But if uncertainty is viewed mostly in a negative light, others have argued that it is a productive resource rather than merely a constraint. "Uncertainty is not always exclusively a problem to be faced and solved," write Elizabeth Cooper and David Pratten in the introduction to a volume on experiences of uncertainty in Africa. "Uncertainty is a social resource and can be used to negotiate insecurity, conduct and create relationships, and act as a source for imagining the future with the hopes and fears this entails" (Cooper and Pratten 2015, 2). Here, uncertainty is taken to be as much about hope and possibility as it is about vulnerability and anxiety. Moreover, uncertainty can become "the basis of curiosity and exploration; it can call forth considered action to change both the situation and the self" (Whyte 2009, 213–14).[16]

Following Susan Whyte (2005) on the subjunctive mood, Cooper and Pratten (2015) argue that "a theory of contingency or uncertainty is best approached as history in the subjunctive mood—action that attends to that yet to happen" (3). They draw particular attention to Whyte's definition of the subjunctive as a mood of action—"doubt, hope, will and potential" (Whyte 2005, 250–51). Cooper and Pratten's recentering of uncertainty as constitutive of the very grounds for action draws on the legacy of John Dewey (1929), specifically his contention that "action and uncertainty are so mutually entwined that they need to be perceived within the same frame" (quoted in Cooper and Pratten, 6).

The structured indeterminacy produced by legal regulations concerning Bulgaristanlı migrants and their accompanying bureaucracies is indeed productive of unexpected initiatives. Bahriye spent weeks and a considerable amount of money on notarized translations and seals for the documents required for her citizenship application, including an extra trip to Bulgaria for her "document of origins" when the association refused to provide her with the document it had promised because her passport carried her Bulgarian name instead of her Turkish one.

After she thought she had everything ready, another problem emerged: the discrepancy between Bulgarian and Turkish conventions of how one's name is written on official documents. In Bulgaria, one's paternal name is listed as the middle name, whereas no such norm exists in Turkey. For the application to be considered, everything needs to be consistent across each document—namely, the document of origins or birth certificate, passport, and residency permit—and even a difference in the spelling of a name can cause trouble. The tiniest correction, such as a letter or a part of a letter—for instance, the s with the cedilla that exists in Turkish but not in Cyrillic (ş)—needs to be authorized by a translator and then a notary needs to provide an official stamp. After discovering all these potential causes of trouble along the way and having spent a whole month's salary on collecting the documents, Bahriye was furious when she realized that the translator had made the mistake of including her paternal surname as her middle name on the birth certificate.

Three more trips to the notary in which she pleaded with the clerk to correct it so that she would not have to start the process from scratch drove her finally to take matters into her own hands. "They are human like you and me. All this uncertainty, lack of clarity. And we keep feeling overwhelmed and intimidated by it. I said this is it. The third time I went back and forth between the Registrar's Office and the notary, I spoke very confidently about my complaint to that director at the Registrar's Office. And she said, 'Just go tell that notary to take care of it and cross it out and stamp it.' I went back to the clerk at the notary and told her what the other clerk had said. I don't know if she was convinced by my story, or if she thought, 'This woman has become a plague and I will not be rid of her if I do not do what she says.' But anyway, the notary clerk simply whited out the middle name. Look!" And proudly she showed me the birth certificate, which bore the official stamp of the notary of that district and contained a rather visible blotch of white right in the middle.

Bahriye Hanım's saga about the vagaries of bureaucracy did not end there. The last step was to have all of the documents reviewed by an official at the Registrar's Office before submitting the application. Her first two attempts failed even though she went to the office at dawn and waited the entire day. "It is all because of the chaos, lack of a proper system," Bahriye said. "The uncertainty around the rules. It is not clear who decides and how they decide to line up the people left over from the day for the following day. It seems to all be arbitrary." After the second day of frustration, Bahriye organized the discontent among the crowd into a modest protest. She convinced the officials—"They all knew me by face and name by that point"—that she would be a fairer judge of whose turn it should be.

The morning after she had told me this story, I got the following message from her at 8:15 a.m.: "Got here at 4:00 a.m., and at 8:00 a.m., it was ME who made the list for the 105 people waiting their turn."

Uncertainty may lead to inventive daily tactics in response to bureaucratic frustrations. Beyond such immediate fixes, uncertainty may also result in people "translating the indeterminacy of existence into a sense of possibility" (Di Nunzio 2015, 139) toward the realization of longer-term commitments and plans. Atiye, a migrant from Zavet, was initially extremely frustrated with the onset of the ninety-day rule. Playing by the rules would have endangered her job as a nanny. Her employer had told her that she would be replaced by someone else if she left. After worrying for weeks, she told me that she had come up with a plan. She was going to work even harder, putting in an extra ironing session here and her special dish there, and make herself indispensable. She already felt confident about how much they trusted her with their five-year-old son. She talked to a friend back in the village who had initially been reluctant to leave for Turkey to work even though her family was financially struggling. Her friend did not want to leave her own daughter, who had just had a baby. So the two women decided that they could alternate every three months. This way, both would be legal in terms of exit and entry. Just before her ninety days were about to end, we met and Atiye was beaming. Her employer had accepted her proposal, and from that time on she would be working for three months here and staying back in the village near Razgrad with her husband for three months, which she said was actually better for their marriage as well.

To the extent that precarity is about being at the mercy of a more powerful other, people's resourcefulness in coming up with creative responses to uncertainty and contingency provides a useful reminder that there is always some room for negotiation and maneuvering within relations of domination, whether it is the relationship between Bahriye Hanım and the notary or that between Atiye and her employer. In that, the recent reappraisal of uncertainty as productive of creativity is useful. And yet some caveats are in order.

It may well be that "contending with [uncertainty], going into the mud, is a different response than gripping on to familiar securities or the authorities that pronounce them" (Allison 2013, 13). Moreover, as Susan Whyte (2009) contends, uncertainty befits the subjunctive mood of doubt, hope, will, and potential. However, the range of resources that one has access to in order to contend with uncertainty in the first place is no small matter. Bulgaristanlı migrants, with their structural position of relative privilege as *soydaş*, can count on being the objects of compassion and solidarity. Furthermore, a Bulgarian passport allows them to reorient themselves toward other geographical locations.

Compare this to migrants from sub-Saharan Africa in Turkey, who are systematically racialized, or migrants from Armenia, who suddenly found themselves threatened with mass deportation by the prime minister in 2000 in retaliation for the law that France passed making genocide denial a crime.[17] Uncertainty, indeterminacy, and unpredictability are often decisively more productive of fear than they are of creativity in situations of profound political inequality and lack of institutional accountability. Broadening the geographical scope, Tobias Kelly (2006) describes how the Palestinian residents of Bayt Hajjar, in each journey across an Israeli checkpoint that might have resulted in being denied entry, or perhaps a fatal gunshot, "wore the uncertainties of their legal status on their bodies as their encounters with the Israeli military became marked by fear and anxiety" (102).

And even where one might have more resources at one's disposal with which to contend with uncertainty, that benefit is perhaps a little too glibly celebrated by those who wish to reappraise it. For uncertainty, even as it enables creative solutions, takes its toll. Kalbiye Hanım, who was in her late fifties, had managed to get citizenship. However, no one else in her family who had applied, including her husband and her daughter and son-in law, had yet been approved. Even though Kalbiye herself had achieved the goal of obtaining citizenship, she continued to work as a domestic without insurance or social security because the pay was good. "I don't mind so much for myself," she said, "but the children, they are young. They have no insurance, no social security. I really worry for them. What will happen to them?" she would ask disconcertedly, more than once in every interaction we had. "I do not consider going back to Bulgaria. I can't get decent employment there. But what will happen in the future? I don't know . . . [I]t is, after all, the Foreigners country [elin memleketi] . . . My grandfather used to say, 'A bird makes a nest on a tree, and once the branch swings, the nest is broken.' 'Our story is just like that,' he used to say."

The worry of uncertainty is often thus projected onto the younger generation, children themselves becoming an embodiment of hope as they represent an insistent connection to the future. Or the worry of uncertainty is articulated through references to the elder generation. In the middle of a particularly merry moment as we were having brunch at their place, Kalbiye Hanım's neighbor had suddenly blurted out, "Last night, in the middle of the night, my father called. 'I cannot fall asleep tonight,' he said, 'from worrying about you. You have been working for eleven years, and it all melts into the air. We retired, we have social security, and it makes me devastated to think you will have none of this.' Hearing him worry like that made my blood pressure soar."

A celebratory vision of "achieving indeterminacy," as Di Nunzio (2015, 153) calls the individual accomplishment on the part of subjects who have been exposed to structural violence and injustice, is bound to be a wanting account without an accompanying analysis of who gets to systematically bear the burden of having to struggle against structural uncertainty. In the move away from structures of domination to lived experience, or away from Marx and

Foucault and toward Dewey, we risk losing sight of uncertainty as an instrument of sovereign power used to keep migrants in their place—as undocumented legal subjects and as informal laborers. It is one thing to account for "the power of the unforeseen and of the unfolding and people's relentless determination to negotiate conditions of turbulence to introduce order and predictability into their lives" (Mbembe and Nuttall 2004, 349) and another to glorify uncertainty as the creative condition of being. The first grants people their dignity and recognizes their will to put up a fight even under the most devastating of circumstances. The second naturalizes and universalizes uncertainty to the point where the analysis of power and structural inequality starts to fade away.

Finally, uncertainty may be productive of hope in ways that benefit an exploitative migration regime rather than securing the individual rights of migrants. Recall the systematic uncertainty that surrounds the expectations of and the ambiguous terms for each of the amnesties for residence permits. The very uncertainty that surrounds the wait for each amnesty raises hope among the undocumented Bulgaristanlı migrants for legalization. The outcome is neither full of disappointment for all concerned nor fulfillment across the board, but instead, selective delivery of the promise. Such selective delivery does not abolish uncertainty but suffices to renew hope by continuing to set the example of the possibility of fulfillment, as Şemsiye so aptly captured with her reference to the "gate of hope" created by the amnesties.

In her depiction of the precarious lives and labor of Rio's urban poor, who collect recyclables in garbage dumps, Kathleen Millar (2014) argues that work in the dumps is in fact a choice of sorts, one that enables the poor to better contend with the multiple fragilities that characterize other aspects of their precarious lives. Against the conventional understanding of the informal economy and unpaid work as the last resort of the poor, Millar suggests that the flexibility of unpaid labor provides a relative degree of control and autonomy over all the unpredictability and the multiple insecurities, from health and environmental hazards to makeshift housing, debt, and incarceration, that already mark the lives of garbage collectors.

Unlike the acontextual revalorization of uncertainty, Millar's argument about the appeal of unpaid labor for the urban poor gives the notion of precarity geographical and historical specificity. She demonstrates how the meaning of and responses to precarity take on different inflections in the global south than they do in contexts characterized by post-Fordist affect. In contrast to the postindustrial societies of Europe, North America, and Japan, where Fordism was strongest and where its demise was therefore also most direly felt, in the global south, "precarious work has arguably always been a part of the experience of laboring poor" (Millar 2014, 34). This contrast leads Millar to reverse the directionality of the argument made by scholars of post-Fordist settings: if for the latter "unstable work destabilizes daily living" (Allison 2012, 349), for the urban poor in Rio this relationship's "unstable daily living destabilizes work" (Millar 2014, 35).

This is where the historical and contextual difference emerges. Precarity as it is experienced and signified with meaning by the Bulgaristanlı migrants, I would argue, is not so much agentic reappropriation of precarious conditions of work. Rather, the experience of precarity goes hand in hand with a sense of entitlement that is rooted in the past as well as in the concomitant expectation that better conditions should be, and are even likely to be, possible. More than other migrants in domestic work who seem pushed into or compelled to accept a range of exploitative and abusive behavior—lower pay, withholding of the weekly day off, humiliating treatment, and occasional sexual advances by a member of the household—Bulgaristanlı feel entitled to a sense of security and predictability.

Precarity, therefore, is not simply about uncertainty, risk, or the "indeterminacy of lived relations *within the present*" (Han 2011, 8, my italics). Precarity also presupposes a sense of security, a relative well-being in the past, or, as Muehlebach has aptly put it, precarity is "increasingly the structure of feeling of the once privileged." If one key source of this sense of entitlement stems from having once been privileged vis-à-vis the historically nurtured expectation by Turkey's migration policies for *soydaş*, another draws on the Bulgaristanlı migrants' past experience with and their recollections of communism. Whether that past is a "really existing" past or a romanticized past is a question I turn to next. I also consider how residual attachments to the Communist past are utilized as a resource to manage the difficulties of the present and manufactured into hopes for a more secure future.

4　NOSTALGIA AS HOPE

"YOU NEVER WORRIED about still having your job the next day, about putting food on the table," Bahtışen said over tea and *simit* (a savory staple of Istanbul) at a Simit Palace shop conveniently located near the police station. It was two in the afternoon, and we were done for the day because the queue number we had been given indicated that Bahtışen would not get a turn before the office closed that day. This meant that she would have to come back early the next morning to submit her application for a three-month resident permit to be granted as amnesty in 2009 for Bulgaristanlı migrants whose visas had expired and who were currently "illegal." Bahtışen was already fretting about the negotiations she would have to engage in with her employer in order to get permission for a second day off.

Having migrated from Ruse six years ago, Bahtışen was working as a live-in nanny for two children, ages eight and ten. They were well mannered, and the job was a breeze compared to what she had done in the past. This was the fourth nanny position that she had had since coming to Istanbul. She had quit two of them within a week of starting—which meant forgoing any wages—because the conditions were unbearable. For the third job, she said, the conditions were decent and she had appreciated the respect shown toward her. "They recognize my worth," she told me several times. But they had let her go anyway. "Unwillingly, *very* unwillingly," she said with pride. They did not want to hire another nanny to cover the three months that she would have to be away in Bulgaria because of the ninety-day rule that had come into effect in 2007. At first, Bahtışen had overstayed her visa in order to keep her job, but after a brush with the police she was no longer willing to risk illegality. "Actually, once [the police] realized I was *soydaş*, they were willing to let me go," she told me. But being stopped in the street like that and the intimidating, unwanted intimacy of the police officers until they marked her as *soydaş* made her shiver each time she recalled the encounter.

"Back in Bulgaria, you never felt this scared as a woman on your own," she said. "Here I have to worry if I am giving the wrong impression with people in general. I have to worry if they will take me for, you know, a natasha. Not that there is anything wrong with Russian women. In fact, I get along best with them, but you know what I mean." Furthermore, her husband back in Bulgaria was missing her too much. He said, "'That is it. No more of this *kaçak* [clandestine] business. Please come back.'" But their daughter needed help with her university studies and their son was getting married. Bahtışen also went on to explain that she just isn't herself when she doesn't work: "Work is the mirror of the person. That is what we were taught, that is what we got used to. First comes your *own* work, outside, only then the work you do at home. I am not myself when I don't work."

The amnesty that she now hoped for would gain her another ninety days. By then, she reasoned, her current employer would not want to let her go and would agree to an arrangement in which she worked every other three months. She had friends who had negotiated similar solutions. Then again, she dreaded even asking for an extra day off in order to be able to return to the police station the next day—especially, she added wearily, so soon into her new job. "You never worried about your job under *komünizma*, never worried about putting food on the table," she said, her tone once again animated, repeating her previous statement almost word for word, but this time adding that critical historical and political layer of experience: communism, or as it is pronounced in its Bulgarian inflection by the Bulgaristanlı, *komünizma*, which, given its nostalgic flavor, they prefer over the Turkish pronunciation, *komünizm*.

In their masterful depiction of landscapes imbued with what Lauren Berlant (2007) has called "post-Fordist affect," Muehlebach and Shoshan (2012) evoke the ways in which people across the globe yearn for aspects of the Fordist dream, particularly its promise of security and relative predictability. "Fordist citizens were thus, in some parts of the world at least, the collective owners of not just a commonly produced prosperity, but of commonly held attachments vis-à-vis the future—a future marked by predictable, measured incrementalism mediated by the state" (333). In certain respects, there are unexpected similarities between what Muehlebach and Shoshan describe as post-Fordist affect and what I explore in this chapter as post-communist affect. The communist attachments sustained by my interlocutors resemble Fordist attachments in the latter's internalization of labor as a collective social act that transcends the individual (Castells [1996] 2011, 619). Dreams "get reactivated and recuperated" and are invoked as residual yearnings for the promises of Fordism (Muehlebach and Shoshan 2012, 326) or, in the context I discuss, for the promises of communism. The yearnings for what Fordism promised constitute a particular experience of precarity, Muehlebach and Shoshan astutely point out, one that is grounded in what could have been. I suggest that post-communist nostalgia similarly sheds light on the precarity experienced by Bulgaristanlı migrants as not just uncertainty in the present but also as a yearning for what once was possible as well as a sense of entitlement to what ought to become possible again.

Muehlebach and Shoshan's depiction of post-Fordist affect is also inspiring because of the differences between what they describe and the post-communist predicament of the Bulgaristanlı migrants. The emphasis in their portrayal is on the "*frustrated* promises" (324, emphasis mine) of Fordism that continue to hold sway over post-Fordist subjects. I consider not just the frustrated but also the actualized promises of communism for my interlocutors, even if they were only partially realized. I also explore what remembering the past, one that is not just about frustrated promises but also actualized ones, means for the cultivation of hope as a collective structure of feeling. I argue that reducing nostalgic yearnings for communism to the melancholic condition risks the same kind of reduction that was all too often made by those who viewed post-communist nostalgia as mere fantasy or strategy.

BETWEEN NORMALIZING AND ORWELLIZING[1] COMMUNISM

Sedanur, a forty-five-year-old woman from Razgrad who worked as a nanny and cleaned houses in Istanbul, said she resented the condescension shown by people she met toward the kind of work she did. "Here they treat me like an inferior human being because I clean houses. In Bulgaria, under *komünizma*, we knew to respect our work, and we were respected for it, no matter what kind it was." Cumasiye, in her late forties, who was a factory worker for years in her town in Silistra and now worked as a live-out domestic, took the comparison further as we waited in line for an inquiry at the Foreigners' Branch: "We were equal there. Employer and worker would sit at the same table. We would joke around. Here they make sure to let you know your place." A month later, this time at her home, she reminisced about life under communism. Sighing over apricot rakiya and pictures of her now deteriorating house back in Silistra, which once had a glorious garden, she said, "We *lived* under *komünizma*. The *gavur* taught us how to lead ethical lives, not to steal, to work for your own bread."[2]

The resentment of the class- and gender-based marginalization they suffered upon coming to Turkey and the nostalgia about how good it used to be in Bulgaria under communism are affective states shared across cohorts of Bulgaristanlı women, whether they migrated in 1989 and were granted citizenship or came as part of the post-1990s economic migration wave and continue to be in irregular immigration status. Such positive recollections of communism, often glossed as "nostalgia" in scholarly and popular discourses, have baffled many. If, as Hannah Arendt (1973) argued, the political system completely colonized the lifeworld under totalitarianism, how is it that the very victims of the system do not display pure joy at its demise? From the particular vantage point of the Turkish minority, the query might become yet more pointed: how is it possible that members of Bulgaria's Turkish minority fondly remember the very regime that subjected them to various degrees of discrimination that culminated in the assimilationist measures of 1984–89?

The more simplistic explanations of the phenomenon branded as "postcommunist nostalgia" posit a resistant, indeed recalcitrant, communist legacy whose heirs lack the capacity to think beyond communism. Economist Georgy Ganev (2005) accounts for the negative public perceptions of Bulgaria's situation after the fall of communism through what he calls the "experience gap"—that is, the gap between the "positive objective experience" (449) in Bulgaria (such as higher GDPs, increased industrial output, sales, and productivity, jumps in foreign direct investment, and decreased corruption) and the "negative changes in perceptions" (the public perception that the situation in Bulgaria is deteriorating). According to Ganev, the gap has emerged because instead of the market price theory of value, people in Bulgaria still subscribe to the Marxist labor theory of value, which blinds them to the empirically improved conditions of the present. A gendered version of the thesis of communism's impervious legacy posits that women in Bulgaria at the close of the twentieth century were trapped in the myths of equality and emancipation. After the fall of communism, they continued to be entangled in communist myths because of their passivity and lack of awareness of their own specific interests (Kotzeva 1999, 96). Alternatively, as Alexia Bloch (2005) demonstrates, neoliberal or conservative perspectives view post-communist nostalgia as a form of "internal colonialism" (554) in which the privileges that were extended to a certain few under communism resulted in their ability or willingness to forget the oppression and humiliation that they had to endure.

Such views exemplify a dominant tendency in the literature on post-socialism to depict the communist experience as irredeemably totalitarian and oppressive regardless of the variations that developed across different communist landscapes or the specificities of subject positions. Former communist subjects who are nostalgic for full employment, access to education, and social security, and who construct a narrative of autonomy about the pre-1989 era are often considered to be hopelessly tainted with Marxist ideals to the point of not being able to discern where their true interests lie. This seems to be the case especially for women. Even some of the critical feminist scholarship in the United States on Eastern Europe exhibits a tendency to gloss over the real gains women made under communism in terms of both economic and social independence. Although women are not reduced to being viewed as having false consciousness, positive legacies of communism tend to be subsumed under the otherwise important "double burden argument": the assertion that the rhetoric of gender equality under communism masked a double exploitation through which the communist state secured women's labor by incorporating them into the workforce while continuing to place traditional demands on them as mothers and wives.

These subtle elisions in the scholarship of positive recollections of the communist experience are significant for probing the question of post-communist affect on the part of Bulgaristanlı migrants. First, the systematic minimization of the substantial gains that women made under communism may be viewed as an enduring symptom of what Katherine Verdery (1996) has called the "cognitive organization of the world" (4) under Cold War ideology. Without denying the complexities obscured by the communist ideal of the woman-as-worker, an ethnographic exploration that takes the emic view seriously contributes to the still-marginal archive on the enabling aspects of the communist experience. Inspired by the pioneering scholarship of Kristen Ghodsee (2005, 2011) and Maria Todorova (2010, 2014) for the Bulgarian context, I highlight the experiences of a minority group in or from Bulgaria to suggest an alternative to normalizing communism, as official communist ideologies have done, or by Orwellizing communism, as Cold War ideologies and scholarship are wont to do. Second, I do not reduce fond reminiscences of communism solely to discursive strategies deployed to ease the difficulties encountered in the present after migrating to Turkey, though they are certainly that, too. Unlike the melancholic attachments that characterize post-Fordist affect, what I call post-communist affect is a resource that Bulgaristanlı migrants draw on to affirm their entitlement to better treatment, including legalization in Turkey, and to sustain their hope for a better future that they firmly believe they deserve.

If up until this point this book has focused on the ways in which a sense of entitlement and deservingness is based on and performed through claims to racial kinship, I now foreground the communist legacy as another key resource for claiming dignity and demanding better treatment. Considering nostalgia as intimately related to hope stresses the need for an intersectional analysis in what often becomes too generalized a depiction of certain shared affective predicaments. To tease apart blanket terms such as "post-communist nostalgia" or "post-communist affect," I turn to scholarship that has focused on the gendered aspects of post-socialist nostalgia (Ghodsee 2004a, 2004b; Rofel 1999) as well as scholarship that has looked at the intersection of gender and minority status (Bloch 2005; Grant 1995) and add to that the significance of yet another category of difference: migrancy. Attending to Bulgaristanlı migrant women's recollections as members of a minority group in Bulgaria and as migrants in Turkey where they confronted a very different gender regime refines our understanding of the post-communist predicament. A simultaneous consideration of subjectivities constituted at the intersections of gender with other relevant categories of difference (Scott 1986)—in this instance, ethnic minority status and migrancy—gives ethnographic and historical substance to affective predicaments like post-communist nostalgia.[3]

The following examination of post-communist affect among Bulgaristanlı migrants as it bears on their hope in Turkey draws to some extent on the presentist focus of the nostalgia scholarship. Various scholars have questioned the limitations of viewing nostalgia as being primarily about the past. They emphasize instead the ways in which nostalgia is a "presentist" act (Berdahl 2000; Ivy 1995; Özyürek 2006), that is, a strategy that serves the present. The presentist emphasis has paved the way for innovative analyses of nostalgia in post-communist contexts as a strategy for coping with the difficulties of the transition period (Berdahl 1999; Grant 1995; Patico 2005).[4] It also draws due attention to the situated nature of the teller and the telling, both of which are inevitably motivated by the (adverse) conditions of the present. Reminiscences of a past in which one fared better are also a way of communicating a sense of dignity for the here and now: I might be undocumented *now*, working as a nanny *here*, but I was respected *then* and had a better job *there*. I would even further extend the presentist argument to suggest that nostalgia about the past is also a claim on the future, and hence intimately related to entitled hope: If I was respected then and lived under better conditions there, I expect the same of my future here.

But I also do not wish to reduce nostalgic memory to an instrument for coping with the present or managing expectations for the future. While the presentist and future-oriented components of nostalgia are also crucial to my analysis, I want to hold on to the claim that in certain cases nostalgia says something concrete about the past that can contribute to the historical record. I find this to be the case with Bulgaristanlı migrants not because they have an inherently more privileged vantage point on the past. Rather, their experience of two diverse geographies, political ideologies, and gender regimes gives their emic point of view the added benefit of the critical perspective of cross-cultural comparison. Such comparisons are based on their first-hand experiences of the distinctive gender regimes on two sides of the border. The cross-cultural perspective afforded by migration enables my interlocutors to critically assess especially the differences between the two regimes in terms of appropriate labor roles for women and gender codes.[5] Post-communist affect, then, is also a critical commentary on the precarious conditions of labor and the predicament of migrant women in contemporary Turkey.

EMANCIPATION OR DOUBLE BURDEN?

Hayriye, a fifty-five-year-old woman working as a live-out domestic in Istanbul since she migrated from a village near Ruse in 1993, told me of an encounter she had on the minibus, the cheapest mode of public transportation in Istanbul. "The money collector in the minibus once asked me," she recalled, "when I was returning very late from work, 'Are you coming from work, *abla* [the honorific kin term for older sister used as a form of address]?' 'Yes,' I replied to him. 'What a pity,' he said. 'Why should it be a pity?' I responded and then asked him, 'Are *you* able to meet your house's needs all on your own with this job? What does your wife do? If only you let her work, you will feel such relief!' 'That wouldn't be by our book' [*bizim kitabımızda yazmaz*], he said. 'Aaah,' I said to him, 'but it is written in other books.'"

"What can you do?" Hayriye asked me, as she concluded her account of the conversation, inviting me to commiserate with her over what she viewed as the irredeemable attitude of the money collector.

Indeed, an explicit refusal to comply with gendered norms imposed on them was the most common response that I came across among Bulgaristanlı women. Rahime, considerably younger than Hayriye, was thirty-five years old and had worked as a nanny since her arrival in 2001 from Haskova, Bulgaria. "I married a local after coming here," she told me. "He is originally from the Black Sea region. They are, you know, conservative people. They are not used to women working. I mean, I also understand that they are jealous; our people do take away their jobs. But then what to do? The Bulgaristanlı are really hardworking and diligent. All the women work. Even my husband, he is getting used to it. Eh, what else can he do but get used to it? I adjusted to so many things to fit in with his family. But on this point, I said to him, 'I will leave you, but I will not quit my job.'"

Whether they arrived in 1989 and received citizenship or after the 1990s and are seeking regularization, Bulgaristanlı migrant women who came of age during the period of communism shared a similar worldview in terms of gender roles and work. Virtually all of the immigrants I met expressed amazement at the low level of women's participation in the workforce in Turkey and described the communist ethos as one that made a life without work unthinkable. In fact, being without work in Bulgaria elicited only scorn or pity. Nezihe, who was pursuing a graduate degree at the time I met her, had immigrated as part of the mass migration of 1989 and therefore automatically received citizenship. She put it this way: "Back in Bulgaria, if someone did not have a job, they would either be scorned for laziness or pitied for being sick. And it wouldn't matter if this person was a man or a woman."

This normative criticism that not working suggests major sickness—or as another woman put it, "a character flaw"—is quickly conjoined with another common reservation, one that is predicated on personal grounds. As Bahtişen said in the quote that I presented at the outset of this chapter, "I am not myself when I do not work." Recall as well Elmas's migration story from chapter 1. Elmas had said that she decided to migrate again in the 1990s because of financial difficulties and also because if "you no longer have anything to put on the table, you start to fall apart." And recall Sevdiye, who had said, "Back in the days of *komünizma*, I knew there would always be bread to put on the table. I did not worry about getting sick, losing my job, not receiving my pay." A woman may marry a local and adjust to familial norms that feel conservative, as Rahime did in accordance with her husband's values, but work is not something that she could easily give up. And returning once again to Bahtışen's words, work was seen as the mirror of a person in communist Bulgaria, where one could count on putting bread on the table. Work was thus a fundamental source of self-esteem. Hatice, who had immigrated in 1989 and was working as a high school teacher in Istanbul, told me with proud defiance: "I had a university diploma, but I was cleaning houses when I first got here. Still, I did my job proudly because we learned in Bulgaria that all labor is worthy of respect."

Are these reiterations of more gender equality, the greater freedom that work provides to women, and the sense of security and dignity that comes from being a worker merely the manifestations of melancholic attachments to an idealized past? Svetlana Boym (2001) defines "nostalgia" as "a longing for a home that no longer exists or has never existed. Nostalgia is a sentiment of loss and displacement, but it is also a romance with one's own fantasy" (xiii). Given this definition, one could argue that the communist past becomes idealized, especially since the conditions of the present tend to be less favorable, if not outright unbearable, for many. In her work on East Germany, Daphne Berdahl (2000) underscores the need to situate practices of *ostalgie*—the term coined to designate the specific manifestation of nostalgia in the German context—within the atmosphere of disillusionment following reunification. Like Boym, Berdahl emphasizes the allusion to and illusion of a lost homeland inherent in nostalgia and suggests that practices of *ostalgie* "can thus be an attempt to reclaim a kind of *heimat* (home or homeland), albeit a romanticized and hazily glorified one" (137). Long ago, Kant (1798) pondered whether "homesickness" (*heimweh*)—the term in use before being replaced by the more medical "nostalgia"[6]—was truly about homesickness or merely about ephemeral time. In that spirit, one may even ask whether postcommunist nostalgia is about communism at all or whether it is simply "a Proustian quest for lost youth" (Alexander Kiossev, June 2016, personal communication; see also Nadkarni and Shevchenko 2004).

Although I agree with the importance of recognizing how slippery the referent of nostalgia may be, I argue against the conclusion that it therefore has no referent at all. Memory inevitably filters the past through the lens of the present. And there is indeed always the gap between the remembering and the remembered. However, why dismiss the materiality of the remembered altogether? In communist Bulgaria, women were guaranteed maternity leave, which began forty-five days before the expected delivery date and could be extended until the child was three years old. The first two years were paid leave and the third was unpaid, and the women were guaranteed that their job would be held for them. Returning to work before the end of the first two years entitled a woman to her prematernity wage and to 50 percent of the national minimum wage for the unused portion of leave. In addition, if the mother chose to return to work early, the father or one of the grandparents could be appointed caregiver and receive the unused portion of the maternity leave.[7]

The legal rights to maternity leave and child support under communism in Bulgaria are significant not only because they exceeded the feminist achievements of some of the most progressive Western capitalist societies. These rights also point to the stark contrast between past experiences and the current predicament of Bulgarıstanlı migrant women. Memories of the sense of security that came from maternity leave and the sense of freedom provided by subsequent free child care were cherished by my interlocutors. Nurgül, a mother of two, had been working as a nanny in Turkey since her arrival from Silistra in 2001. She said she felt "her heart go stiff with sadness" each time she let herself think about not getting to see her younger child grow up. He was just ten when she left him behind in Bulgaria. While many women risked clandestine border crossings to bring their children along, others left them in Bulgaria, sometimes as toddlers, to be tended to by relatives. In Turkey, these same women care for the children of middle- or upper-middle-class women, who, in turn, rely on migrant women to allow them to keep up with their own careers, given that Turkey currently offers only four months of maternity leave.

These facts cast a different light on the idea of nostalgia as mere fantasy. Furthermore, they provide an important corrective to the "double burden argument," possibly the most influential perspective in the scholarly literature on socialism and gender. The double-burden argument contends that under communism the rhetoric of gender equality masked a double exploitation. By seemingly ensuring women's right to work, the state actually secured women's labor while continuing to place traditional demands on them as mothers and wives. In their seminal work on the politics of gender during and after socialism, Susan Gal and Gail Kligman (2000) point out the contradictory goals of various communist regimes for the policies that were enacted across Eastern Europe: "They wanted workers as well as mothers, token leaders as well as obedient cadres" (6).

A key merit of the double burden argument is its critical distance from the rhetoric of state socialism, especially the claim that socialism has emancipated women by ensuring their participation in the labor force. The argument exposes instead the more complex and contradictory realities of everyday experience. Gal and Kligman (2000) offer a detailed assessment of the ways in which socialism reconfigured the public-private distinction and the extent to which gender roles were transformed in the process. They acknowledge positive outcomes, including women's reduced dependence on husbands and fathers because wage work established a direct relationship to the state that was not mediated through men. This led to a more autonomous sense of self-worth for women, and "despite discriminatory wages and excess of hours of labor, many came to take seriously the communist ideal of equality between men and women" (53), sentiments that were repeatedly articulated by my interlocutors.

Despite such positive outcomes, Gal and Kligman note, there were also setbacks. Perhaps most important, the strategic deployment of gender equality as an official discourse in the public realm masked the less visible forms of inequality that were reproduced in the private one. Gal and Kligman write that despite the ideal of equality, "the conditions of work, low wages, and the magnitude of demands on [women] produced a sense of victimization and perennial guilt at their never being able to do enough of anything, especially mothering" (53). Furthermore, they point out that the image of the competent mother and worker presented by magazines went hand in hand with the omission of sexualized beauty in the pursuit of femininity (54). They suggest that even some of the aspects that were hailed as positive had negative consequences. For example, the generous child care payments and maternity leave arrangements reinforced women's subordinate position in the labor force, feeding into their image as less-reliable workers (49). Likewise, the legal measures that rendered women more autonomous, such as the "relative ease of divorce and the guarantee of state support for single women and children," reinforced the "extreme fragility" of marital ties (54).

A balanced assessment of the communist experience is crucial, no doubt. But the substantial gains women made under communism tend to be overlooked in the double burden argument. Discussion of the merits of the double burden argument has to be sufficiently qualified to avoid replicating, even if in a feminist inflection, any assumption that the capitalist first world is superior to the communist second world. Kristen Ghodsee (2004a, 2004b, 2005), for example, meticulously depicts the institutionalized benefits and advantages that the communist regime provided for women in Bulgaria and offers a timely critique of the unqualified importation of cultural feminism to postsocialist contexts. She argues that focusing exclusively on gender at the expense of class fails to address the local histories, debates, and understandings of the "woman question" in formerly communist societies. With the alleged intention of "saving women"—to borrow from Lila Abu-Lughod's trenchant critique (2002) of a parallel discourse deployed by U.S. liberal feminism about Afghan women—such imported feminism either hardly acknowledges legacies of socialism or does so only in negative ways.

Even the local NGOs funded primarily by Western cash sources assume that Bulgarian women are willing to borrow or work to pay for basic needs that were once provided by the socialist state. Under socialism, these needs once existed as the basic rights and entitlements of the communist citizen. Indeed, one of the most lauded achievements of the communist countries was the high level of human development that they achieved. This was particularly true for women. In Bulgaria, women greatly benefited not only from generous maternity leave but also from free education, free health care, free subsidized child care, communal kitchens and canteens, communal laundries, subsidized food and transport, and subsidized holidays on the Black Sea (Ghodsee 2004a, 747).

Not surprisingly, the assumption of total oppression by the communist state, accompanied by either the thorough indoctrination of or the wholesale resistance by its citizens, is central to Turkish nationalist representations of Turkish women in Bulgaria. Turkish nationalist historiography regards the communist period in Bulgaria as the most sinister phase in that country's oppression of the Turkish minority, especially women. According to Turkish nationalist historiography, one of the particularly insidious ways in which communism sought to destroy what is regarded as an essential and invincible "Turkishness" was through the indoctrination of Turkish children. Hapless children were left to the mercy of the communist state because their mothers were forced to work.

In the day care centers and kindergartens that surrounded Bulgaria like a spider's web, history was taught to babies in distorted ways, and hatred of Turks was injected into children in a systematic way. Turks were made to follow the same mandate as Bulgarians and send their children to these crèches and kindergartens so that Turkish children would be prevented from learning their own language, religion, customs, and mores. (Konukman 1990, 54, translation mine)

Another Turkish author bemoans the inability of the family, viewed as the fortress of ethnic preservation, to withstand the attacks by communists:

He [the Bulgarian], under the guise of ensuring mothers' work, meticulously began to subject the Turkish population to the regulation that children were to be given to crèches and kindergartens. It has been observed that their goal was to minimize the children's contact with their families and that by and large they succeeded. Thus, we saw during those days [of the 1989 immigration] that little children who arrived in Turkey could barely speak Turkish. (Toğrol 1991, 69, translation mine)

When my interlocutors referred to the equality of men and women in the workplace and at home, were they merely continuing to parrot party propaganda? When they viewed having access to free child care as allowing them a certain freedom, were they still so entrenched in a distorted vision of the past that they were unable to assess how the state conspired against them? How can one go beyond the simplifications of the communist indoctrination argument to probe the nebulous boundary between the lived and the remembered?

Instead of choosing between the view that the communist imperative to work was experienced as just another burden and the view that it meant total emancipation, I point to the multifaceted nature of socialism as it was experienced by women who belonged to the Turkish minority in Bulgaria. Ethnic discrimination against the remaining Turkish minority in Bulgaria began immediately after the founding of the Bulgarian nation-state in 1878. In fact, the repression that took place during the fascist regime (1941–44) right before the advent of communism was so severe that the initial policies of communism offered a respite. After the severe isolation and deprivation of the fascist era, the experience of communism for members of the Turkish minority meant opportunities for education, health care, and welfare. For women especially, educational opportunities and the requirement that they join the workforce marked a radical break with a past that offered virtually no education and no prospects of a career besides work in the fields. The immigrant women I met who had come of age during the communist era emphasized two points of contrast between themselves and their mothers. First, although they came from rural backgrounds, they had had access to at least eight years of schooling in the standardized communist system, whereas their mothers had had only a few years at Turkish religious schools and often could not read. Second, unlike their mothers, who had primarily taken care of children and made unpaid contributions to family farms, many of these women earned degrees and found jobs in the professions of health care and education, thanks to their exposure to the standardized system. The latter is often dismissed by the double burden argument as employment limited to lower-paid and lower-prestige jobs. Nevertheless, these jobs were esteemed by these women and their communities. The day care centers and kindergartens that are painted as hotbeds of pernicious communist propaganda in the accounts of Turkish nationalists were regarded by many women as resources that afforded them some autonomy.

"Why should I lie?" asked Emine, who had come of age during the communist era. "We really had it good under *komünizma*. Yes, there was still a certain amount of discrimination against us, but we never worried about a roof to stay under or our stomachs going hungry or our children's schools. Not to mention the quality of education." I was privy to these confidences only after we had met several times. Her preemptive preamble "Why should I lie?" reflects a degree of anxiety over social disapproval other than the one related to being a working woman: that of saying something positive about communism. Saniye, who was bewildered upon her arrival in 1989 at the expectation that she would stay at home now that she was in Istanbul, prided herself on the exceptional education that she received growing up in a village near Razgrad. But, she said, she soon learned that her positive evaluations of the communist system were best left unexpressed. "If it was so good over there, why did you bother to come?" she was asked by a neighbor who would have preferred to listen to narratives of deprivation and suffering of ethnic kin. One tacit prerequisite of social acceptance was acquiescing to the image of the persecuted *soydaş*, and neither the working woman nor the immigrant who spoke favorably of communism suited that image.

GENDERED VIOLENCE AND
RELATIVE IMMUNITY

Bulgaristanlı women fit uneasily into the moral economy of gender in Turkey because they defied gendered expectations of work, a defiance that was certainly prompted by monetary need. But beyond monetary need, this defiance should also be considered in conjunction with what Bourdieu (1990a) calls "durable dispositions"—ways of acting in, seeing, and making sense of the world that are transmitted through a particular cultural and class milieu, and acquired and embodied by the individual starting with childhood socialization, and that are "classificatory principles as well as being the organizing principles of action" (Bourdieu 1990b, 12–13). The durable dispositions evidenced by Bulgaristanlı migrants, who acquired them as a minority group under a communist regime, rendered life without work quite unthinkable. My interlocutors paid less heed to the kinds of negotiations in which their local neighbors so carefully seemed to traffic if they had to work. In chapter 3, I discussed how the segmentation of the feminized domestic market in terms of live-in and live-out nannies is a result of these considerations: local women were not allowed to or preferred not to work as live-in domestics, an arrangement in which one's exposure is enhanced, while Bulgaristanlı women did not find it a breach of one's reputation to work as a live-in. In fact, they made it a point of pride to take jobs considered unsuitable for women. Recall how proud Elmas was that she worked as a welder alongside men. Or recall Vasfiye, who had worked as a crane operator in her native Kirdjali in Bulgaria: she often boasted that the "local women" she met in Istanbul could not fathom the idea that operating a crane could be a woman's job.

Within the hegemonic moral economy of gender and work in Turkey, migrant men "who let their women work" fell short of the ideal, too. Ahmet, a thirty-eight-year-old man who arrived in Istanbul in 1999, found a much-coveted arrangement: a position with his wife in a villa. "This neighbor who was just visiting," he told me, when I was called on him and his wife where they worked and lived, "he came to vent off steam because he was furious his wife had gone out without his permission. Poor woman, no chance for her but to be a housewife." Another Bulgaristanlı man, twenty-eight-year-old Seyhan, said, "I am good friends with the guys at work. So they can take it when I tease them. I tell them, 'You don't let your wives work because you are jealous. You don't trust them. I don't mind my wife going to work, even overnight, because I trust her.'" Besides revealing differences in attitudes toward women's work, these remarks suggest ways of coping with the local construction of hegemonic masculinity. The emphasis on trust and lack of jealousy may also be a way of negotiating the perceived challenges to their honor, which is potentially compromised by having working wives whose chastity may be suspect.

Bulgaristanlı women rejected the norms of femininity associated with job choice and were taken aback by the convention that they affirm their modesty through their attire. As we traveled from one legal office to another, my informants and I would often take the bus, a notorious public venue for harassment of women in Turkey through leering looks, groping, and even physical assault. After a necessary adjustment of one's position to avoid contact with a man or turning one's head to avoid a lewd glance, we would almost invariably discuss the difference between Bulgaria and Turkey. "There, you can be up and about any time of the day, and no one will stare at you like this," a frustrated Necmiye, mother of a daughter who had just turned twenty, often griped.

> Here the default assumption is that you are looking for something. And even more than that. You know how when you address someone, you smile, you meet their gaze. To show that you are actively listening, to show that you care about what you are saying. Ah, but here, even that gets misinterpreted. I keep having to warn my daughter, don't smile at people warmly like that, don't dress like that. But of course she does not get it. She got used to something else growing up there. Or take me, at this age. Suppose I meet a buddy of my husband's on the way. We would say in Bulgaria, come let us get a cup of coffee. But here, oh no, that would instantly be read in a malevolent way.

Sevdiye, who at the time was working as a nanny in an upscale neighborhood, underscored the class element of these gendered negotiations of one's honor and chastity.

> As dinner was about to be ready, I realized that we are missing the dill to add to the dish. I said to Sevda Hanım, "I will go get it in a minute." And as I made [my way] toward the door, she stopped me: "Are you going out like this?" And I had on the same kind of shirt I have on me right now, only with stripes. Sevda Hanım said, "Please put something else on, there is the fruit seller, there is the grocer." So I said, "Look, Ms. Sevda, this is who I am. I don't engage with that fruit seller or the grocer in the way you insinuate, but this is

how I dress." And I went out just like that. And the thing is, she herself wears those super minis.[8]

Though they challenge conventional codes of attire, Bulgaristanlı migrants have to and do make adjustments. "I am not entirely without religion," the defiant Saniye said when talking about her great-uncle, who had become a citizen and very conservative after his immigration in 1989. "He is disapproving of the way I dress, the way I go out, but in fact I am always trying to be considerate when I go visit them. Whenever I stay with them, I am always rushing down the stairs so as to avoid meeting any of the neighbors so that they won't speak ill of my uncle, saying, 'What kind of relatives come to visit you!'" And Reyhan, who came to Turkey in 2005 with a scholarship to pursue a master's degree, observed a shift among the young Bulgaristanlı: "Some of our girlfriends have changed their attitudes a bit. For example, they warned one of our friends at the language course we were taking that she shouldn't wear transparent things. And she stopped wearing them. Things like that add up, and they adapt. Once you cross the border, things change."

But even as they made small and reluctant compromises to adapt to the moral economy of gender in Turkey or continued to defy it, it is important not to lose sight of Bulgaristanlı women's distinction vis-à-vis other migrant women. Notwithstanding their discomfort as women who had to occupy public spaces that might not have been welcoming, Bulgaristanlı women still had a better shot at fitting in than did undocumented migrant women who could not claim the status of *soydaş*.

TROPES OF HONOR AND THE DIFFERENCE *SOYDAŞ* MAKES

Narine committed suicide on November 24, 2012, after being blackmailed by her lover's brother. He sought sex in return for not revealing "compromising" visual evidence of her affair. Jesca was thrown out of a window on September 6, 2014, after being raped by an acquaintance. The murderer's attorney premised his defense on his client's honor and Jesca's lack of chastity, alleging that Jesca was a sex worker. A., whose full name did not appear in any news or court records, withdrew her complaint against the police officer who, under the auspices of taking her into custody for illegal status, kidnapped and raped her in a private house. Her body was never found, so there was no court case and no name mentioned in the news. Narine was from Armenia, Jesca from

Uganda, and A. from Turkmenistan. All were residing and working in Istanbul without papers.

The short trial that was held regarding Narine Mıkırdciyan's case ended with the release of the two brothers, who had been charged with blackmail and coercion. Narine's brother, Zhora Mıkırdciyan, a key witness in the court hearings, was abruptly deported before he could testify at the trial.[9] Though Narine's case was sensationalized in the media with laudatory references to her "decision" to preserve her honor by braving death, it was not taken up by feminists or migrant activists.[10] Jesca Nankabirwa's lawsuit, on the other hand, garnered more publicity as well as support from the Women Without Borders feminist activist network and legal support from a group of feminist lawyers who were intent on bringing Jesca's murderer to justice. The trope of honor would play a leading role during the trials.

Jesca was missing for four days before her body was found. After repeated inquiries, her friends finally located her in the morgue of the Yenisbosna hospital. Jesca had been residing in Istanbul for more than a year. She was working in a textile factory for 900TL a month (about $250) and sent money back home for the three children she had left behind with her mother and sister after her husband's death. Jesca had visited the man referred to as E.D. on the day of her murder. He had allegedly told the janitor who spotted the lifeless body on the pavement, "We had a fight; I threw her out and killed her." But during the first hearing, E.D. rejected the charges, and the defense attorney suggested the possibility of suicide. The initial forensic report supported his statement, as it suggested that Jesca could have fallen out of the window or killed herself. The possibility that she had fallen on her back was added to the forensic report only later through the perseverance of Jesca's lawyers. It was also subsequently documented that E.D. had raped Jesca before the murder.

The defense attorney pushed for suicide or accidental falling instead of murder as the explanation for her death through a line of reasoning in which he took no pains to mask his racism and sexism. He alleged that his client would not have been physically capable of throwing Jesca out the window by stating that "blacks are the strongest people on earth." When asked why Jesca did not walk out the door, he responded, "Well, naturally, my client carries with him the honor of a man." The word "honor" was mentioned even more vociferously in relation to Jesca's "compromised sexual honor" through allegations of sex work. "Once the blind girl dies, she is remembered as the one with almond eyes," the attorney said, citing a well-known Turkish idiom and insinuating that Jesca's tragic end was now garnering undeserved sympathy for her and obscuring what was in reality a tarnished past with regard to her chastity. Although the accused was convicted, he received a significantly reduced sentence based on his repentance, good behavior, and lack of premeditation. The defense attorney further charged, "Why should my client engage in premeditated murder? She was, after all, not his girlfriend."

Perihan Meşeli, the attorney who argued on behalf of the victim, asked, "And suppose she was a sex worker, what does that have to do with her murder?" But despite these feminist interventions, without which a corrected forensic report, an indictment, and even a reduced sentence would most likely not have come about, Jesca's sexual honor was the key trope that was paraded even by the feminist activist network Women Without Borders. The group's website declared: "The murderer is trying to devalue the rape and the murder by claiming Jesca was doing sex work. We will not buy it!" Regardless of their own convictions as to the irrelevance of Jesca's involvement in sex work, it is poignantly telling that even the feminist migrant solidarity campaign had to appropriate the discourse of honor and chastity to some extent in order to appeal to the Turkish public.

It is indeed common in Turkey to view migrant women, including those who work in domestic services, as potential sex workers or as sexually available, as I have already discussed in chapter 3. The stereotype of the natasha was referred to by my Bulgaristanlı interlocutors, too, although they said that they themselves did not agree with it, qualifying it with statements such as "I actually have many Russian friends, they are great women" or "It is unfair that they get called natashas." Still, they used the term as a reference point to mark their own distinction. "I have to be especially explicit and direct about my Turkishness because of my looks; otherwise people easily take me, you know, for a natasha."

Being taken for a natasha is a perilous affair. It renders the undocumented woman immediately deportable for engaging in "unregistered" sex work in a country where registered prostitution is legal (Çoskun 2014). Even the accusation that she carries an STD is legal justification for deportation, according to Passport Law No. 5682/1950. The only way out is to claim to be a victim of sex trafficking. However, the existing perception that undocumented women from Africa and the former Soviet Union are engaging in or are prone to engage in sex work coupled with the fact that any evidence of payment can legally act as proof of consent almost invariably leads to deportation.[11]

Over the course of more than a decade of work in this field, I never encountered or heard of a Bulgaristanlı migrant woman who had been detained or deported on charges stemming from sex work. This is not only because Bulgaristanlı women have other options that allow them to avoid it. It is also because they are able to ward off the suspicion that follows all undocumented migrant women in Turkey by performing their *soydaş* status. In fact, not only do they hold the pervasive perception of migrant women as sex workers at bay through claiming racial kinship, they can also perform gendered intimacy as they move through legal space. Such intimacy ranges from appeals to kinship terms as "sister" or "mother" to measured flirtatious gestures. Recall Hoşgül's flirtatious giggles when responding to the chief at the police station she had walked into as an undocumented migrant and Nurcan's demure appeals to her role as a daughter tending to a sick mother. Vasfiye, the proud crane operator, got a kick out of describing in detail the strategies she resorted to in trying to speed up her citizenship application and to smooth out the bumps along the way. In particular, she established a fictive kin relation with one of the clerks, urging him, as she recalled, to treat her like he would his own mother.

Mirem, who is in her early thirties and is used to attracting unwanted attention because of her "Russian looks," was stopped by two police officers once for an identity check. One of them clearly had bad intentions, she said, judging by how close he stood and the way he looked at her. She let him know that she was Turkish right away. *"Ha, kusura bakma bacım"* (Pardon me, my sister), he said, pulling back quickly and retreating to the language of kinship. "I think he was too taken aback and embarrassed to ask for a bribe after that," she said, in reference to a time when she had been stopped and then waved away only after having handed over all of her cash.

The most reliable way to compensate for suspicions of gendered impropriety is through appeals to Turkishness, which are sometimes enacted on one's behalf by someone else. Hazel, a sassy senior in high school, always had a story to tell about the latest abuse she had had to ward off at school, primarily by other girls who tried to bully her through accusations about how she went around *"açık saçık"* (dressed too skimpily). Once, during a routine verbal brawl, a teacher overheard one of the girls taunt her with the words "What would *you* know, you Bulgarian girl?" Hazel explained to me that this was one the few teachers who actually had her wits about her. The teacher intervened and shut them up: "Hazel, these girls might not know their history, but you are more Turkish than the rest of us." They were dumbfounded, Hazel said, reliving and relishing their stupefaction as she told the story.

By foregrounding performances of racial kinship as a resource to which only some migrants can resort, I do not intend to suggest that the landscape is on the whole safe for women in Turkey if only they can be appropriated as kin. On the contrary, rather than being the exceptions, the treatment of undocumented migrants at the hands of men, the police, and the judiciary renders in its most unbridled visibility the inscriptions of gendered morality and violence in Turkey. Feminist and legal scholar Dicle Koğacıoğlu (2007) has described the plight of women in Turkey thus:

> We all know that if we don't act "properly" with regard to honor, something might happen. No matter how we might trivialize the significance honor has in our lives, we still adjust our behavior accordingly. Despite all the differences and inequalities between us, honor plays a major role in many of the choices we make, from how we sit and stand to which parts of the city we travel, which mode of transportation we choose, when we make love. We live in Turkey under a regime where women's bodies are disciplined through the construct of honor and where women discipline themselves through this construct. (My translation)

Being a woman acts as an unforgiving equalizer when it comes to the threat and experience of gendered violence, as Koğacıoğlu's use of the inclusive "we" implies. Nonetheless, even then, there are degrees of protection and immunity depending on one's class position, ethnic identification, and legal status. Undocumented status constitutes the most brutal, unshielded layer of vulnerability in increasing the likelihood of sexual violence and impunity for the perpetrators. By contrast, Bulgaristanlı migrants have relative recourse to protection because they are considered *soydaş*. This does not mean, however, that they are not vulnerable to harassment, threats, and violence, just as women who are citizens of Turkey are also vulnerable. The balancing act here is in recognizing the ever-present vulnerability inflicted on all women by Turkey's gender regime at the same time as acknowledging the differential distribution of that vulnerability.

CROSS-CULTURAL ANALYSIS FROM THE OTHER SIDE OF THE BORDER

The first civil and penal codes of Turkey have often been celebrated as paragons of women's equality and as progressive benchmarks in the history of the Republic of Turkey. But in fact both the Turkish Civil Code (Law No. 743/1926) and the Turkish Penal Code (Law No. 65/1926) were replete with instances of gender inequality and considered honor and chastity as relevant criteria in determining the nature of a crime and its appropriate punishment. Until its reform as late as 2001, the Turkish Civil Code (Law No. 743/1926) defined the husband as "the head of the household" with final say over domicile and children. The Turkish Penal Code (Law No. 65/1926), less obviously and perhaps more insidiously, entrenched norms of gendered morality through its monopoly over the appropriate comportment of women's bodies and sexuality.

Until 1990, sentences for those convicted of rape were reduced through the infamous Article 438 of the Turkish Penal Code Law No. 65/1926 if the victim was a sex worker. Until its comprehensive reform in 2004, the partially revised Turkish Penal Code (Law No. 5237/2004) classified sexual assaults against women under the category of "Felonies against Public Decency and Family Order," not as "Felonies against Individuals," as is the case with all other assaults against individuals. Regulated under the "Felonies against Public Decency and Family Order" laws were also acts deemed to constitute "shameless behavior in public." Feminist lawyer Pınar İlkkaracan (2007) notes that the idea of *hayasızlık* (shamelessness) was used to exonerate police who engaged in violence against LGBTI persons. If an abducted woman was unmarried, the minimum sentence of seven years could be reduced to three. A rapist would be exempt from criminal charges if he agreed to marry the woman he had raped. The terminology itself revealed the morals underlying the legal norms. The term used in the law for "rape" was not the more literal *tecavüz* (violation and attack) but *ırza geçmek*. *Irz* is the Ottoman word for "honor." *Irza geçmek* is the transgression of one's honor. Sexual abuse of minors was defined as an act against honor, while marital rape or state-enforced virginity examinations did not find a place in the law at all.

Abolishing male supremacy in the civil code and redefining sexual and bodily rights of women as individual rights in the penal code and not as part of societal honor were achieved through a long struggle by feminist and LGBTI groups in Turkey. Their sustained work and campaigning were aided by the EU accession process, international lobbying, and networking. In an ironic twist, their victory was also helped by the egregiousness of the antifeminist rhetoric of the Justice and Development Party (Adalet ve Kalkınma Partisi, JDP) government. In 2002, the campaign of the Women's Platform, the umbrella group under which all feminist and LGBTI groups gathered, had reached full speed in its demand for the most major revision of the penal code in Turkey's history. The same year, the JDP rose to power as the first Is-

Iamist party in the history of the Turkish republic to gain an overwhelming majority in parliament and thereby rule without a coalition. The pervasive feeling across the Women's Platform was that "all hopes for the reform of the penal code regarding gender equality were lost" (İlkkaracan 2007, 13). There was to be, however, an unexpected twist. First the conservative and government sympathizer Turkish daily, *Vakit*, ran the headline "The Shameless Proposal" in reference to one of the key demands of the Women's Platform: eliminate all terminology related to *haya* (shame) and *namus* (honor) in the penal code. The Minister of Justice Doğan Soyarslan went on to make the following statement:

> The draft law defies the realities of Turkey. No man would like to marry a woman who is not a virgin. Marrying one's rapist is a reality of Turkey [that we must accept]. The brother of a girl or the father of a girl who has been raped would want her to marry her rapist. In fact, those at this meeting who are seemingly taking issue with what is our reality, let me tell you, they also would like to marry virgins. And if they claim the opposite, they are lying.

The minister's rant had the effect of tipping what was a divided public in favor of the reform campaign. The European Union issued an ultimatum, stating that it would refuse to start negotiations if the proposed draft law was not immediately accepted and adopted. The government yielded and the new penal code was accepted in 2004 (Law No. 5237/2004).

This was a major victory for the Women's Platform. The majority of its demands were met: the demand to end the categorization of sex crimes as crimes against society and moral customs; their recognition instead as crimes against individuals; and the elimination of all references to chastity and honor from the law. Recep Tayyip Erdoğan, who was the prime minister at the time (and then became president), retaliated, accusing the platform of being "a marginal group who does not represent Turkish women." Erdoğan directed his invective particularly toward the placards that had been paraded in front of the Parliament and that read, "Our bodies and sexuality belong to ourselves." "These placards are not appropriate for Turkish women," he fumed. "They do not represent the moral values and traditions of Turkish women."

If the prime minister's remarks came across like petulant complaints uttered in defeat, it would soon be clear that this was not the case. Since its rise to power, the JDP has consistently tried to repeal the feminist advances that were enacted through legal reform. As Simten Coşar and Metin Yeğenoğlu

(2011) put it, "The party's stance gradually evolved from an expressed willingness for cooperation to lack of interest and an intense hostility toward feminist demands" (10).

While the laicist/Kemalist perspective reads the current repressive turn in Turkey as an Islamic one, the vigilance over women's chastity in Turkey is not a story that can be contained under the rubric of Islam. It was the republic, the very secular state taking such pains to distance itself from Islam, that originally laid the groundwork for a legal code premised on the notion of women's honor and chastity. The motion that had caused such fury was in fact part of the penal code until 1994 and was repealed only through the persistent efforts of feminist groups. That it was being brought back to the table by an Islamic government that was also conservative and authoritarian—certainly qualities not reducible or intrinsic to Islam—only attests to the fact that the feminist struggle is always a struggle against different forms of patriarchy, whether secular or religious. But it is certainly the case that the JDP has finessed its own brand of anti-feminism, one that is exclusively family-oriented, openly hostile to any sign of women's autonomy in the public sphere and vengeful at even a hint of defiance.

When I use the overburdened term "honor," therefore, I am not referring to a cultural or religious essence or to that catch-all word "tradition." Rather, I am referring to "honor" as the discursive practices enacted by a complex array of institutional structures, including law, medicine, education, and the family (see also Koğacıoğlu 2004, 121).[12] But despite feminist and scholarly calls to abandon the concept altogether, "honor" has proven to be hard to dispose of. It continues to carry emic relevance and tremendous legal power. Feminist and LGBTI movements in Turkey invest enormous energy into continuing the fight against the cultural impositions and legal ramifications of the honor concept.

Within this cultural, legal, and political landscape in which everyday and legal acts of violence continue to be enacted in the name of honor, the ideal of the woman as worker-citizen promoted in communist Bulgaria reemerges as cherished memories and as an alternative paradigm for Bulgaristanlı migrant women. As they alternate between, on the one hand, passing as Turkish-Muslim ethnic kin who can be absorbed into the national family and, on the other hand, being viewed as formerly communist citizens whose gendered morality is suspect, they utilize post-communist nostalgia as a resource for dignified survival. They defend their own norms about work, propriety, and gender roles through an appeal to the communist ethos and through an appeal to the way things were on the other side of the border. Rather than merely a melancholic attachment to an idealized past, post-communist affect is thus a resource that they draw on to manage their uneasy reception. It also grounds their sense of entitlement to dignified treatment in the present. Collapsing temporalities, residual attachments to the communist past in Bulgaria are manufactured into hopes for a more secure and hospitable future in Turkey.

Contrast this with the "frozen hopes" of Omnia, a Palestinian woman in the refugee camp in Gaza, as depicted by Ilana Feldman (2016) in her brilliant analysis of the temporalities of hope. Omnia, who Feldman describes as being very much engaged in the life of the refugee camp, with a leadership role in a local organization, spoke of her hopes for Palestine's future as being held in abeyance: "I made a term for my hopes. I said they are frozen now. Frozen hopes because—frozen means they still exist but I am not using them now. One day I will get them out of the freezer" (Feldman 2016, 418).

Feldman writes that the imagination of the future is always grounded in the present condition, which in turn delineates and delimits the realm of possibility. In this chapter, I have also emphasized the weight of past experience on the maintenance of hope in the present. But in this case, unlike Omnia's experience, hope does not get deferred or renounced. The contrast between the frozen hopes of Omnia and the expectant hopes of Bulgaristanlı women points as well to the critical role played by different contexts of hoping for the production of hope as a political category. In the conclusion to this book, I explore the implications of the hopes of the Bulgaristanlı for the realm of migrant politics.

CONCLUSION

Troubling Hope

IN THE EXCHANGE that opened this book, Nefiye, one of the sassiest women I have gotten to know over more than a decade of fieldwork among the Bulgaristanlı, had admonished me for not unequivocally affirming her hope for the approval of her citizenship application. A few days later, this time in a queue at the Foreigners' Department, I was waiting with Nefiye and her sister to see whether we could plead a case for Nefiye's sister to take advantage of the amnesty being offered. The catch was that Nefiye's sister had not currently overstayed her residence permit. Ironically, her "legal" status disqualified her from the amnesty, and along with it, the prospect of a citizenship application that was premised on receiving the amnesty, since only those currently in "illegal" status could take advantage of it.

As we waited, the sisters spotted an acquaintance of theirs, Gülcan, who looked to be in her late forties or early fifties. She waved to us and stepped out of the adjacent line to briefly keep us company, entrusting her spot to a friend she had come with. Gülcan was exhilarated about this latest 2011 amnesty and the prospect for citizenship that it promised. She carried on with great animation about the document of origins she had finally procured back in Ruse, Bulgaria, and the notarized translation of her certificate of marriage that she was about to obtain to complete her application. Nefiye interrupted her, pointedly asking about the duration of her last overstay. When Gülcan muttered something vague, Nefiye said with impatience, "Just give me that passport." Glancing over the passport, Nefiye shook her head with disapproval and said, "That's too long. Not six months, not one year, but three years! I doubt they will approve your application with that kind of length of illegal stay." Gülcan became agitated and offered a string of explanations as to why it should not matter under the new amnesty. Nefiye simply listened, without saying a word, until Gülcan's friend called her back to their line.

At the end of the day, we ran into one another again and exchanged results. On our end, the efforts to coax and convince the officers had failed, and Nefiye's sister, because she was currently "legal," would not qualify for the amnesty. Meanwhile, Gülcan had calmed down, assured by her friend that she indeed had reason to hope. The conversation strayed to the birth of a mutual acquaintance's granddaughter in Bulgaria, wedding preparations in a village close to the one where Nefiye's sister used to live, and other aspects of everyday life. Everyone hugged while saying their good-byes. As her parting words, Gülcan turned to Nefiye and said, in a conciliatory tone, "But don't say things like that again to make my hope empty."

*   *   *

Hope is a fundamental tenet of being in the world. The psychoanalytic perspective would even posit that the hopeful disposition is necessary to be able to sustain an attachment to the business of living. One can presumably go through the day without other emotions such as anger, or fear, or, for that matter, happiness, but hardly without some minimal hope. Perhaps because it is so critical to survival, hope is just as fragile. In that regard, the defensive gesture is not peculiar to the condition of the Bulgaristanlı. Most of us, most of the time, want to cling to our hopes, whether for a residence permit or citizenship or a more secure and fulfilling existence. We are likely to be resistant to having our personal hopes scrutinized, let alone challenged.

And yet, even as hope produces perseverance and provides "the energy, the petrol" that enables people to "live sanely" (Zigon 2009, 267), hope may also be troubled and troubling. In this conclusion, I return to the political and epistemological implications of Crapanzano's (2003) prescient and deceptively simple proposition to treat hope critically as a category of analysis and as experience. Approaching hope in this way sounds like an obvious enough proposition. But it is precisely the pervasiveness of the impulse to shield hope against criticism that makes the proposition more toilsome than it appears at first glance.

It is not just in the realm of the ordinary and the everyday that we tend to be defensive about our hopes. Expansive affective energies are invested as well into the political work that hope is expected to do. Especially in times of political and social turmoil, critical inquiries into the grounds or consequences of a particular politics of hope can trigger an accusation of intellectual cynicism or pessimism. The exemption of hope from critique may also take on more sophisticated philosophical or theological justifications whereby hope is elevated from being one among many emotions or dispositions to something higher—a virtue or a method of being/living.

Anthropologist Hirokazu Miyazaki, as a sequel to his compelling exploration of hope as method (2004), has also proposed that hope cannot quite be analyzed but can only be "replicated on another terrain" (2017), namely that of the quest for knowledge—whether it is the quest of the social scientist or of the people with whom the social scientist interacts. Miyazaki's theoretical leap has led Annalise Riles to suggest that perhaps "there is really no critical study of hope" (Riles 2017, 133). This book, however, has followed a different path, insisting that the hoper, particular hopes, and even hope itself are, at least in certain circumstances, apt for criticism.

THE POLITICS OF HOPE

The central role of hope was a prominent discursive trope throughout Barack Obama's campaign for the U.S. presidency, an effort that is still recalled affectionately by his supporters and scholars alike. Pondering the role played by hope in Obama's presidential campaign, Miyazaki foregrounds the "positive" work that hope did, including, in his rendition, reducing millions of Americans to tears as they listened to Obama's speech and "in crying, became the substance of their own hope" (Miyazaki 2017, 185). Regardless of what disappointments Obama's presidency itself may have brought after his campaign of hope, Miyazaki concludes, Obama had already made a major contribution to the public's participation in politics through his invitation "to reorient ourselves, to endure one more time, and hope" (186).

In a similar spirit, some on the left have been insisting on the urgent need to learn to hope again in order to salvage critical social science. This position contends that late capitalism kills hope of the possibility of an alternative system. If only we can recover and relocate hope, we will also be better equipped to continue the battle against that which ravages it.[1] Jessica Greenberg provides an excellent depiction of the affective landscape of this recent scholarship that laments the absence of hope: "Hope has become an aspirational horizon in which scholars are increasingly invested: if the world gives us disappointment, we might anecdotally (or ethnographically) locate hope in unlikely places" (Greenberg 2016, 20). In a perfect illustration of Greenberg's diagnosis, David Harvey (2000) posits capitalists and their speculative spirit as a model for despondent social scientists to emulate so that the latter may reclaim hope for their own critiques of capitalism.

Much of the contemporary thinking on hope as a horizon of possibility that is utopian and emancipatory draws on the legacy of Ernst Bloch, who has been called "the" philosopher of hope (Eagleton 2015). In his magnum opus, *The Principle of Hope* ([1947] 1995), Bloch posits hope as the core of humankind. If for Marx the act of labor is what defines our species-being, for Bloch our distinguishing characteristic is the act of hoping. According to him, humans possess an ontologically prospective orientation that automatically produces "hoping" because the act of living itself is about striving and striving is necessarily oriented toward the future. However, even as hope constitutes the essence of mankind, Bloch goes on to argue, something has gone fundamentally wrong with the way we hope. Again, in the spirit of the Marxist tradition that locates the alienation of species-being as alienation from its own labor in class-stratified societies, Bloch believes that the bourgeois class is guilty of having contaminated hope by emptying out its prospective and revolutionary potential. Hope, in its bourgeois guise, has been reduced to petty daydreams. However, for Bloch this is still no cause for despair. On the contrary, because hoping is the very basis of being and striving, even in petty daydreams, there remains extractable that other part, which is "provocative, is not content just to accept the bad which exists, does not accept renunciation. It can be extricated from the unregulated daydream and from its sly misuse, can be activated undimmed" (Bloch [1947] 1995, 4).

In his *Hope without Optimism*, Terry Eagleton (2015) takes no pains to hide his irritation with Bloch's "excessive cheerfulness" and "oracular prose." Eagleton points out that in Bloch's universe, hope takes on a cosmic quality such that Bloch finds "hope in the world as if there is uranium" (95). Now, as already pointed out, psychological approaches to hope, too, deem hope as an objective and necessary relation to the world, one that enables us to go on getting up in the morning and getting through the day. But the crucial difference with Bloch's take on hope, as Eagleton astutely points out, is that Bloch seems to be assured that this objective dynamic of hope "has the backing of the universe in unfolding its inherent purpose towards perfection" (102). Eagleton also finds Bloch's ontologizing of hope to be ultimately antithetical to the historical materialism to which Bloch so fervently adheres. For Marx, a belief in progress or in the evolution of productive forces resides in the material practice of human affairs. But in Bloch's universe, hope takes on the qualities of a metaphysical claim about the nature of matter. Even his prose adopts mystical terms: Bloch writes, "there is good that is making its way through" (Bloch [1947] 1995, 198). Hence Eagleton's verdict that the hope posited by Bloch "is one that no mere empirical defeat could rebuff" (2015, 104).

Some have insisted that there is a major difference between hope for a specific object and unspecified or "open-ended" hope (Turner 2014). A similar logic underlies the distinction that Bloch makes between expectant and filled emotions, except that for Bloch hope can be only an expectant emotion in the first place. Filled emotions such as joy or greed are emotions "whose drive object lies ready, if not in respective individual attainability, then in the already available world" (Bloch [1947] 1986, 74). Bloch then contrasts these filled emotions with what he calls "expectant emotions," such as hope and fear, which do not target particular obvious objects. Rather, expectant emotions, in Fredric Jameson's explication, are steered toward "the configuration of the world" and through it, the "configuration of the self" (Jameson 1971, 127). This is why expectant emotions rank incomparably higher in Bloch's hierarchy of emotions: "Whereas the filled emotions only have an unreal future, i.e., one in which objectively nothing happens, the expectant emotions essentially imply a real future" (Bloch 1986, 75). The qualifier "real" is crucial here. What Bloch means by "real future" hinges on the filled vs. expectant emotion distinction. In Fredric Jameson's gloss again, if filled emotions "ask for fulfillment in a world at all points identical to that of the present, save for the possession of a particular object desired and presently lacking," they partake of "a kind of provincialism of the present, into which we are plunged so utterly that we lose the very possibility of imagining a future which might be radically and constitutively other" (Jameson 1971, 126). Expectant emotions, on the other hand, entail "a kind of ethics, a keeping faith with the open character of the future, a life in time which holds to the prospect of the absolutely unexpected as the only expectation" (127).

As normatively alluring as this distinction may be in paving the path for a revolutionary ethics through hope, I find that the ethnographic lens blurs the analytic clarity promised by such distinctions between filled and expectant emotions or between goal-oriented and open-ended hope. This is especially so when the lens is trained on those who do not struggle for a grander cause or cultivate an ethics of imagining a radically different future, but who instead wage their daily battles in the realm of the mundane and hope for the reasonably expected rather than desire the wildly unexpected.

Saniye, in her fifties and working as a nanny with the same family, taking care of their boy since he was two years old, never really considered settling in Turkey. Her husband, to whom she was much attached, was in Bulgaria, and unable to work because of his health, had acquiesced to this "migration business" unwillingly. Saniye had been hoping during these last four years that she could at least acquire a renewable residence permit. To that end, she pursued every amnesty between 2006 and 2010. Even if she did not particularly care for obtaining citizenship, she wanted to be free of the perpetual anxiety of being undocumented as she went about her work and saved up for the family. She wanted to stop having to hold her breath when crossing the border, worrying whether she would be questioned by an officer who might ask why she traveled back and forth so often. She wanted to stop being "at the mercy of that sigh of relief" that she would let out when she found out after the amnesty in 2009 that she could count on three more months of salary. That income, she calculated, would be used up by making much-needed repairs in their house in Sliven, Bulgaria. But she hoped to save up enough for their daughter's university expenses and perhaps even her wedding.

As specific as goals like these may be, together they constitute hope for a less precarious future, which certainly does not measure up to the "real future" envisioned by Bloch. Ethnographic attention to the prosaically profound everyday reality of migrants, who are caught up in the unrelenting rhythms of continuous work punctuated by daylong queues in pursuit of legalization documents, renders less palatable the distinction between "a prospective orientation" that will reconfigure the world and "a provincial presentism" that leaves little impact.

PROBABILITIES, POSSIBILITIES, AND MIGRANT ACTIVISM

There is a danger to the critique of Bloch's idealized revolutionary hope through the lens of everyday ordinary hope, of course. In honoring the primacy of the ordinary, one may unwittingly end up justifying the status quo of an unequal world, where some people are limited by certain hopes precisely because of colossal inequalities in access to legalization or capital. Still, the insistence on authentic and utopian hope, while pointing toward the possibility of another world, also tends to unhelpfully reinscribe a series of binaries, as insightfully identified by Jessica Greenberg (2016): hope and hopelessness; apologia and utopia; moral purity and compromise.[2] I want to add yet another problematic opposition to that list, one that has become quite fashionable in the recent turn to thinking radically about hope: the distinction between probability and possibility.

"If we follow probability there is no hope, just a calculated anticipation authorized by the world as it is," states Isabelle Stengers in an interview with Mary Zournazi (2002, 245). Stengers's absolute dismissal of considerations of probability has been influential for a particular politics of hope that glorifies the notion of "hope against hope." In fact, this perspective would posit that we come all the more near the essence of hope precisely when we hope "in spite of the evidence, in spite of probabilities and in spite of reason" (Smith 2008, 10). The influence of Stengers's intervention has extended to anthropology as well: in her introduction to a recently curated collection on the politics of refusal in the flagship journal *Cultural Anthropology*, Carol McGranahan writes: "Hope combines with will to refuse authorized anticipations, thus moving away from the probable into the possible" (McGranahan 2016, 325).

In chapter 2, I addressed the possibility/probability distinction on ethnographic grounds to show that the hope I describe in this book is one that resonates more closely with the rationalistic approaches to hope. In concluding, I inquire into the political implications of the stance that draws a strict separation between hope and expectation. This separation would disqualify, or at least devalue, the hope of the Bulgaristanlı migrants for legalization, given that their hopes are produced by and implicated in authorized anticipations about what *soydaş* can hope for from the Turkish state in terms of belonging. A cavalier dismissal of probability assessments not only devalues ordinary hopes, in much the same way that the goal-oriented versus open-ended hope distinction did. The approach to hope that purifies it, as it were, of any considerations of likelihood and probability also calls attention to the disparate stakes and worldviews that are often at work in the encounter between, on the one hand, dispossessed groups, and, on the other hand, the ethnographers, activists, or theorists who advocate on their behalf. Going against the grain of this incitement away from the probable, I want to pause and take to task the competing kinds of hope I witnessed during ethnographic research among Bulgaristanlı migrants and the hopes we performed as members of the Migrant Solidarity Network. In rethinking how the possibility/probability distinction is being used to measure what constitutes meaningful politics, I take up as well Greenberg's query as to "what has been the toll on activists who live and work under the shadow of such binaries" (Greenberg 2016, 19).

The Migrant Solidarity Network was established in February 2010 by a group of academics and activists who first came together in the summer of 2009 during the protests of the larger anti-globalization platform Direnİstanbul (resIstanbul), which was formed in opposition to the International Monetary Fund (IMF) summit held in October 2009 in İstanbul. While the platform dissipated after the IMF protests were over, a smaller initiative endured, one that had coalesced specifically around the question of undocumented migrants in Turkey and their lack of rights. The Migrant Solidarity Network came into being in a context of virtually no existing institutional channels through which undocumented migrants could advance collective claims. Trade unions have been indifferent at best to the question of undocumented migrants. Worse, they have participated in nationalist protectionist rhetoric, perceiving migrant labor to be a threat to the local labor force, and they have occasionally been instrumental in inciting local police to crack down on migrants working without permits in the neighborhoods where unions organize (Erder 2015). As for the considerable number of existing NGOs concerned with migration, they tended to limit their area of concern to asylum seekers and refugees (Balta 2010).[3] It was precisely this void that the Migrant Solidarity Network sought to fill.

In a retrospective piece, one of the members of the network, Fırat Genç (2017), provides a balanced and thoughtful assessment of what the network was able to achieve during its four years of activity as well as the shortcomings that eventually led to the group's dispersal. It emerges from Genç's account that in some ways it was precisely the original strength of the founding motivations of the network that eventually became its weakness. Rather than abide by existing legal categories that differentiated among migrants, the network subsumed all migrants as subjects who waged the same struggle and embraced the principle to "construct a solidarity network confronting the cycle of uncertainty, futurelessness, and precariousness that defined *the* migrant experience" (121, italics mine). But, Genç goes on to acknowledge, "under conditions where effective and egalitarian social policies were not present to meet the urgent daily needs of migrants, the gap between the expectations of migrants and the solidarity perspective put forth by us continued to widen" (127).

I want to build on Fırat Genç's insight to further probe this gap through the lens of divergent hopes. That lens exposes a gap not only between migrants and activists but also among variously positioned migrant groups. I start with an absence, one that became increasingly glaring to me as I navigated the terrain of ethnographic fieldwork and the terrain of migrant activism.

The Bulgaristanlı migrants, including those whom I knew intimately from my fieldwork, never attended any of the meetings or events of the Migrant Solidarity Network or even showed the slightest interest in participating. Worried about the ethics of field research and about compromising my interlocutors, I, too, refrained from making comments that might have come across in any way as a demand that they participate. The one instance in which this general mutual avoidance was unintentionally breached and the topic broached directly was during a trip to the Foreigners' Department with Halime, who was on a companion permit through her children and had been trying to obtain citizenship for the whole family for five years. Her hope had been renewed with each amnesty that afforded temporary legalization. On one of the many visits to the Foreigners' Department for submitting paperwork, I had to leave early. I apologized for leaving her on her own in the queue we had been standing in for four hours. I explained that I had to go to an important Migrant Solidarity Network meeting. In previous conversations, Halime had asked a few questions about our activities but had tactfully steered away from the topic after hearing that we worked with undocumented migrants regardless of their country of origin and subscribed to the political demand for open borders. When I had to abruptly leave that day, Halime seemed to feel the need to offer an explanation: "All right! Off you go," she said. After a brief pause, she added, "Once we get this *kimlik* [identity card], maybe then we will come to one of your meetings."

At the moment, I assumed Halime's remark to be an expression of anxiety and precariousness. And this, of course, was true. Over time, however, I have also come to understand her reluctance as part and parcel of her hope. Given her hope for legalization, there was too much at stake to take a risk that would jeopardize the chances of success for her and her family. Her cautious hope for legalization in a nation-state to which she strove hard to prove she belonged did not lend itself to easy translation into one of the recurrent, daringly hopeful slogans we shouted in each of our protests: "No border, no nation, stop deportation."

What to make of those moments and ways in which the hope that circulates among one's interlocutors in the field and sustains them in their struggles is at odds with the hope propounded by the politics of collective organizing? To what extent do critics and activists too easily presume to know the world and its possibilities, even while often arriving after the fact or speaking from positions of relative safety in dismissing probability as an adequately pure grounding and motive for hope?

A critical analysis of hope, though, has to go both ways and not stop at the tension between the collective solidarity perspective put forth by activists and self or family interest prioritized by migrants. Within "the" migrant experience that we as the Migrant Solidarity Network sought to address, there was in fact far too great a differentiation among migrant groups in terms of divergent hopes. The Bulgaristanlı migrants' hope was structured around cultural and legal privilege, which complicated potential solidarities with other migrant groups that were more vulnerable. My interlocutors, even if they might occasionally appeal to territorial presence and their hard labor in grounding their right to legalization, would quickly steer away from a broader identification as undocumented migrants and instead latch on to the distinction of being *soydaş*. This strategy was entirely different, for example, from asserting territorial presence as the justification for rights claims, which is how a group of undocumented migrants in France famously formulated their demands for belonging and consolidated the sans-papiers movement (McNevin 2006). By contrast, the Bulgaristanlı migrants anchored their entitlement in an appeal to the ethnicity privileged by Turkey's citizenship regime. If nationalism is at the same time a "kind of affect productive of a community of belonging" (Rafael 1997, 267), hope worked to foster emotional legitimacy for Bulgaristanlı migrants' investment in social norms for inclusion and exclusion.

The vexed relationships across differently positioned groups in inegalitarian societies also complicate the use of precarity as a political concept that asserts the unity of those who are compromised by different modes of labor exploitation, as I addressed in chapter 3. What Thorkelson nicely phrases as an "overcommitment to a redemptive reading of precarity," (2016, 476), is belied by the experience of precariousness among the Bulgaristanlı, which tends less toward emergent possibilities of class recomposition (Allison 2016; Campbell 2016). Rather, precarity aligns with an insistent hope for (a return to) security, which gets projected onto the promise of citizenship. Thus, precarity as a shared predicament does not necessarily and always foster class awareness and solidarity; it may spur a fragmented, individualized struggle for a return to a previously experienced, more secure status.

If an ethnographic account should not shun the ways in which the hope of Bulgaristanlı migrants is implicated in the discriminatory criteria of Turkey's migration and citizenship regime, it is also important to take responsibility for the complicity of our own politically progressive hope as activists or critical theorists. The trouble with the Blochian universes of hope is the ease with which they locate the pettiness of hope in the everyday, the routine, and the ordinary but refrain from a similar confrontation with the immediate untranslatability of utopian hope that favors the dimly possible to the exclusion of the probable.

A compelling account of how the probability/possibility distinction might bear on qualifying hope is offered in Peter Redfield's (2013) description of the humanitarian workers from Medecin Sans Frontiere/Doctors without Borders. Redfield identifies the trademark of their stance as its moral minimalism. Against the stereotype of the humanitarian vision as morally righteous, Redfield exposes the scrupulously nursed moral discontent of MSF volunteers with the world and with themselves. Through their disaffected compassion for the work they do, these actors go against the grain of the maxim that has acquired the status of scripture in contemporary Western public culture, namely that "action demands hope and hope demands optimism if not a fully articulated utopia" (229). Instead, the MSF worker acts with a disillusioned awareness of the immediate limits of humanitarian deeds when measured against the structural injustice that pervades the world. Such awareness results not in a total abandonment of hope and action but in a major modification to the category of hope, which Redfield captures in the evocative phrase "residual hope."

Redfield's notion of residual hope invites us to think about hope in ways that might not aim for a radical reconfiguration of the world. It also points to the importance of trimming grand gestures and injecting more minimalism into our moral claims as activists and critical theorists. I have tried to cast a certain amount of doubt on triumphant claims of hope that seamlessly equate it with collective goals and political solidarities. This is not to lapse into full-fledged relativism that renders impossible any distinction between the consequences of different hopes in terms of exacerbating existing structural violence. Nonetheless, the experiences of one migrant group whose relative privilege mediates in a particularly thorny manner the relationship between individual and collective struggles beckon us to be less confident of the seeming simplicity of hope as a call to political action.

ONLY HOPE DID NOT ESCAPE
PANDORA'S BOX

It is not only in the realm of the political that hope occasionally takes on a sacrosanct quality. In a certain philosophical approach, too, hope is elevated to the status of a principle. As an interpretive exercise in what he calls philosophical anthropology, Jonathan Lear (2008) ponders the possibilities that may exist for maintaining hope under conditions of cultural devastation so extreme that the epistemological tools for making sense of one's existence have all but disappeared. This, in Lear's rendition, was the predicament faced by the Native American Crow tribe. Threatened by ecological scarcity and their mightier rival, the Sioux, the chief of the Crow, Plenty Coups, decided to align with the U.S. government against the Sioux. On behalf of his tribe, he accepted reservation life in exchange for basic securities and survival. This agreement would mean gradual dispossession of their land and loss of all meaningful cultural activities. The loss of resources and traditions, in turn, meant the loss of the very concepts around which life used to be organized and through which life acquired meaning, including courage and perseverance. But even in this extreme case of epistemic rupture, the Crow, surprisingly, did not despair. Instead, thanks to the guiding vision that visited Chief Plenty Coups and was collectively interpreted with the elders, the tribe was shepherded through this chasm under the chief's leadership. Rather than trying to have his tribe survive under deteriorating environmental conditions or persist in their traditional ways, Plenty Coups cleared the path for a new way of life by acknowledging and coming to terms with the death of the former Crow traditions. What Lear calls radical hope, then, is this kind of orientation to the future in the face of extreme cultural devastation and conceptual loss.

Much of the hope that floats in the world, including the hope of the Bulgaristanlı that this book has depicted, falls short of the severe epistemological rupture that Lear's assessment of radical hope seems to require. For many, lives are lived under routinely compromised conditions of possibility rather than epistemic ruptures that force encounters with ontological vulnerability. And yet, Lear's formulation of radical hope continues to have significant appeal. I suspect that one reason for how widely Lear's radical hope has been brought to bear on conditions that do not seem all that radical is that his poignant and compelling formulation of radical hope can also be read as a story of compromise.

The other protagonist of Lear's story is the Sioux chief Sitting Bull, who had been present until then only as Plenty Coups's nemesis. Unlike Plenty Coups's reaction, Sitting Bull's response to the ecological and military threats to his people's way of life is to defy the U.S. government. He meets with Plenty Coups to discourage him from reaching a compromise with the white man and considers Plenty Coups a sellout because of his alliance with the U.S. government. In Lear's interpretation, Plenty Coups is the wise one because he is able to "thin out" the traditional understanding of courage: that is, rather than limiting courage to a question of warfare and masculine bravado, Plenty Coups resignifies courage to mean being able to live with anxiety and uncertainty. Releasing courage from its confines in warfare, the only realm in which it was previously imbued with meaning, Plenty Coups reframes it so that it makes sense as a way of confronting an entirely unfamiliar life. Sitting Bull, on the other hand, is unwilling to risk such malleability and clings to the traditional notion of courage. Lear also tells us that there was a rebellion within the Crow tribe that was crushed after Sitting Bull's visit, indicating that there were other Crow who shared Sitting Bull's perspective. (And one wonders if there were indications in the opposite direction among the Sioux.)

Which is the radical gesture here, the hope sustained by Plenty Coups or its refusal by Sitting Bull? Or perhaps the question needs to be posed differently: what exactly does the qualifier "radical" mean? Given the alternative possibilities presented by the text itself, one could read the story that Lear tells as one of compromise without its politically negative connotation. One could, as Lear seems to be ultimately doing, reinterpret compromise as the courageous thing to do under the circumstances.

ORDINARY HOPES

This ethnography of a routinized, almost prosaic quest for legalization has sought to convey that it is not only crisis-laden hope that carries legal and political significance. I also suggest that the ordinariness of the Bulgaristanlı migrants' hope captures something of the increasingly shared predicament of more and more people around the world, which the constant emphasis on crisis has a tendency to obscure. A hope that verges on expectation, one that is emboldened by a sense of entitlement but nonetheless remains precarious in terms of economic security, speaks to a larger predicament in which increasing numbers of citizens grapple with a relentless anxiety that is barely held in balance by the structural production and collective cultivation of hope.

My focus on the importance of ordinary hopes is not meant as a depoliticizing move. In that, the usage of the term "ordinary" nods to but also departs from hermeneutical approaches deployed to theorize the "ordinary" as it applies to the realm of ethics, morality, and virtue. Michael Lambek's influential discussion of the realm of ethics as ordinary is evocative for also thinking about the realm of hope: "I think the ethical is immanent," writes Lambek. "It is immanent to the existential condition of human thrownness to our life in the world" (2010, 16). Like the ethical, hope suffuses life and is a way—according to some, the only way—of being in the world. I follow the hermeneutical approach to theorizing the ordinary insofar as it tends to our "sense of respect for and obligations to others, . . . the range of notions concern[ed] with dignity, and the ethnographic quest to do justice to the living of human lives by providing analyses and interpretations of the art of living" (Lambek 2015, 10; Nehamas 1998). I have, however, more hesitations about the political implications of embracing "the art of living" as the primary task of ethnography. The hesitations concern the danger of equalizing all individual acts of living ethically—and one can substitute acts of living hopefully—in the presence of profound structural inequality, relations of domination, and the use and abuse of privilege, entitlement, and distinction.[4] If hope is virtuous in that it imparts the necessary perseverance and courage to pursue one's aspirations and, more generally, to have a purposeful life, the thornier question concerns the complicities of hope. When do appeals to hope start to obscure the work of subjection and subjectivation? To what extent does hope subject one to institutionally or politically produced identities and goals that may prevent one's self from flourishing (Berlant 2011), or under what circumstances might the hope of some detract from the hope of others (Hage 2003, 2016)?

I have argued that the hope for legalization provides a resource for the Bulgaristanlı migrants to persevere in their legalization quest, one that subjects them to the ordeals of bureaucracy *and* mitigates its indignities. But I have also recognized how these particular hopes reproduce the logic of the broader migration regime that rewards and discriminates on the basis of a rigid hierarchy of belonging based on racial and religious kinship. Given the pervasiveness of ethnoreligious nationalism in Turkey, the aspiration to uniformity, and the often violent domestication and elimination of difference, the hope of legalization can become a scarce good that one keeps for oneself and shields from others.

In attending to the political economy of hope, and more specifically, the principle of distribution in the Bulgaristanlı migrants' chances of legalization, I have tried to sustain the tension between understanding and critique, between acknowledgment and confrontation, between living as best one can in the world and being complicit in relations of power. Hope is a way of resisting immobility and marginalization as it is a tool of governmentality. It provides an orientation to struggle with dignity and perseverance for legal inclusion, but one that is not immune to acts of exclusion at the expense of less-privileged migrants. It may enable the migrants to break through the constraints of the regulations through their perseverance but without necessarily delivering the promise even when the object of hope is attained. In the spirit of the legend of Pandora, I have not sought to solve the ambiguities inherent to hope. Attributing neither inherent virtue nor inevitable complicity to hope, I've tried instead to contribute to the expanding "archive of public feelings" (Cvetkovich 2012) in contemporary times by capturing the ambivalence of hope through various qualifiers: entitled hope, precarious hope, troubled and troubling hope.

* * *

Hope—without a qualifier—is the title of an 1886 oil painting by the English painter George Frederic Watts. The painting, which is alleged to have influenced Martin Luther King Jr.'s sermon "Shattered Dreams," features a single female figure. She is blindfolded and sits, lonely and towering, on the globe. She is playing a lyre that has only one string left. At the time of its exhibition, many critics disliked the painting, mostly, it seems, because of its ambiguous message.

Why was hope, one of the three fundamental Christian virtues, depicted as a blindfolded woman? Was it hope that blinded her, or did the painting suggest the disappearance of hope from the world? Some viewers called attention to the only other figure in the sparse painting, a star in the distance, to suggest that the painter did indeed believe in the continued existence of hope. It was, they surmised, the blindfolded figure who had lost hope because she was no longer capable of seeing it. Some theologians favored the interpretation that the central figure personified not hope but rather a humanity horrified by the sight of the world that was its own doing. While the painter donated a reproduction of the painting in support of London dockworkers, some within the socialist movement were dissatisfied with what they found to be the inertia and lack of commitment to praxis in Watts's depiction.

There does not seem to be a consensus among art critics as to why exactly

Watts painted two other versions of *Hope* before his death. It may merely have been due to financial considerations, but the fact remains that the spirits of the two subsequent versions seem to be diametrically opposed. In one of them, the star in the distance, which was deemed to be the sole symbol of optimism in the original version, is expunged entirely. In the other, the forlorn blindfolded figure is nestled in a rainbow.

EPILOGUE

A Note on Method, or Hopeful Waiting in Lines

In his brilliantly provocative *Anthropology and Egalitarianism*, Eric Gable (2011) writes of the experience of standing in lines—whether for a movie ticket, or at the grocery store, or during a museum visit— as a democratic one.[1] Lines are equalizers. But, Gable goes on to note, there is also something troubling about that equality, at least as far as American public culture goes: "Standing in line is an act fraught with the paradox of American egalitarianism that we should all be treated the same, yet we should also each be different, individual, or special" (2011, 54–55).

My ethnography of the legalization quest of the post-1990 Bulgaristanlı migrants could be described for the most part as an ethnography of waiting in lines. But the lines *we* waited in—whether at the Foreigners' Branch of the Istanbul Police Department, the City Registrar's Office, or various local police stations—hardly resemble the lines in Gable's description of the line that is supposed to have its self-regulating rules: a line in which everyone is stuck but has to wait patiently and where one tends to get annoyed if someone cuts in. The lines in which we sometimes spent an entire day were often disordered, if not chaotic. People cut in all the time to come stand next to an acquaintance, a norm violation that rarely triggered any protest. The unruliness of lines, especially the lines at local police stations, where amnesty applications were made, was a fact taken for granted and even systematically manipulated to one's advantage if one had the savvy and skills to negotiate a better spot through an acquaintance or a police officer sympathetic to the plight of those who were *soydaş*.

Though Gable's analysis uses a different operational logic, there is something that carries over to the Turkish context in his point about the paradox of the line. The lines in which we waited were simultaneously an individual and a collective affair, and the two planes did not always converge. Lines were where hopes of legalization were kindled, challenged, reassured, and collectively cultivated by *soydaş* who felt entitled to legalization. But in the words of Şemsiye, the lines were also "gates of hope" created by the government. "Every single person in this line thinks they will get citizenship," she said bitterly, "but they will not give it to everyone in the end, will they?"

The fieldwork for this book was conducted primarily in Istanbul over forty-eight months between 2007 and 2011 and an additional twelve months of follow-up in 2013. I followed the legalization attempts of post-1990 Bulgaristanlı migrants who have been moving to Turkey from Bulgaria to work in the informal labor market. But the analysis presented here also draws on insights from earlier fieldwork that I had conducted between February 2001 and September 2002. This early work was among the prior wave of migrants from Bulgaria: the 1989 migrants who arrived as part of a politically framed migration and who were automatically granted citizenship in Turkey as refugees who were escaping the persecution that the Bulgarian regime directed at its Turkish minority between 1984 and 1989. While the book depicts the legalization quest of the post-1990 migrants, my earlier research among the 1989 migrants provided the crucial background that enabled me to trace continuities across these two cohorts, who are different in terms of their legal status upon migration to Turkey but who share much more in terms of the prehistories and motivations for their migration than the hierarchical distinction of political migrants versus economic migrants would suggest.

Between 2010 and 2012, I was also a participant in the Migrant Solidarity Network, an activist group established in 2010 that sought to draw public attention to and politicize the predicament of undocumented migrants in Turkey, mostly through protests and solidarity events. I kept the field of activism and the field of research as separate as possible, a task in which I was greatly aided by the fact that my Bulgaristanlı interlocutors showed no interest—and even assiduously avoided—such efforts at collective organizing. My work with the migrant network nonetheless informs my analysis of the ethnographic field by providing invaluable points of comparison between the Bulgaristanlı and the plight of other, less privileged undocumented migrants in Turkey.

Though the fieldwork was, for the most part, based in Istanbul, I also crossed the Turkish-Bulgarian border several times, mostly by bus, which was the preferred mode of transport by Bulgaristanlı, and once by the notorious train, a choice my interlocutors found absolutely appalling and substandard. These trips to the Razgrad and Silistra regions in northern Bulgaria, when I had the chance to visit the villages of those among my interlocutors to whom I had grown particularly close, gave me a deep appreciation of the beauty of the rural Bulgarian landscape and the air that almost hurt one's lungs with its fresh sweetness. They also gave me a chance to see the places about which my interlocutors spoke so fondly and then to reminisce with them once I returned to Istanbul. I lounged in the gardens they tended to with enormous care and yearned for in their city apartments or the cluttered rooms they occupied while working as a nanny. "I miss my garden the most," was a phrase I heard often. I drank *rakiya,* an alcoholic beverage they brewed from the fruits in those gardens. I witnessed firsthand the torment of saying good-byes and leaving behind their children or grandchildren to tend to the children of their employers in Istanbul.

Even as these trips remained peripheral to my primary field site, the experiences of the everyday on the other side of the border illuminated how hope for legalization was cultivated in Turkey. Being able to talk about those experiences with my interlocutors also distanced me, as I very much wished it would, from the assumptions about a researcher identified as being from Turkey. The Bulgaristanlı feel they have to prove their credentials of ethnic identity, religiosity, and even language proficiency to longtime residents, whom they suspect, with good reason, of measuring them against a true standard of Turkishness. Instead, they could relate to me as someone who was genuinely appreciative of their attachments to Bulgaria, shared their appreciation for aspects of the communist experience, and was often even more critical of Turkish nationalism than they were, not to mention someone who enjoyed *rakiya* and pork, habits for which they often got grief from their more conservative neighbors.

Fieldwork in Istanbul encompassed those neighborhoods that host significant Bulgaristanlı populations, including Sultanbeyli, Avcılar, Sefaköy, and the migrant settlements in Kurtköy as well as the upper- middle-class neighborhoods of Bebek, Etiler, Nişantaşı, and Bahariye, where they worked as domestics. Although much time was spent socializing in these neighborhoods, the spaces where encounters with the law took place were the locations that I placed at the core in framing both my ethnographic design and my analysis. First and foremost, these included institutional sites such the Foreigners' Branch, the City Registrar's Office, social security offices, and local police stations. I then tracked how these legal spaces spread into expanding adjacent spaces: migrant associations, public transportation to reach various offices in the city; the *simit* (pastry) shops around these offices that were a favorite meeting place before or after submitting an application; photocopy shops that sprang up near police stations to provide assistance with making online appointments in return for small fees; the exchange shops that would "informally" produce a receipt for $3,000—one of the documents required for a residency application—without any money actually changing hands. Pioneering work in the scholarship on law and society insists that one not distinguish strictly between legal and personal spaces (Sarat and Kearns 1993) or, more broadly, between law and society (Calavita 2010)—a proposition that Elif Babül (2017) masterfully demonstrates in her rendition of how human rights training in Turkey is (mis)translated into the everyday practices of government workers.

One other key motivation for prioritizing legal sites within an amorphous ethnographic field was that legal spaces provided spontaneous opportunities for me to be useful to my interlocutors. I was able to help fill out applications, make appointments, ask questions, request documents, and sometimes negotiate—though not necessarily with more savvy than my migrant friends—with police officers, state bureaucrats, and migrant association staff. These opportunities offered a modest degree of reciprocity, ameliorating a long-standing moral dilemma for anthropologists, who worry, as they should, about the disproportionately one-sided nature of their exchanges with the people they meet in the field.

In foregrounding my zeal to be as useful as I could in the field, I do not want to idealize the ethnographic encounter and imbue it with more reciprocity than it entails. I knew Nefiye's sister well, and we had already met several times in various offices in pursuit of amnesties. But the first time Nefiye herself called me, after her sister had repeatedly urged her to do so since she thought Nefiye could really "aid me with my research," she was blunt about her own priorities: "Now, will *you* be able to help me? If you tell me that, I will continue this conversation accordingly." It turned out that she knew more than I did about the documents, online appointment forms, queues, and even which government employees were more agreeable than others. Still, she saw in me an opportunity to play it safer because of my "university connections" and because, she said, "You still manage to communicate a bit better in Turkish with them, and there is less chance of making a mistake on the forms."

Sometimes migrants' ideas of what "a researcher" would be like involved expectations of a certain stature or physical appearance more than any pragmatic considerations for assistance with paperwork. I will never forget the crestfallen expression on Vasfiye Hanım's face when she first opened the door of the house where she worked as a caretaker. She turned to the mutual acquaintance who had brought me there, and said, right there on the threshold before she let us in, "I thought you had said you were bringing your professor!" Her disappointment was visible, and she did not even try to hide it. After her initial upset that her limited available time was potentially being wasted on someone she considered too young to be entrusted with her story or to write a book, we actually ended up really taking to each other. Indeed, the long-term fieldwork led to several enduring friendships that have stood the test of time and distance. But rather than regard these as evidence of reciprocity and thus fall into the danger of romanticizing the fieldwork condition, I prefer to consider such intimacies as gifts to be cherished.

In designing my research, I took to heart anthropologist Susan Coutin's evocative phrase "legalizing acts." Coutin (2000) highlights the contingent nature of il/legality. Arguing against the assumption that undocumented migrants form hermetically sealed communities, she describes her research on the legalizing acts of Latin American immigrants in the United States as the "ethnography of a legal process rather than of a particular group" (2000). I follow in Coutin's footsteps in conceiving of my field site as the entire range of legalizing acts undertaken by migrants. Unlike her, however, I could not avoid focusing on a particular ethnic group. This is because I was also seeking to show how ethnic privilege makes a difference for this group of migrants. Notwithstanding the additional risk of a design bias, whereby the significance of ethnicity is overdetermined as a finding precisely because the initial design of the research has the ethnic group built into it (Glick Schiller and Çağlar 2010; Wimmer 2008), conceiving my research as the ethnography of a legal process for a particular group best suited my key research questions, which address both legalization and the role of ethnic privilege.

It has variously been noted that within the participant observation dialectic, the weight continually shifts between participation and observation (O'Reilly 2004). I retreated to the role of "participating observer" (Bernard 2011) in more formal interviews with migrant association representatives and when I recorded life stories at length. But the latter did not always occur in prearranged, sealed-off settings. In the spirit of researchers who have highlighted the significance of life stories as particularly revealing of the multiple identities that individuals can hold, create, and manage over time and in different contexts (Das 2000; Narayan and George 2012; Polkinghorne 1995), the life stories I narrate in this book were mostly compiled over several sittings and often in surroundings that bled into the activities of daily life (Rapp 2000), "co-constructed" (Ochs and Capps 1996) while on long bus rides from one state institution to another or while waiting in queues.

I moved to the "observing participant" (Bernard 2011) end of the spectrum while accompanying my interlocutors to state institutions, assisting with the filing of forms, helping them to claim a place in queues in disarray, or demanding clarification for outrageously unclear document-requirement instructions. Such active participation allowed me to witness and experience firsthand the elusive boundaries between formality and informality. An amnesty that did not apply to a particular person if days of entry were abided by, might, at the discretion of an officer, be tailored to fit; another sympathetic official might be cajoled into substituting the application requirement of a bank account balance with a more dubious form of proof of savings; depending on one's charms or the disposition of the police officer on duty that day, an applicant might be granted a better spot in the queue for the following day's line. Even access to legal information on a particular amnesty or an individual was dependent on the specific whims and varying levels of knowledge of the clerks. I also observed how migrants, in navigating what they duly recognized as an arbitrary legal system, came to rely on personal skills that were often gendered, using their femininity or appealing to kinship terminology in culturally appropriate ways. Such performances of the "affective features in language" (Ochs and Schieffelin 1989, 90) abounded in my fieldwork, as attested to by Vasfiye's address to the official in the idiom of maternal kinship.

Delineating the contours of an initially vast field site was a relatively easier task compared to the more knotty process of selecting what would eventually constitute data that would make its way into the book. My long-term fieldwork led to relationships in which I was privy to very personal aspects of people's lives. Though everyone to whom I refer in this book was informed about the reasons for my presence, the line between ethnographic research and intimate conversation often became blurred, especially when we stood for hours together in a line and had all the time in the world to flit from one topic to another. At some points, I pondered the notion of consent in the fieldwork encounter. When the conversation strayed too deeply into personal detail, should I have interrupted it? Should I have warned the speaker by asking whether this was still considered part of the data for the research? In the end,

I opted to filter out the personal as much as possible. A son lost to a childhood accident, a son lost to political violence, a marriage kept out of sight and mind until it was forced into view by an application requirement, or a sickness kept from family—such life events were expunged from the field record. I included personal details only to the extent that they came to bear on the realm of the legal in the most direct ways or were part of a public performance or utterance. I kept only those personal stories that were obviously rehearsed and retold for public consumption. I can only hope that I have been a good judge of where those slippery lines lie.

The last thorny question that haunted my research was the relation between epistemology and methodology. How *does* one ethnographically discern and locate hope? The twin problems of transparency and access have always been present in the study of emotions. Any study of emotions is plagued by what Lutz and White have called "common-sense naturalism" (1986, 114–16)—namely, the assumption that emotions can be read from individual utterances or bodily experiences in ways that are transparent and translatable across cultural lifeworlds through empathy or shared experience (Lutz and White 1986; see also Leavitt 1996). The danger of projecting one's own categories and experiences onto others is ever present in ethnographic research and perhaps exacerbated by the assumption of empathy in the field. Lutz and White warn against empathy as a method of understanding other people's emotions because it assumes that feelings are universal (115). I have discussed how these pitfalls may become exacerbated in the hard version of affect theory in chapter 2.

While acknowledging that there is no absolute way to circumvent the problem of transparency as long as ethnography continues to aspire to a dialectic between the emic and the etic, I nonetheless discerned hope in this book by following in the footsteps of the anthropology of emotions. That is, I paid simultaneous attention to how hope was expressed, performed, and embodied. The most immediate and visible level on which I detected hope was in the locutionary act. Typical recurrent utterances I concentrated on included: "I have hope" (*umutluyum*); "I have hope this time" (*bu sefer umutluyum*); "this time I have hope that X will come about" (*bu sefer olacağına ümidim var*). I also included idiomatic expressions, such as the one Şemsiye used in her criticism of government: the "gate of hope" (*umut kapısı*). However, I refrained from counting another extremely widespread idiomatic usage, *inşallah*, as instances of hope. *İnşallah*, literally "God willing" in Arabic, is a generic term employed by users of the Turkish language, including the most secular among them. It is less an expression of religious piety—although it can certainly be that—than an ingrained cultural utterance to express a whole range of attitudes from having faith in destiny to trying not to jinx things. It is used so often in daily conversation that if one tracked its prevalence as evidence of hope, all ethnographies of Turkey would emerge as also ethnographies of a particularly religious kind of everyday hope. Following Crapanzano's Whorfian emphasis on how language shapes the parameters of thought and culture (2003), one could presumably make an argument about how Muslim societies are characterized by an understanding of hope that is marked by the notion of fate. But that is not the direction I have taken here. I do not explore hope as having a uniquely Islamic inflection in the Turkish context. In fact, I have resisted a culturalist explanation of what I emphasize to be an equally historically, legally, and politically inflected phenomenon.

Finally, hope made some of its most conspicuous appearances and surfaced most clearly as a discernible affective state in the moments when it was challenged, when the grounds for hope's existence were called into question by a more skeptical interlocutor. Tracing this cycle of how hope is contested, defended, and affirmed in everyday interactions, I suggest that hope's very fragility provides an important yet hitherto understudied vantage point from which to discern, locate, and critically analyze it.

I did not begin this project with hope as an a priori category of analysis. Instead, hope emerged as central to the bureaucratized existence of Bulgaristanlı migrants. It was revealed inductively over the course of five years of fieldwork. As I waited in lines with my interlocutors to file an application for the extension of a permit or to submit the final dossier of a citizenship application, hope manifested itself in direct and oblique articulations. Hope also manifested itself as a practice of waiting—of pushing forward in the line and in life. For some, it was hope for amnesty that fees owed for overstaying a visa for months, sometimes years, would be waived. For others, it was hope for a renewable residence permit that might lead to citizenship. For those already residing in Turkey on intermittent permits, it was hope that a window would open up for citizenship applications. But regardless of its object and regardless of how each individual quest for legalization played out, hope was not just an individual matter. Rather, it was an "emergent product of social life" (Lutz 1988, 5), collectively enacted and reaffirmed during long hours of waiting in government office queues, visits to migrant associations, conversations with other undocumented migrants, and systematically kindled by the law.

Kirin Narayan, in a groundbreaking essay that has become a classic of the anthropological method, asks, "How native is the native anthropologist?" Hers is a sarcastically rhetorical question that undercuts the colonialist and dyadic vision of anthropologists as either insiders or outsiders to the culture they study. Instead, Narayan argues, most anthropologists operate on some-times crosscutting, sometimes contradictory planes of identification with the places where they do fieldwork, even if they have birth or kinship ties to those places. When we acknowledge the fact that all of us belong to several commu-nities at once, we can become more aware of the fact that whichever "facet of our subjectivity we choose or are forced to accept as a defining identity can change, depending on the context and the prevailing vectors of power" (Na-rayan 1993, 674).

Another corrective to the insider-outsider dichotomy that Narayan takes to task is that degrees of insiderness/outsiderness pertain not only to the an-thropologist but also to the people we write about. Our interlocutors, too, for-mulate fine distinctions between degrees of insiderness and outsiderness. When introduced to a Bulgaristanlı through a mutual acquaintance, I would frequently be told right away, "But I don't think I am one of the migrants you are looking for." I soon came to realize that the disavowal often had to do with an assertion of distinction from others or an assumption of authenticity. If uttered by someone who migrated in 1989 and settled without going back to Bulgaria, the disavowal might indicate a distance from those who migrated after 1990 and thus were not considered equally legitimate in their migration in the eyes of some of the 1989 migrants. Or, conversely, it might indicate that the speaker had in mind someone more authentic than herself that I should be talking to, a *muhacir*, someone who had migrated much earlier and was a true immigrant who had entirely embraced Turkey rather than someone who sustained dual attachments on both sides of the border. Early on in my field-work, a Bulgaristanlı to whom I was introduced gently told me to reconsider my categories. She was speaking from the position and experience of being a minority within a minority in Bulgaria growing up as Alevi. She felt that the Alevi/Sunni distinction had been more definitive for her and her family than the ethnonational distinction between Bulgarian and Turkish.

I was also often warned of another divide, one framed in geographical terms between the south and north of Bulgaria. My interlocutors, most of whom tended to be from the north, would point out that they were far more integrated into Bulgarian culture, while those in the south were more isolated. The implication of this distinction might be accompanied by positive and negative judgment: in the eyes of many northerners, migrants from the Kırdjali region were less modernized and westernized, but in the eyes of some others, they were also more authentic in having kept to Turkish traditions. Those who had become members of the Communist Party might be frowned upon by others who felt that an active level of political participation was a betrayal of Turkishness. But even as these internal negotiations over the definition of who was the real insider proliferated, there were simultaneously recurrent declarations of cultural intimacy that bound the Bulgaristanlı together: "We can immediately spot one another," I would often be told. "We can just tell another Bulgaristanlı from one hundred meters away, just from the way she carries herself or just from the way he gestures."

That the term *Bulgaristanlı* is at best an approximation of a historically constructed, politically instrumentalized, socially idealized, and yet somehow culturally intimate category was most playfully brought home to me by Ayşe, whom I met only once, by chance, waiting in line. She came over because she recognized the people I was with, and she ended up waiting with us. She was an extremely jovial woman, witty, quick to retort, and with a ringing laugh that made people in the room turn and stare at us. When the day was done and it was time to part, she wanted to exchange phone numbers. After I gave her mine, I started to type in hers. I typed her name and then paused, not sure if I should ask her surname. I had, after all, just met her and there is always a precariousness to sharing identifying information for those of undocumented status even if one has been introduced through mutual acquaintances. Ayşe seized on my hesitation, and with that resounding laugh, said mockingly, "Put me down as 'Ayşe the *kaçak*.'" That is, Ayşe the illegal, or Ayşe the fugitive.

But *kaçak* is not quite captured in either of those translations. *Kaçak* means "the one who escapes." Ayşe's playful and masterful appropriation of a term that has negative connotations in public discourse, an appropriation that perhaps was also meant to underscore the difference in precarity between herself and me despite the coincidence of our sharing the same first name, has served as a witty, and sobering, reminder for me of how even the seemingly most straightforward designations escape full capture.

NOTES

INTRODUCTION

1. While some of the amnesties were made available to the general public, others circulated only among migrant networks and through the handful of active migrant associations established by earlier migrants from Bulgaria. The full informal regularity of the amnesties was thus discernible only through the proximity provided by ethnographic fieldwork. I was able to discern the informal regularity of the amnesties only because I was constantly present in the field. The lack of official visibility and transparency surrounding them also probably accounts for the fact that they have gone unmentioned in overviews of migration policy in Turkey penned by less ethnographically inclined observers.

2. Three key moves undertaken by this groundbreaking scholarship on anthropology of emotions inform my analysis of hope in this book. First, against much of Western political thought that considers emotions to be inner states of being that reside in the individual and against nineteenth-century psychologists' view of emotions as psychophysiological in nature, anthropological work on emotions reclaimed the crucial significance of culture—understood in its broad sense as a set of norms and practices that include the legal and the political—for how emotions are experienced, articulated, and performed. Second, it underscored the interpersonal nature of emotions, focusing less on how emotions indicate personal states and more on how they are indices of social relationships. Finally, this pioneering body of work in the anthropology of emotions emphasized the relationship between the distribution of power in society and the ideological structuring of emotion (see Lutz 1988).

3. Philosopher Joseph Patrick Day, in a lucid defense of the rationalist and empiricist analysis of hope (1991), locates the kernel of this approach in the Hobbes-Locke-Hume tradition. Hope always involves both a conative aspect (the desire for something) and a cognitive aspect (a subjective belief in the attainability of the desired object that is based on estimations of probability). The advantage of this approach, as elaborated by Nicholas Smith (2008), is that it offers a scheme for tracking and assessing degrees of intensity (conative level) as well as degrees of likelihood and probability, and by implication, an assessment of whether particular hopes will be realistic, compromised, or irresponsible, etc. (cognitive level).

4. While Patricia Williams's (1992) approach resonates with that of Raymond Williams (1977) in emphasizing the collective and differentiated nature of feelings,

Patricia Williams additionally foregrounds the *racialized* hierarchies that constitute the institutional underpinnings of hope: in the United States there are certain hopes, Patricia Williams writes, that whites can take for granted in their daily, mundane encounters with the law, but blacks cannot exercise that same expectation.

5. As an interpretive exercise in what he calls philosophical anthropology, Jonathan Lear (2006) pondered the possibilities that may exist for maintaining hope under conditions of cultural devastation. Lear reconstructs the predicament faced by a Native American tribe whose chief aligns with the U.S. government to accept reservation life in exchange for basic securities and at the expense of land, tradition, and the tools for making sense of existence. He argues that this predicament gives rise to radical hope, a future-oriented stance for survival in the face of material and conceptual loss.

6. One comes upon this earlier variant of the term *ırkdaş* in publications and parliament discussions during the early years of the nation-state. The root word *ırk* instead of *soy* leaves no leeway for interpretation, as *ırk* exclusively means "race." But even without such evidence of deployment of the literal term for race, I would still insist on thinking about *soy/ırk* (ethnicity/race) together, given that the former often becomes a euphemism for the latter, as Etienne Balibar and Immanuel Wallerstein (1991) have argued. My approach is also similar to the integrative approach advanced by Andreas Wimmer (2008), who consciously rejects a definitional ontology of ethnicity. One might argue that in refusing the ontological primacy of race, Wimmer takes the more radical step of proposing that we view race and racial identification as a subset of ethnicity and expose how ethnicity gets variously and contingently operationalized.

7. Azat Zana Gündoğan (2018) has recently translated *soydaş* as "consanguines." Gündoğan's excellent rendition of the term is in the same spirit as my own emphasis on the importance placed on blood. I have opted for "racial kin," however, in order to preserve the sentiments evoked through explicit references to kinship made by both officials and migrants themselves.

8. Following Kirişçi's pioneering article (2000) on the links between immigration law and Turkey's citizenship regime, migration scholars refer to the Settlement Law as a key legal text regulating both migration and settlement, including the displacement and resettlement during the early years of the republic of ethnic groups deemed to be difficult to assimilate. In a very important overview of migration and settlement policies in Turkey's changing political landscape (2014), Sema Erder calls the Settlement Law a foundational and understudied text, one that gives critical indication of the content and scope of how citizenship is defined in Turkey. Through meticulous analysis of the range of regulations that fall under its rubric, from the right to use land to the distribution of property, Erder suggests that the Settlement Law reflects the general fear of "the foreigner" in Turkey's political culture and the concomitant instinct to close inward. It is also important to note that veteran sociologist İsmail Beşikçi, imprisoned for years for his research and writing on Kurds in Turkey, called the Settlement Law "a racist Exile Law" (Beşikçi 1977) in a book that was in-

stantly banned and described it as a law that was primarily used to colonize what was deemed an unruly and threatening Kurdish population (see Martin van Bruinessen 2005 for an excellent discussion of the significance of this work within Beşikçi's larger work as a persecuted scholar).

9. See Kadirbeyoğlu's 2010 *Country Report: Turkey* for EUDO Citizenship Observatory. For a more detailed breakdown of migrations since the nineteenth century according to country of origin, the two most precise and reliable sources I have come across are Ferhunde Özbay and Banu Yücel (2001) and İlhan Tekeli (2002).

10. According to the 1992 consensus, as cited in Eminov (2000, 139), Turkish speakers constituted the majority of the population in the district of Kurdzhali in southeastern Bulgaria at 65.7 percent, and in northeastern Bulgaria Turkish speakers accounted for 47.4 percent of Razgrad's population. Other districts that host significant Turkish populations are Silistra (33.5%), Turgovishte (32.8%), Shumen (30.3%), Dobrich (14.7%), Burgas (13.8%), Ruse (13.0%), Haskovo (11.4%), and Blagoevgrad (11.3%).

11. See Bilecen 2006 and Dündar 2008 for archival-research-based accounts of the settlement policies for the migrants arriving from the Balkans during the first decades of the twentieth century.

12. In contrast to Kemal Karpat (2004), who uses the term "founding cadres" and subscribes to the aptness of this designation, historian İlhan Tekeli (2002) analyzes these migrations with far more scholarly detachment and describes their logic as part and parcel of the violent processes of becoming a nation-state.

13. The expression was used by Reşat Yavaş, a presenter at the International Symposium on the 20th Century of the 89 Exodus, organized by Mehmet Hacısalihoğlu and held at Yıldız Technical University in Istanbul in December 2009.

14. See Kristen Ghodsee's (2010) incisive analysis of the political and gendered causes for a return to Islamic education and practice among the Pomak, a Bulgarian-speaking Muslim minority in Bulgaria, after the fall of socialism and subsequent rampant unemployment. Though claimed by different groups as their own, the Pomak self-identify as either Turkish or Bulgarian.

15. Before the fieldwork conducted between 2007 and 2013, which forms the basis of this book, I had also conducted eighteen months of fieldwork specifically among the Bulgaristanlı who came to Turkey in 1989 as part of the massive 1989 migration (see Parla 2006).

16. While the Turkish government misses no opportunity to boast of this fact—one that has also been recognized by the first World Humanitarian Summit, which Turkey was chosen to host—Ataç et al. (2017) note with due sarcasm that Turkey also issues fewer grants of refugee status to its asylum applicants than any other country in the region.

17. For the six million figure, see http://data2.unhcr.org/en/situations/syria. For the three million figure, see http://www.goc.gov.tr/icerik6/gecici-koruma. My thanks to Ayşe Şanlı for singling out these sources as the most reliable data on statistics that are inherently difficult to pin down. It should be noted that the UNHCR data do not reflect those Syrians who have been able to make it to Europe.

18. On women who engage in the shuttle trade, see Yükseker (2003); on migrants from Moldova, see Keough 2006 and Eder 2015; and on the field of domestic migrant work in general, see Akalın 2007 and Erder 2007.

19. An early piece that diagnosed this situation in the Turkish context is Danış, Perouse, and Taraghi 2009. For an excellent critical take on the problems with the term "transit," see İkizoğlu Erensü and Kaşlı 2017. They show how Turkey gets designated as a "transit" country for migrants from the global south trying to cross to Europe. However, the phrase "transit country" fails to reflect not only the empirical complexity of fragmented, interrupted migration journeys but also neglects to identify important distinctions in migration pathways within the same country. For example, İkizoğlu and Kaşlı demonstrate how transit plays out differently in the city of Edirne, with its immediate physical border with Bulgaria and Greece, and in Kayseri, which has no geographical proximity to Europe.

20. When Brewer and Yükseker wrote their survey of the field of African migrants in 2006, virtually no ethnographic research had been conducted among this group. Since then, several ethnographically informed analyses have refined the analytic scope of the field of migration studies in Turkey: Mahir Saul (2014)'s work on sub-Saharan migrants from Africa dispels the common assumption that the poorest are the ones who migrate; Kristen Biehl (2015b) demonstrates the increasing visibility of and marginalization faced by African migrants in the hub of Kumkapı; and Emel Coşkun 2018 exposes the sexual violence that targets African women in particular.

21. Erder and Kaska 2012 note the difficulty with exact estimates. This is not only because of the well-known unreliability of statistics on undocumented migration, where the clandestine nature of many border crossings makes it impossible to pin down exact figures, It is also because differently motivated groups are likely to cite different figures, inflating or deflating them in line with their pro or con migration agendas. The approximate figure of 1 to 1.5 million seems to be a reasonable estimate.

22. In July 2016, Recep Tayyip Erdoğan, the president of Turkey, declared without offering details that those Syrians who qualified would obtain citizenship. The statement was enough to unleash and exacerbate anti-immigrant sentiment among broad segments of the population. People from wide-ranging class and ethnic backgrounds, including my Bulgaristanlı interlocutors, all too readily assumed that Syrians had been granted citizenship in exchange for voting for Erdoğan and his party, when this was not the case. Just before the 2018 elections, an unannounced number of Syrians in fact were granted citizenship, lending support to Didem Danış's insight that the Syrians are the first ethnically non-Turkish group to be accommodated in such numbers in Turkey (Danış 2016). But it remains to be seen whether the Syrians, until now one of the most socially vulnerable migrant groups in the country, will eventually emerge as another group with relative legal privilege. Even if they do, it seems extremely unlikely that this will come close to the cultural privilege of the Bulgaristanlı, who are viewed as religious and racial kin.

23. Among theoretically sophisticated and ethnographically rich elaborations

of the mechanisms of "inclusive exclusion" in various geographies, see Balibar 2004; Coutin 2000; De Genova 2006; Khosravi 2010; Ticktin 2011; and Willen 2007.

24. Acquisition of citizenship through marriage was rendered more difficult in 2003 when a waiting period of three years was introduced, during which the partner whose application is pending is not eligible for work.

25. The 1951 Convention itself was initially restricted to "persons who became refugees due to events occurring in Europe," but the 1967 Protocol Relating to the Status of Refugees was passed in part to remove the geographical and time limits of the original convention. Turkey signed on to removing the time limit but retained the geographical one. Since becoming a party to the convention, Turkey has officially accepted a total of only forty-three people as refugees (Erdoğan 2015, 45). In an earlier publication, Kirişçi 2012 cites this number as thirty.

26. In practice, migrants from Afghanistan, Iran, Iraq, and increasingly Africa have been applying for refugee status in Turkey, doing so through the United Nations High Commissioner for Refugees, which has an agreement with the Turkish state. If the UNHCR approves a refugee's application and that person qualifies for refugee status, he or she must then wait for approval for settlement from a third country. The applicant is granted temporary protection so long as the application is pending. In this way, legal status can be obtained temporarily through applying for asylum and gaining the temporary right to stay while the application is processed. Even if the application is approved, an applicant may wait up to three years for a third country of settlement, an outcome that itself is by no means guaranteed (Biner 2016). By the end of 2011, more than 14,000 outstanding applications had been filed with the UNHCR (Soykan 2012); by 2014, that figure had more than doubled, to 33,000 (K. Biehl 2015). Even when these applications are approved—approval rates are low: around 1,000 per year (UNHCR 2009, cited in Soykan 2012)—and a third country is found to accept the applicant as a refugee, there is no possibility of legalization in Turkey.

27. See legal scholar Lami Bertan Tokuzlu (2013) and also personal communication, April 6, 2010.

28. But see Ataç et al. (2017), who underscore the importance of not signaling EU's design to externalize its border regime as the sole explanation for current migration policy and practice in Turkey when policy is also affected by Turkey's own local dynamics and peculiarities.

29. See Soykan (2012) for an early and thorough assessment of what the 2013 Law on Foreigners and International Protection changed in the field of migration governance and what it left untouched. For a detailed account of the specific problems that continue to plague the asylum regime in Turkey, even after the implementation of the Law on Foreigners and International Protection no. 6458/2014, see Sarı and Dinçer 2017. On the basis of interviews with relevant NGO workers and lawyers, Sarı and Dinçer provide convincing fresh evidence that continuing restrictions exist on freedom of movement for applicants who are to reside in designated satellite cities and that the numerous state actors that are now supposed to be coordinating the process,

such as the Ministry of Health, the Ministry of National Education, and the Bar Association of Turkey, are unaware of one another and of their own responsibilities and duties. Sarı and Dinçer also see signs that the now centralized Directorate General of Migration Management is sharing less with the UNHCR and its Turkish counterpart and implementing partner ASAM (Association for Solidarity with Asylum Seekers and Migrants) and is even taking over the interviews for refugee status determination despite its personnel being unqualified for the task.

30. My reading of the new law on this issue was confirmed by Veysel Eşsiz, human rights advocate at the Istanbul branch of Helsinki Citizens Assembly Refugee Advocacy and Support Program, an NGO that was an active participant in the drafting of the 2014 Law on Foreigners and International Protection to push the government to try to make the law as comprehensive as possible (personal communication, April 2014).

31. This would put Turkey in closer proximity to countries like Japan and Israel, for example, where racialized notions of belonging underlie legal formulations of citizenship. See Tsuda (2003) for Japan and Nadia Abu El Haj (2010) for Israel.

32. Kirişçi 2000. Also see Tekeli 2002.

33. See Akçam and Kurt 2015; Üngör and Polatel 2011.

34. The first systematic exposition of Kemalism as a rightist, solidaristic-corporatist ideology with strong militaristic overtones and totalitarian tendencies, one that resists both the unbridled individualism of liberalism and the class struggle of socialism, was undertaken by political scientist Taha Parla in the 1980s (T. Parla 1991; see also T. Parla and Davison 2004). Since then, excellent critical engagements with Kemalism and its authoritarian legacy include a variety of disciplinary perspectives from anthropology (Navaro-Yashin 2002; Özyürek 2006), political theory (Bargu 2014), and sociology (Tuğal 2009; Turam 2007).

35. Atatürk's famous dictum "how happy s/he who says I am a Turk" is the quintessential slogan that is often cited as proof of Turkish nationalism's inclusiveness and its civic rather than ethnic underpinnings. The dictum is also the last line of the oath recited in unison by elementary school students across the country as an everyday ritual. But the realities of belonging in Turkey are better captured in the twist that political scientist Ahmet Yıldız brings: "How happy s/he who is able to say I am a Turk" (2001).

36. Members of the Jewish minority avoided such explicit policies of violence in the Turkish context but were subjected to pogroms in 1934 that were tolerated by the state. They faced additional taxes levied on minorities and continue to be targets of sudden bursts of anti-Semitism.

37. Anthropologist Hirokazu Miyazaki is a key figure in this field and the most eloquent proponent of hope as a method for self- and scholarly knowledge (Miyazaki 2004); see also Riles's (2017) excellent and sympathetic account of hope studies.

38. For an examination of the role of hope in Greek philosophy that offers a reappraisal of Plato on hope, see Vogt (2017).

39. "[Fear and hope] are bound up with each other, unconnected as they may

seem. Widely different though they are, the two of them march in unison like a prisoner and the escort he is handcuffed to. Fear keeps pace with hope. Nor does their moving together in such a way surprise me; both belong to a mind in suspense, to a mind in a state of anxiety through looking into the future. Both are mainly the result of our projecting our thoughts far ahead of us instead of adapting ourselves to the present" (Seneca, Letter 5.7–8, quoted in Bloeser and Titus 2017).

40. A different translation of Spinoza renders the same ambivalence in this way: hope is "an inconstant joy" aroused by "the image of a future or past thing whose outcome we doubt" (Spinoza 1994, 165).

41. For some, like Miyazaki (2004, 2017a), this paradoxicality of hope makes it unique among the emotions, giving it a distinctive reflexivity and openness. While I do not refute the analytic and experiential potential of hope to be distinctive, the analysis in this book does not rest on the attribution of such special potential to hope even as I try to do full justice to its paradoxical and ambivalent nature.

42. I thank Amanda Schaffer for critically fine-tuning the formulation of this point.

43. There are different analytical and political commitments to hope, and these are reflected in both how it is defined and how it is then assessed. Often the two converge in interesting ways; that is to say, efforts at delineation may go beyond mere concerns of analytic precision (although they are that, too) and indicate something of the analyst's own normative commitments to the utility and consequences of hope for the individual or the collective good.

44. In later work, Butler (2012) develops a more nuanced formulation of the relationship between ontological and political analyses of vulnerability and precariousness, arguing that precarity is political precisely because we are vulnerable and socially dependent upon one another. Tadeusz Rachwal (2016) pursues the Butlerian argument to claim that *precarity* is a political issue and *precariousness* is an ontological one. He adds a third element, stating that the two "cannot really be untangled" because "the need for existential security is paired with epistemological security." I thank Theresa Giroux-Gischler for alerting me to Butler's subsequent iterations on the precarious and Rachwal's elaboration on Butler. However, my analytic preference remains for retaining a distinction between precariousness and vulnerability rather than allowing them to bleed into each other, for reasons that I explicate in chapter 3.

45. My take here is parallel to Muehlebach and Shoshan's (2012) evocative depiction of post-Fordist affect: it is the promise of security and predictability offered by the Fordist vision that causes many who experienced it to mourn its loss and yearn for its revival.

46. I narrate some of these clandestine border crossings in detail in chapter 3.

CHAPTER 1

1. The association faded mysteriously away toward the end of my fieldwork. It first closed its centrally located headquarters and moved to the outskirts of the city.

Then its active website shut down and the newsletter went out of print. My interlocutors and I speculated, on the basis of our impressions formed over time and during many visits, that the president had political aspirations, and we wondered whether he was finally running for office.

2. Citizenship Law 5901, 29/5/2009 Sayı (no.) 27256: cilt 48. The exceptional acquisition as migrants, i.e., those of Turkish origin, is explained in chapter 12, article d.

3. For a comparison of Balkan Turks associations with Iraqi Turks associations in their deployment of "kin-state politics," see Güldem Baykal Büyüksaraç (2017); see also Danış and Parla (2009).

4. For an excellent recent historiography along these lines, see Bedross der Mateossian's *Shattered Dreams of Revolution* (2014).

5. The contemporary ramifications for dissident politics in Turkey of this mostly overlooked aspect of foundational dispossession have been explored elsewhere (Parla and Özgül 2016).

6. "Kazanızda Bulgaristandan getirilecek temiz Türk kanı muhacirlerle nüfus kesafeti husule getirilmesi düşünülürken oraya yerleşmiş bu gibi Turk muhacirlerinin kaçırılmasına elbette zatı alieri de razı olamaz" (quoted in Çağaptay 2009, 92).

7. See T. Parla and Davison (2004) for a critique of the simplistic secular/religious binary that pervades much of the scholarship on Turkey.

8. The inveterate propinquities between Sunni Islam and Turkishness surface most clearly when it comes to joining forces with regard to who is to be excluded or kept at bay. Historian Yekten Türkyılmaz , who in a recent provocation takes a jab at what he calls "the unfortunate narrative spun around an exaggerated tension between Sunniism and laicist Turkism," insists that the ways in which the two have coalesced during at least the past 150 years is key to understanding how the proponents of both categories have invariably united over who the outsiders or enemies are. Political factions identified with Sunnism have lent their support to the bloody policies undertaken by the various Republican regimes against the Sunni Kurds. The Christianity of the ethnically Turkish Gagauz and the Alevi identity of the Turkic-speaking Kızılbaş have been enough reason to categorize them out of Turkishness.

9. See Çağaptay (2003) for a detailed list and discussion.

10. I thank Merav Shohet for helping me make this point explicit.

11. TBMM (Turkish Grand National Assembly), 1933. *Zabıt Ceridesi*, devre 4, içtima 3, cilt 23/24.

12. Law No. 2510/1934 on Settlement. The Council of Ministers was in charge of determining which groups were considered to be of Turkish descent.

13. The only adjustment to the most contemporary 2006 Law, in order to make it ostensibly more compatible with EU accession demands for multiculturalism, was the omission of exclusionary references to the Roma.

14. This is my translation. The original states: "Türk soyundan ve Türk kültürüne bağlı olmayan yabancılar ile Türk soyundan ve Türk kültürüne bağlı olup da sınır dışı edilenler ve güvenlik bakımından Türkiye'ye gelmeleri uygun görülmeyenler göçmen olarak kabul edilmezler." In a parliamentary meeting when the most recent version of the Settlement Law was being debated, an expert insisted on the problem-

atic nature of the formulation that equates migrants with those who are of Turkish origin. The expert's proposal for an alternative formulation—namely, "they will not be accepted as migrants of Turkish origin,"—was rejected (see Erder 2014, 165).

15. Turkey's migration regime thus flips the hierarchy of desirability common to most other migration regimes, where (political) refugees are considered more deserving than (economic) migrants. By contrast, in Turkey, "migrant" acquires a higher status than "refugee," but precisely because of the already historically particular and favorable connotations of the term "migrant," which, at least until recently, has been legally and culturally subsumed under *soydaş*. I thank Nihal Kayalı for her insightful question on this point that led me to this formulation.

16. The full name of the Treaty in Turkish is: "Türkiye Cumhuriyeti ile Bulgaristan Halk Cumhuriyeti Arasında Yakın Akrabaları 1952 Yılına Kadar Türkiye'ye Göç Etmiş Olan Türk Asıllı Bulgar Vatandaşlarının Bulgaristan Halk Cumhuriyetinden Türkiye Cumhuriyetine Göç Etmeleri Hakkında Anlaşma."

17. This is a significantly low rate in comparison, for example, with that of the Armenians, another minority population in Bulgaria, for whom it was more than 30 percent.

18. Ali Eminov (1997), who provides one of the most thorough accounts of the repressive policies directed at the Turkish minority, espouses this latter view.

19. See Amnesty International (1986).

20. Such use of the Cold War rivalry through the movement of migrants resonates with the German case as well, in which ethnic German immigration was cited by West German politicians as proof of the superiority of the West German nation-state and economic system (Münz and Ohliger 2003, 189).

21. The "negative" Schengen list singles out those countries whose citizens must have a visa to enter the EU. The "positive" list consists of countries whose citizens are exempt from the requirement of having a visa to travel within the Schengen area. The positive list at the time of this writing includes twenty-five European countries.

22. A news piece in *Milliyet* designated the Bulgaristanlı migrants as Bulgarians and caused an angry outpouring of letters to the editor by the Bulgaristanlı in Turkey. The author of the piece issued an apology that included all of the reactions as well as his own compassionate sentiments of ethnonationalist fervor on the plight of these "ethnic kin."

23. The scholarship that tears apart the economic and political migrant distinction is vast. See the excellent collection curated by Fernando and Giordano (2016) for a discussion that continues to take this distinction to task in relation to refugees and the crisis in Europe.

24. *Shalvar* (long, loose pants) were considered too traditional and rural by the measures of modernity at the time. They are, however, extremely convenient and comfortable for work in the fields and at home, and incidentally, as a few of my interlocutors also liked to point out, the *shalvar* style has become a trend across the Western world with the rising infatuation with yoga and meditation.

25. For decades, the MRF was the only party representing the Turkish vote, along with the majority of the Pomak and the Roma, the two other significant minorities

in Bulgaria. However, in 2016, after the party founder and leader, Ahmet Doğan, expelled Lütfi Mestan, a longtime politician, member of the National Assembly of Bulgaria, and chairman of the MRF, Mestan and his followers founded a new party, Democrats for Responsibility, Solidarity, and Tolerance, which now also competes for the Turkish vote. In 2013, Turkey's president banned Ahmet Doğan from entering the country, and since then Mestan has been the closer ally to Turkey.

26. I thank Candice M. Lowe Swift for alerting me to the relevance of this specific piece by Aihwa Ong.

CHAPTER 2

1. As explained in chapter 1, until 2009, Citizenship Law 403/1964 made an exception for individuals of Turkish origin by allowing them to apply for citizenship after two years of residence instead of the standard five. The new Citizenship Law No. 5901 accepted in May 2009 eliminated this ethnic privilege with regard to residency and established a single rule for all foreigners; however, it granted a two-year grace period in which those of Turkish origin would continue to be processed according to the old law.

2. While the immediate comparison is with other migrants in Turkey, the comparative analytic lens I pursue here would also include a conversation with perspectives on hope among groups who are not migrants in Turkey but who are uneasily positioned vis-à-vis the law of the Turkish state. In a powerful analysis of hope and despair in the courtroom during the political trials of oppositional Kurdish youth, Serra Hakyemez (2018) shows how their families' assertions of hope, instead of display of tears and the admission of despair, become a political and honorable performance in defiance of the violence enacted by the law and its enforcers.

3. See section 3, "The Standard Account and the Rationality of Hope," and section 4, "Analyses of Hope in the Psychological Literature," in Bloeser and Titus (2017) for an excellent overview of the discussions on the probability requirements for hope. The preference for possibility over probability in defining hope does not dominate the realm of psychology, either. In fact, in Charles Snyder's theory of hope, (minimal) probability rather than possibility is the defining element: "Within a goal-setting framework, we propose that there are two major, interrelated elements of hope. First, we hypothesize that hope is fueled by the perception of successful *agency* related to goals. The agency component refers to a sense of successful determination in meeting goals in the past, present, and future. Second, we hypothesize that hope is influenced by the perceived availability of successful *pathways* related to goals" (Snyder et al., quoted in Bloeser and Titus 2017; italics in the original).

4. The insightful distinction Rebecca Bryant (2012) makes between anticipation and expectation would be interesting to pursue in terms of its potential ramifications for the probability/possibility distinction in relation to hope and the question of agency. Bryant suggests that expectation "involves a patient waiting for a future whose parameters are already in some sense known," while anticipation "implies an orientation to a future that may require our own action in order to realize or obviate it" (340).

5. https://en.oxforddictionaries.com/definition/hope. Most recently, Terry Eagleton (2015) has reiterated expectation as key to hope against the stance that asserts "hope only in the face of unlikelihood." Instead, Eagelton suggests that "hope involves a degree of expectation" (52).

6. My reading of Aquinas is ultimately different from the compelling nuance offered by Smith 2008. Focusing on Aquinas's use of the word "arduous" and on "possibility" (rather than probability," Smith states that the connection with expectation is less obvious in Aquinas and goes on to make a case for a different approach to hope that is more phenomenological. Smith also concedes that "the Aquinas definition does not directly contradict the Hobbes–Locke–Hume definition," but he concludes that "it does suggest a different strategy for explaining the meaning of hope." Bruce Robbins's recent interpretation of Aquinas (2017) is far more absolute: he positions Aquinas under a single theological tradition that he then squarely opposes to the attribution of any rationality to hope whatsoever.

7. For an overview of the trial, which dragged on for years, see http://www.hurriyetdailynews.com/new-probe-launched-into-fatal-shooting-of-nigerian-refugee-at-istanbul-police-post-71063.

8. I talk at more length about the significance of the Migrant Solidarity Network in the concluding chapter, "Troubling Hope." Here I should simply like to note that my exposure to the structural vulnerability of migrant women and men during my activist work with the Migrant Solidarity Network, which overlapped temporally with ethnographic research, informs my thinking about the field and is integral to developing my conceptualization of relative privilege.

9. In her book *Partial Connections* (2004), Marilyn Strathern takes the notion of comparison compellingly further. She describes the ethnographic endeavor as one that is inevitably comparative, regardless of explicit intentions on the part of the ethnographer, given that any description of specificity relies on an implicit comparison.

10. Her friends later figured out, Emine told us, the reason for the unexpected police visit: she had given the address of the house where she worked as a domestic on her application for a residence permit. "You never do that," they warned her, "when you are applying as someone who has overstayed her visa. Because then they know where you are working and without a permit."

11. Many did win, however, in the European Court of Justice. Personal communication with Veysel Eşsiz, Helsinki Citizens Assembly Refugee and Advocacy Program, May 12, 2013.

12. The maximum detention time is forty-eight hours.

13. Personal testimony of an unnamed UNHCR worker, narrated during a meeting of the Migrant Solidarity Network, 2011.

14. For details of this case, see Begüm Özden Fırat's searing analysis (2011) of the multiple vulnerabilities that migrants, especially women migrants who are undocumented, are exposed to, as well as her nuanced critique of feminist activist intervention only in the case of rape, and not, for example, routine labor exploitation.

15. The move from experience and interpretation is viewed by Clifford (1986), in a hugely influential take on the relationship between methodology and epistemology,

as compromising the dialogic richness that abounds in experience. While certainly much of that experiential dialogy gets lost in the act of inscription, I would also suggest that there are ways in which one's already partial understanding of the field can benefit from the retrospective analysis enabled by the separation of the field and of writing.

16. I elaborate in chapter 3 on the significance of these amnesties and their exceptional and indeterminate nature.

17. I was told by a member of the other major Balkan migrant association, BAL-GÖÇ, that the actual number of people on "the list" was four thousand, including people who had filed petitions through the Bursa and İzmir branches of their association. The BAL-GÖÇ member was insinuating that the Istanbul-based association, Balkan Turks Solidarity Association (BTSA), was citing only the nine hundred people who had filed through BTSA so as to overplay its own importance.

18. Erikson (2000) develops the term "maladaptive optimism" from the infant's failure to see the limits of the possible because it is not able to register that the desires of those around it are incompatible with its own.

19. The petitions were signed individually, but the act was a collective one, carried out under the rubric of the Migrant Solidarity Network and with the goal of making the transgressions in the legal process publicly visible.

20. The Contemporary Lawyers Association is a leftist lawyers' group in Turkey that is famous for taking on politically charged cases of leftist and Kurdish dissidents. Several members of the association were imprisoned on subsequent allegations of working against the interests of the state. I am grateful to Alptekin Ocak, the lawyer who gave me the opportunity to see the court records. At the time of writing, Ocak had still not given up on the case. In fact, as of January 2019, he has reopened the case by getting the court to consider the testimony of Festus's brother, after the case was stalled following a procedural decision by the Supreme Court of Appeals to overturn the guilty verdict.

21. Hope has alternatively been designated by recourse to a third term: "disposition." One of the features of confidence as a virtue, in Aristotle's elaboration, is that it evinces a hopeful disposition.

22. While scholars who argue for the radical separation of affect and emotion are many and come from numerous disciplines, perhaps the most vocal and most frequently cited proponent of this perspective is Brian Massumi, who squarely states his position for the necessity of such a theoretical program: "It is crucial to theorize the difference between affect and emotion" (Massumi 2002, 28).

23. Contemporary writers who explicitly identify themselves as "affect theorists" point to a wide range of philosophical, psychological, and physiological underpinnings and vocabularies that inform their work. Some of the common classical sources that they draw on for establishing this core lexicon on affect are psychologist Silvan Tomkins (1962, 1995) and philosophers Baruch Spinoza, William James, and Gilles Deleuze.

24. Some also find that the hard version of affect theory misappropriates Spinoza

and point to Gilles Deleuze's (1988) culpability in this misappropriation. According to this criticism, Spinoza has a far more cognitivist account of affective life. This reading of Spinoza posits a rational kernel to affective states. And as far as Spinoza's ethical program is concerned, that rational kernel is to be maximized to the furthest extent possible. Thus the converse insistence on a radical separation between cognition and affect does not do justice to Spinoza's intentions (see Zerilli 2015).

25. In one of the most evocative ethnographic discussions of affect as transmitted by the phantomic landscape of Northern Cyprus, a landscape whose affect is mediated by the inhabitants in accordance with their own historically shaped subjectivities, Yael Navaro-Yashin (2012) criticizes precisely this drive for absolute choices between paradigms, suggesting that under such pressure, theory building itself becomes a project of ruination. See also Lutz (2017) for a similar and eloquently articulated refusal to subscribe to the dictates of affect theory.

26. Ngai (2005) makes only a minimal distinction that pertains to the degree between affect and emotion: "My assumption is that affects are less formed and structured than emotions, but not lacking structure or form altogether; less 'sociolinguistically fixed,' but by no means code-free or meaningless; less 'organized in response to our interpretations of situations,' but by no means entirely devoid of organization or diagnostic powers" (27). In a recent intervention, Catherine Lutz (2017) pointedly states that she will use the terms interchangeably, underscoring that the rigid conceptual distinction often seems to come at the expense of turf claims and disregards existing valuable work.

27. Allen's incisive analysis (2017) underscores the enormity of the political stakes that accompany different kinds of authority. Investigative commissions in Palestine took it for granted that commissioners could read Arabs' feelings, and that conclusion formed at least part of the basis on which commissioners justified their refusal to grant Palestinians rights and political entitlements, since they deemed the Palestinians' emotions not to be sufficiently fervent or compassionate.

CHAPTER 3

1. http://www.balgoc.org.tr/arsiv2009.html.

2. See Kaşlı 2016 for an analysis of how the core members of the association, former migrants who now have citizenship, monopolize access and decision-making powers vis-à-vis the post-1990 migrants, who are expected to pay fees to become members but are not granted equal participation.

3. Such six-month permits had also been granted through a previous amnesty in 2007.

4. One year later, another representative at the same association would correct me during a conversation, saying that the list actually comprised four thousand people and not nine hundred; there were nine hundred people who had petitioned through this association only. The correct figure, he said, also included people who had petitioned through other migrant associations.

5. Three full-fledged military coups, in 1960, 1971, and 1980, and two military

memorandums have taken place in Turkey since the founding of the republic in 1923. The 1960 coup entailed the summary execution of the prime minister, who was overthrown by the military, and the 1980 coup, which involved thousands of tortured and disappeared persons, resulted in a highly militarized revision to the constitution that is still in effect in Turkey today. For an evaluation of the detrimental effects of these coups on Turkey's democracy and political culture, see Taha Parla (1991) and Banu Bargu (2014). It is also important to underscore that states of emergency have periodically been sustained in southeastern Turkey even during "democratic" governments, these being justified by the state's declared threat of Kurdish insurgency.

6. Beller-Hann notes that this designation is nurtured by bias against Christians as well as communists (1995, 230–31).

7. Jesca Nankabirwa was thrown out of the window after being raped by an acquaintance in April 2014. https://m.bianet.org/bianet/kadin/173925-ugandali-jesca-nankabirwa-nin-katil-zanlisina-muebbet-hapis-istemi. Beatrice Babiry was deported before she was able to testify in the trial of the death of her sister, who was murdered in December 2016 while trying to save Beatrice from the two men who raped her. https://m.bianet.org/bianet/toplumsal-cinsiyet/181448-kardesi-olduruldu-tecavuze-ugradi-sinirdisi-edildi-dava-yarin-caglayan-da.

8. See Lauren Collins's journalistic essay, "Europe's Child-Refugee Crisis," *New Yorker*, February 27, 2017, for a chilling account of the plight of unaccompanied minors in the makeshift camp in Calais, an exposé that does a formidable job of avoiding sentimentalization or victimization.

9. While criminals no doubt abound in smuggling networks, scholars have also pointed out that the smuggler as the quintessential villain is a stereotype that does not capture the full range of smuggling practices, some of which are embedded networks of various degrees of intimacy. See the article "Smugglers," by Jason De León (2017).

10. For a comprehensive report on undocumented children's access to education in Turkey, on the whole a neglected area of research, see Atasü-Topçuoğlu (2013).

11. To give a broader picture of the checkered access to education for undocumented children, it should also be noted that semiformal access was granted to children from Armenia through a 2012 circular that allows them to enroll in Armenian minority schools, albeit only as "guests" (Özinian 2009). Preliminary fieldwork that I conducted with school principals at two Armenian minority schools shows that educators find this provision entirely inadequate: it keeps the children off the street, but its failure to provide any official document for schooling leaves their future in limbo. More recently, the formal granting of protection to Syrians has allowed Syrian refugee children access to compulsory education. However, initial research suggests that this has not resulted in easy access for Syrians: the legal basis of access is shaky because it rests on the ill-defined principle of temporariness, and Syrians, in contrast to the Bulgaristanlı, are likely to face resistance from school administrators, who will come up with excuses to turn them away from registering in their school (Şanlı 2018).

12. In fact, the phrase *çabuk çabuk* had acquired such colloquial obviousness that

during a solidarity event organized by the Migrant Solidarity Network for migrant men from Sierra Leone who were trying to earn a daily wage by collecting plastic cans from the city's garbage, and where I acted as translator, those who offered testimonies would use the phrase frequently in their (English) speech, not feeling the need to explain what it meant until a journalist in the audience asked for clarification.

13. Demirdizen (2013) also provides a thorough account of various other constraints, such as the maximum number of times that work permits may be renewed and dependence on the employer for obtaining a permit. At the time of my fieldwork, the new regulation had not gone into effect. In fact, until 2003, the law even stipulated that domestic work was one of the occupations in which foreigners were not allowed to work at all. In 2003, however, given the undeniable increase in demand for workers in that sector, the Law on the Work Permits of Foreigners (Law No. 4817/2003) was passed, lifting the restriction on foreigners in the domestic work sector. Given the difficulty of negotiating the hurdles of the bureaucracy for this kind of permit and the overwhelming number of rejections, legalization was not a path pursued by migrant women and their employers; only forty-five such work permits (a ridiculously low figure) were ever granted.

14. The second on the list were the Azeris, another Muslim ethnonational group who are considered culturally closer, with 11,000 permits granted.

15. According to a key analytic distinction made by de Genova and one that has marked critical migration studies, while deportation is an effective tool for border enforcement, it is *deportability* that has historically had by far the greater disciplinary power and efficacy. The main thrust of de Genova's argument for foregrounding deportability is that, unlike deportation, deportability "has historically rendered undocumented migrant labor a distinctly disposable commodity" (438). What makes deportability so decisive in the legal production of migrant illegality and the militarized policing of nation-state borders is that some are deported in order that most may remain (undeported) as workers whose particular migrant status may thus be rendered "illegal."

16. Whyte's discussion of uncertainty is interesting to read with and against Bonnie Honig's mobilization of Hannah Arendt's sites of vulnerability and dependence in her critique of Judith Butler's work on vulnerability and precarity. See in particular Honig 2015, 44. https://muse.jhu.edu/.

17. For international coverage of the prime minister's threat, see https://www.theguardian.com/world/2010/mar/18/turkey-threatens-expel-armenians-genocide.

CHAPTER 4

1. My thanks to Alexander Kiossev for this phrase. Personal communication.

2. *Gavur* is a term historically used by Muslims to refer to non-Muslims, but colloquially it is used to refer to foreigners.

3. While the fashionable term for this kind of analysis is now "intersectionality," I follow Joan Scott's original formulation (1986) in her field-defining piece "Gender: A Useful Category of Historical Analysis," which, in its insistence on viewing gender

in relation to other categories of difference, had opened up and set the terms of this broad vision well before the arrival of the concept of intersectionality.

4. In their critique of the transitology literature, Michael Burawoy and Katherine Verdery (1999) question those analyses that represent the disordered and inadequate character of transition processes as "socialist legacies" (1). Instead, they invite analysis of the ways in which "the past enters the present not as legacy but as novel adaptation" (4). Some have taken the presentist focus further to question the adequacy of the very designation "nostalgia": the feeling of wistfulness connoted by the term obscures the pragmatism of practices of remembering (Pilbrow 2010); or when paired with the adjective "post-socialist," the term "nostalgia" delegitimizes—and at best domesticates—expressions of discontent regarding the injustices of the current situation (Creed 1999). Finally, in a thorough review that catalogs and differentiates among various practices that get subsumed under the umbrella of nostalgia, Maya Nadkarni and Olga Shevchenko (2004) drive home the point that rather than assuming an internally coherent body of cultural practices, one can decipher the meaning and logic of nostalgic practices only by paying meticulous attention to the specific social contexts in which those practices are embedded.

5. I owe my inspiration here to Lynne Haney (1999), who has argued that the protests of mothers to the proposed liberal restructuring of the welfare system in Hungary were not mere expressions of dissent but were actually a comparative analysis of different historical regimes in Hungary.

6. See Boym 2001 and Boyer 2006 for the interesting genealogy of the term.

7. See Ghodsee 2005 for a detailed account of the benefits that the state provided for women under communism in Bulgaria.

8. Sevdiye's insightful point here parallels Potuoğlu-Cook's (2006) eloquent analysis of the neoliberal gentrification of belly dancing in Istanbul. Questions of sexual honor can sometimes be bracketed by the privilege of class. The wealthy elite and the upwardly mobile professional youth indulge in belly dancing for leisure even though the sexuality of the professional working belly dancer continues to be suspect in the public eye and closely monitored by the state.

9. See the report in the Armenian-Turkish weekly *Agos*. http://www.agos.com.tr /tr/yazi/2302/narine-ye-santaj-yapan-kardesler-tahliye-edildi.

10. For example, a columnist who writes for a popular news tabloid, *Yeniçağ*, stated rather rapturously: "She did not succumb to momentary anger, no, she did not! Instead, it was with obstinacy, with insistence that she chose death." http://www .yg.yenicaggazetesi.com.tr/yazargoster.php?haber=2222.

11. See IOM (2008) report on migration in Turkey.

12. Recent critical scholarship on gender and honor in Turkey has thus been careful not to reproduce the dichotomies of the traditional-modern, whether concerning the state's routine intrusions into women's bodies via virginity examinations (Parla 2001), the reproduction of the concern with women's honor by judicial authorities who simultaneously decry the honor crime as an obsolete and barbaric tradition (Belge 2008; Koğacıoğlu 2004), or Islamist and secularist renditions of female mod-

esty that define and delimit an acceptable gendered presence in post-1990s Istanbul marked by market-driven gentrification (Potuoğlu-Cook 2006).

CONCLUSION

1. Those on the left who lament the loss of hope in the realm of the political and press for its recuperation include a diverse set of thinkers from Chantal Mouffe to J. K. Gibson-Graham to David Graeber.

2. Refusing to be bound by these forced oppositions where the negative affects are relegated to the status of loss, Greenberg (2014) offers instead the politics of disappointment as also a space of action and one that does justice to the complexity of the political agency and self-awareness on the part of student activists in Serbia in navigating a political landscape marked by state violence and corruption. In resisting the intolerance with expressions of skepticism, disbelief, and disappointment that pervaded the politics of hope espoused by the opposition to the current regime in Turkey's 2017 referendum, I have in turn made a plea, following Walter Benjamin and Patricia Williams, for a backward- looking and less triumphant politics of hope (Parla forthcoming).

3. This is not to say that many people working in these NGOs are unconcerned with the exclusion of undocumented migrants who are not refugees from their field of activity. To the contrary, those working at the Helsinki Citizens' Assembly Refugee Advocacy and Support Program, for example, have repeatedly voiced their discomfort with the refugee and economic migrant distinction in various forums, and a representative for Mülteci-Der acknowledged the problem at the latest convention of MigrEurope, in May 2010. But the point here is not about the sensibilities of various individuals working in these organizations. Rather it is about institutional limits that currently preclude addressing the plight of the undocumented.

4. Urging that "anthropologists must find the right balance between critique and understanding," Lambek rightly cautions that "the literature at present is replete with important enactments of critique with respect to forms of racism, sexism, colonialism, military and so forth, but these become complacent if they do not fully acknowledge their own contingent position" (2015, 12). Lambek's reminder about a deeper acknowledgment of the "modesty about our own abilities and claims, the limits of our positionality and justification for critique" is one that I take seriously and aspire to bear in mind throughout my analysis. However, this is accompanied by a worry that the effort to recalibrate the balance of understanding and critique runs the risk of a certain depoliticization of the everyday.

EPILOGUE

1. My thanks to Joanna Davidson for bringing Gable's essay on lines to my attention.

BIBLIOGRAPHY

STATUTES

Vatandaşlık Kanunu (Citizenship Law) No. 403/1964
Vatandaşlık Kanunu (Citizenship Law) No. 5901/2009
İskan Kanunu (Settlement Law) No. 885/1926
İskan Kanunu (Settlement Law) No. 2510/1934
İskan Kanunu (Settlement Law) No. 5543/2006
Yabancılar ve Uluslarası Koruma Kanunu (Law on Foreigners and International Protection) No. 6458/2013
Türk Ceza Kanunu (Turkish Penal Code) No. 65/1926
Türk Ceza Kanunu (Turkish Penal Code) No. 5237/2004
Türk Medeni Kanunu (Turkish Civil Code) No. 743/1926
Pasaport Kanunu (Passport Law) No. 5682/1950
Yabancıların Türkiye'de İkamet ve Seyahatleri Hakkında Kanun (Law on the Residence and Travel of Foreigners) No. 5683/1950)
Yabancıların Çalışma İzinleri Hakkındaki Kanun (Law on the Work Permits of Foreigners) No. 4817/2003

PUBLISHED SOURCES

Abu El-Haj, Nadia. 2010. "Racial Palestinianization and the Janus-Faced Nature of the Israeli State." *Patterns of Prejudice* 44 (1): 27–41.
Abu-Lughod, Lila. 1986. *Veiled Sentiments: Honor and Poetry in a Bedouin Society.* Berkeley: University of California Press.
———. 1991. "Writing against Culture." In *Recapturing Anthropology: Working in the Present,* edited by Richard G. Fox, 137–54. Santa Fe: School of American Research Press.
———. 2002. "Do Muslim Women Really Need Saving? Anthropological Reflections on Cultural Relativism and Its Others." *American Anthropologist* 104 (3): 783–90.
Agergaard, Sine, and Christian Ungruhe. 2016. "Ambivalent Precarity: Career Trajectories and Temporalities in Highly Skilled Sports Labor Migration from West Africa to Northern Europe." *Anthropology of Work Review* 37 (2): 67–78.
Ahmed, Sara. 2004. *The Cultural Politics of Emotion.* New York: Routledge.
———. 2010. *The Promise of Happiness.* Durham, NC: Duke University Press.
Akalın, Ayşe. 2007. "Hired as a Caregiver, Demanded as a Housewife: Becoming a

Migrant Domestic Worker in Turkey." *European Journal of Women's Studies* 14:209–25.

———. 2015. "The Lie Which Is Not One: Biopolitics in the Migrant Domestic Workers' Market in Turkey." In *The Post-Fordist Sexual Contract: Working and Living in Contingency,* edited by Lisa Adkins and Maryanne Dever, 195–211. London: Palgrave Macmillan.

Akçam, Taner. 2014. "Önsöz." Introduction to *Türkiye ve Ermeni Hayaleti: Soykırımın Izinde Adımlar,* by Laure Marchand and Guillaume Perrier, 9–18. Istanbul: İletişim.

Akçam, Taner, and Kurt Ümit. 2015. *The Spirit of the Laws: The Plunder of Wealth in the Armenian Genocide.* New York: Berghahn Books.

Akpınar, Taner. 2009. "Türkiye'ye Yönelik Düzensiz Göçler ve Göçmenlerin İnşaat Sektöründe Enformel İstihdamı." PhD diss., Ankara Üniversitesi.

———. 2010. "Türkiye'ye Yönelik Kaçak İşgücü Göçü." *SBF Dergisi* 65 (3): 1–22.

Aktar, Ayhan. 2000. *Varlık Vergisi ve Türkleştirme Politikaları.* İstanbul: İletişim.

Allen, Lori A. 2017. "Determining Emotions and the Burden of Proof in Investigative Commissions to Palestine." *Comparative Studies in Society and History* 59 (2): 385–414.

Allison, Anne. 2012. "Ordinary Refugees: Social Precarity and Soul in 21st Century Japan." *Anthropological Quarterly* 85 (2): 345–70.

———. 2013. *Precarious Japan.* Durham, NC: Duke University Press.

———. 2016. "Precarity: Commentary by Anne Allison." Curated Collections. *Cultural Anthropology.* https://culanth.org/curated_collections/21-precarity/discussions/26-precarity-commentary-by-anne-allison.

Altınay, Ayşe Gül. 2004. *The Myth of the Military-Nation: Militarism, Gender, and Education in Turkey.* New York: Palgrave Macmillan.

Altuğ, Yılmaz. 1991. "Balkanlardan Anayurda Yapılan Göçler." *Belleten* 55 (212): 109–20.

Amnesty International. 1986. "Bulgaria." *Amnesty International Annual Report,* 272.

———. 2014. "Struggling to Survive: Refugees from Syria in Turkey." *Amnesty International Report.*

Aquinas, Saint Thomas. (1274) 1971. *Summa Theologica.* Translated by Fathers of the English Dominican Province. Chicago: William Benton.

Arendt, Hannah. 1973. *The Origins of Totalitarianism.* Boston: Houghton Mifflin Harcourt.

Ataç, İlker et al. 2017. "Contested B/Orders. Turkey's Changing Migration Regime: An Introduction." *Movements. Journal for Critical Migration and Border Regime Studies* 3 (2): 9–21.

Atasü-Topçuoğlu, Reyhan. 2013. *Profiling Migrant Children in Turkey: Social Policy and Social Work Suggestions.* Sweden: International Organization for Migration (IOM).

Babül, Elif. 2017. *Bureaucratic Intimacies: Translating Human Rights in Turkey.* Stanford: Stanford University Press.

Baer, Marc. 2004. "The Double Bind of Race and Religion: The Conversion of the

Dönme to Turkish Secular Nationalism." *Comparative Studies in Society and History* 46 (4): 678–712.

Bakan, Abigail, and Daiva Stasiulis. 1997. *Not One of the Family: Foreign Domestic Workers in Canada.* Toronto: University of Toronto Press.

Bal-Göç Resmi. N.d. Balkan Göçmenleri Kültür ve Dayanışma Derneği. http://www .balgoc.org.tr/.

Bali, Rıfat. 1999. "Cumhuriyet Yıllarında Türkiye Yahudileri: Bir Türkleştirme Serüveni (1923–1945)." İstanbul: İletişim.

Balibar, Etienne. 2004. *We, the People of Europe? Reflections on Transnational Citizenship.* Princeton, NJ: Princeton University Press.

Balibar, Etienne, and Immanuel Wallerstein. 1991. *Race, Nation, Class: Ambiguous Identities.* Radical Thinkers. New York: Verso.

Balta, Ayşegül. 2010. "The Role of NGOs in the Asylum System in Turkey: Beyond Intermediation." Master's thesis, Sabancı University, İstanbul.

Bargu, Banu. 2014. *Starve and Immolate: The Politics of Human Weapons.* New York: Columbia University Press.

———. 2017. "The Silent Exception: Hunger Striking and Lip Sewing." *Law, Culture, and the Humanities.* https://doi.org/10.1177/1743872117709684.

Barkan, Ö. L. "Osmanlı İmparatorluğunda bir İskan ve Kolonizasyon Metodu Olarak Sürgünler." *İstanbul Üniversitesi İktisat Fakültesi Mecmuası* 11 (1–4) (1949–50): 524–69; 13 (1–4) (1951–52): 56–78; 15 (1–4) (1953–54): 209–37.

Bates, Daniel. 1994. "What's in a Name? Ethnicity and Community among the Turks of Bulgaria." *Identities* 1 (2–3): 201–25.

Bauman, Zygmunt. *Liquid Times: Living in an Age of Uncertainty.* Cambridge, UK: Polity Press.

Beatty, Andrew. 2005. "Emotions in the Field: What Are We Talking About?" *JRAI: Journal of the Royal Anthropological Institute* 11 (1): 17–37.

Beck, Ulrich. 1992. *Risk Society: Towards a New Modernity.* London: Sage.

Beirens, Hanne, and Paul Clewett. 2016. "Children: The Forgotten Aspect of the EU-Turkey Deal." Migration Policy Institute. http://www.migrationpolicy.org/news /children-forgotten-aspect-eu-turkey-deal.

Belge, Ceren. 2008. "Whose Law? Clans, Honor Killings, and State-Minority Relations in Turkey and Israel." PhD diss., Department of Political Science, University of Washington.

Bellér-Hann, Ildikó. 1995. "Prostitution and Its Effects in Northeast Turkey." *European Journal of Women's Studies* 2 (2): 219–35.

Benjamin, Walter. 1968. "Franz Kafka: On the Tenth Anniversary of His Death." In *Illuminations: Essays and Reflections.* New York: Schocken.

———. (1968) 2007. *Illuminations: Essays and Reflections.* New York: Random House.

Berdahl, Daphne. 2000. "'Go, Trabi, Go': Reflections on a Car and Its Symbolization over Time." *Anthropology and Humanism* 25 (2): 131–41.

Berlant, Lauren. 2007. "Nearly Utopian, Nearly Normal: Post-Fordist Affect in La Promesse and Rosetta." *Public Culture* 19 (2): 273–301.

———. 2011. *Cruel Optimism*. Durham, NC: Duke University Press.

Bernard, H. Russell. 2011. *Research Methods in Anthropology: Qualitative and Quantitative Approaches*. 5th ed. Lanham, MD: AltaMira Press.

Beşikçi, İsmail. 1977. *Kürtlerin `Mecburi İskan'ı*. Ankara: Komal.

Biehl, João. 2013. "Ethnography in the Way of Theory." *Cultural Anthropology* 28 (4): 573–97. https://doi.org/10.1111/cuan.12028.

Biehl, Kristen. 2015a. "Governing through Uncertainty: Experiences of Being a Refugee in Turkey as a Country for Temporary Asylum." *Social Analysis* 59 (1): 57–75.

———. 2015b. "Spatializing Diversities, Diversifying Spaces: Housing Experiences and Home Space Perceptions in a Migrant Hub of Istanbul." *Ethnic and Racial Studies* 38 (4): 596–607.

Bilecen, Tuncay. 2006. "Balkan Harbi Yılları Rum Yerleşimlerine Muhacir İskanı." *Toplumsal Tarih* 156:32–37.

Biner, Özge. 2016. *Türkiye'de Mültecilik: İltica, Gecicilik ve Yasallik: Van Uydu Şehir Örneği*. İstanbul: İstanbul Bilgi Üniversitesi Yayınları.

Bloch, Alexia. 2005. "Longing for the *Kollektiv*: Gender, Power, and Residential Schools in Central Siberia." *Cultural Anthropology* 20 (4): 534–69.

Bloch, Ernst. (1947) 1986. *The Principle of Hope*. Oxford: B. Blackwell.

———. 1995. *The Principle of Hope*. Reissued ed. Vol. 1, translated by Neville Plaice, Stephen Plaice, and Paul Knight. Cambridge, MA: MIT Press.

Bora, Aksu. 2005. *Kadınların Sınıfı*. Istanbul: İletişim.

Bora, Tanıl, and Bayram Şen. 2009. "Saklı bir ayrışma ekseni: Rumelililer-Anadolulular." *Modern Türkiye'de Siyasi Düşünce* 9:348–55.

Bourdieu, Pierre. (1963) 1979. *Algeria 1960*. Cambridge: Cambridge University Press.

———. 1977. *Outline of a Theory of Practice*. Cambridge: Cambridge University Press.

———. 1990a. *In Other Words: Essays toward a Reflexive Sociology*. Stanford: Stanford University Press.

———. 1990b. *The Logic of Practice*. Stanford: Stanford University Press.

Boyer, Dominic. 2006. "Ostalgie and the Politics of the Future in Eastern Germany." *Public Culture* 18 (2): 361–81.

Boym, Svetlana. 2001. *The Future of Nostalgia*. New York: Basic Books.

Brennan, Teresa. 2004. *The Transmission of Affect*. Ithaca, NY: Cornell University Press.

Brewer, Kelly, and Deniz Yükseker. 2006. "A Survey on African Migration and Asylum Seekers in Istanbul." İstanbul: Migration Research Program at the Koç University. http://portal.ku.edu.tr/~mirekoc/reports/2005_2006_kelly_brewer_deniz_yuksekeker.pdf.

Briggs, Jean L. 1971. *Never in Anger: Portrait of an Eskimo Family*. Cambridge, MA: Harvard University Press.

Brink-Danan, Marcy. 2011. *Jewish Life in Twenty-First-Century Turkey: The Other Side of Tolerance*. Bloomington: Indiana University Press.

Brown, Wendy. 1999. "Resisting Left Melancholy." *Boundary 2* 26 (3): 19–27.

Bryant, Rebecca. 2012. "Partitions of Memory: Wounds and Witnessing in Cyprus." *Comparative Studies in Society and History* 54 (2): 332–60.

Buğra, Ayşe, and Çağlar Keyder. 2006. "The Turkish Welfare Regime in Transformation." *Journal of European Social Policy* 16 (3): 211–28.

Burawoy, Michael, and Katherine Verdery. 1999. Introduction to *Uncertain Transition: Ethnographies of Change in the Post-Socialist World*, edited by Michael Burawoy and Katherine Verdery, 1–19. Lanham, MD: Rowman and Littlefield.

Butler, Judith. (2004) 2006. *Precarious Life: The Powers of Mourning and Violence*. London: Verso.

———. 2012. "Precarious Life, Vulnerability, and the Ethics of Cohabitation." *Journal of Speculative Philosophy* 26 (2): 134–51.

Büyüksaraç, Güldem Baykal. 2017. "Trans-Border Minority Activism and Kin-State Politics: The Case of Iraqi Turkmen and Turkish Interventionism." *Anthropological Quarterly* 90 (1): 17–53.

Cabot, Heath. 2014. *On the Doorstep of Europe: Asylum and Citizenship in Greece*. Philadelphia: University of Pennsylvania Press.

Çağaptay, Soner. 2003. "Kim Türk, Kim Vatandaş? Erken Cumhuriyet Dönemi Vatandaşlık Rejimi Üzerine Bir Çalışma." *Toplum ve Bilim* 98:166–85.

———. 2009. *Türkiye'de İslam, Laiklik ve Milliyetçilik: Türk Kimdir?* İstanbul: İstanbul Bilgi Üniversitesi Yayınları.

———. 2014. "Race, Assimilation, and Kemalism: Turkish Nationalism and the Minorities in the 1930s." *Middle Eastern Studies* 40 (3): 86–101.

Çakir, Aslı. 2004. "Moldovların Tahtına Bulgarlar Oturdu." *Milliyet Pazar*. www .milliyet.com.tr/2004/03/31/pazar/paz05.html.

Calavita, Kitty. 1998. "Immigration, Law, and Marginalization in a Global Economy: Notes from Spain." *Law and Society Review* 32 (3): 529–66.

———. 2005. "Law, Citizenship, and the Construction of Some Immigrant 'Others.'" *Law and Social Inquiry* 30 (2): 401–20.

———. 2010. *Invitation to Law and Society: An Introduction to the Study of Real Law*. Chicago: University of Chicago Press.

Campbell, Stephen. 2016. "Everyday Recomposition: Precarity and Socialization in Thailand's Migrant Workforce." *American Ethnologist* 43 (2): 258–69.

Canefe, Nergis. 2002. "Turkish Nationalism and Ethno- Symbolic Analysis: The Rules of Exception." *Nations and Nationalism* 2 (8): 133–55.

Carter, Donald. 1997. *States of Grace: Senegalese in Italy and the New European Migration*. Minnesota Archive Editions. Minneapolis: University of Minnesota Press.

Castells, Manuel. (1996) 2011. *The Rise of Network Society*. Vol. 1 of *The Information Age: Economy, Society, and Culture*. 2nd ed., Hoboken, NJ: Wiley Blackwell Publishing.

Cessario, Romanus. O. P. 2002. "The Theological Virtue of Hope." In *The Ethics of Aquinas*, edited by Stephen Pope, 232–33. Washington, DC: Georgetown University Press.

Chavez, Sergio. 2009. "The Sonoran Desert Domestic Bracero Programme: Institutional Actors and the Creation of Labor Migration Streams." *International Migration* 50 (2).

Chindea, Alin, Magdalena Majkowska-Tomkin, Heikki Mattila, and Isabel Pastor. 2008. *Migration in Turkey: A Country Profile 2008.* Geneva: International Organization for Migration.

Clifford, James. 1986. "On Ethnographic Allegory." In *Writing Culture: The Poetics and Politics of Ethnography,* edited by James Clifford and George Marcus. Berkeley: University of California Press.

Clough, Patricia Ticineto. 2007. Introduction to *The Affective Turn: Theorizing the Social,* edited by Patricia Ticineto Clough with Jean Halley, 1–33. Durham, NC: Duke University Press.

Collins, Lauren. 2017. "Europe's Child-Refugee Crisis." *New Yorker,* February 27. http://www.newyorker.com/magazine/2017/02/27/europes-child-refugee-crisis.

Connolly, William E. 2002. *Neuropolitics: Thinking, Culture, and Speed.* Minneapolis: University of Minnesota Press.

Cook, Ian, and Mike Crang. 2007. *Doing Ethnographies.* Thousand Oaks, CA: SAGE Publications.

Cooper, Elizabeth, and David Pratten, eds. 2015. *Ethnographies of Uncertainty in Africa.* London: Palgrave Macmillan.

Coşar, Simten, and Metin Yeğenoğlu. 2011. "New Grounds for Patriarchy in Turkey? Gender Policy in the Age of AKP." *South European Society and Politics* 16 (3): 555–73.

Coşkun, Emel. 2014. "Türkiye'de Göcmen Kadınlar ve Seks Ticareti." *Çalışma ve Toplum* 3:185–206.

———. 2018. "Criminalisation and Prostitution of Migrant Women in Turkey: A Case Study of Ugandan Women." *Women's Studies International Forum* 68:85–93.

Courbage, Youssef, and Philippe Fargues. 1997. *Christians and Jews under Islam.* Translated by Judy Mabro. London and New York: Tauris

Coutin, Susan Bibler. 1993. *The Culture of Protest: Religious Activism and the U.S. Sanctuary Movement.* Conflict and Social Change Series. Boulder: Westview Press.

———. 2000. *Legalizing Moves: Salvadoran Immigrants' Struggle for U.S. Residency.* Ann Arbor: University of Michigan Press.

———. 2005. "Contesting Criminality: Illegal Immigration and the Spatialization of Legality." *Theoretical Criminology* 9 (1): 5–33.

Crampton, R. J. 1997. *A Concise History of Bulgaria.* Cambridge: Cambridge University Press.

Crapanzano, Vincent. 2003. "Reflections on Hope as a Category of Social and Psychological Analysis." *Cultural Anthropology* 18 (1): 3–32.

Creed, Gerald W. 1999. "Deconstructing Socialism in Bulgaria." In *Uncertain Transition: Ethnographies of Change in the Post-Socialist World,* edited by Michael Burawoy and Katherine Verdery, 151–88. Lanham, MD: Rowman and Littlefield.

————. 2004. "Constituted through Conflict: Images of Community (and Nation) in Bulgarian Rural Ritual." *American Anthropologist* 106 (1): 56–70.

Cvetkovich, Ann. 2007. "Public Feelings." *South Atlantic Quarterly* 106 (3): 459–68.

————. 2012. *Depression: A Public Feeling*. Durham, NC: Duke University Press.

Damasio, Antonio. 1994. *Descartes' Error: Emotion, Reason, and the Human Brain*. New York: G. P. Putnam.

Danış, Didem. 2016. "Türk Göç Politikasında Yeni Bir Devir: Bir Dış Politika Enstrümanı Olarak Suriyeli Mülteciler." *HYD Saha Dergisi* 2:6–12.

Danış, Didem, and Ayşe Parla. 2009. "Nafile soydaşlık: Irak ve Bulgaristan Türkleri örneğinde göçmen, dernek ve devlet" *Toplum ve Bilim* 114:131–58.

Danış, Didem, Jean-Francois Perouse, and Cherie Taraghi. 2009. "Integration in Limbo: Iraqi, Afghan, and Maghrebi Migrants in Istanbul." In *Lands of Diverse Migrations*, edited by Ahmet İçduygu and Kemal Kirişçi, 443–637. Istanbul: İstanbul Bilgi University.

Das, Veena. 2000. "The Act of Witnessing: Violence, Poisonous Knowledge, and Subjectivity." In *Violence and Subjectivity*, edited by Veena Das, Arthur Kleinman, Mamphela Ramphele, and Pamela Reynolds, 205–25. Berkeley: University of California Press.

Day, Joseph Patrick. 1991. *Hope: A Philosophical Inquiry*. Helsinki: Philosophical Society of Finland.

De Genova, Nicholas. 2002. "Migrant 'Illegality' and Deportability in Everyday Life." *Annual Review of Anthropology* 31:419–47.

————. 2005. *Working the Boundaries: Race, Space, and "Illegality" in Mexican Chicago*. Durham, NC: Duke University Press.

————. 2006. "The Production of Mexican/Migrant 'Illegality.'" In *Latinos and Citizenship: The Dilemmas of Belonging*, edited by Suzanne Oboler. New York: Palgrave Macmillan.

De León, Jason. 2015. *The Land of Open Graves: Living and Dying on the Migrant Trail*. Berkeley: University of California Press.

————. 2017. "Smugglers." Theorizing the Contemporary. *Cultural Anthropology*. https://culanth.org/fieldsights/1155-smugglers.

Deleuze, Gilles. 1988. *Spinoza: Practical Philosophy*. San Francisco: City Lights Books.

Demirdizen, Derya. 2013. "Türkiye'de Ev Hizmetlerinde Çalışan Göçmen Kadınlar." *Çalışma ve Toplum* 38:325–46.

Deringil, Selim. 1998. *The Well-Protected Domains: Ideology and the Legitimation of Power in the Ottoman Empire, 1876–1909*. London: I. B. Tauris.

Der Matossian, Bedross. 2014. *Shattered Dreams of Revolution: From Liberty to Violence in the Late Ottoman Empire*. Stanford: Stanford University Press.

Descartes, René. (1649) 1985. "The Passions of the Soul." In *The Philosophical Writings of Descartes*, 1:325–405. Translated by J. Cottingham, R. Stoothoff, and D. Murdoch. Cambridge: Cambridge University Press, 1985.

Dewey, John. 1929. *The Quest for Certainty*. New York: Minton, Balch.

Di Nunzio, Marco. 2015. "Embracing Uncertainty: Young People on the Move in Addis Ababa's Inner City." In *Ethnographies of Uncertainty in Africa*, edited by E. Cooper and D. Pratten, 149–72. London: Palgrave Macmillan.

Doğan, Mustafa Görkem. 2010. "Labor Resistance against Neoliberal Challenges to the Traditional Trade Unionism in Turkey, 1986–1991." PhD diss., Boğaziçi University, İstanbul.

Dündar, Fuat. 2001. *İttihat ve Terakki'nin Müslümanları İskân Politikası (1913–1918)*. İstanbul: İletişim.

Durkheim, Émile. (1893) 1960. *The Division of Labor in Society*. Translated by George Simpson. Glencoe, IL: Free Press.

———. (1893) 2014. *The Division of Labor in Society*. Edited by Steve Lukes. Translated by W. D. Halls. New York: New Press.

Durkheim, Émile, John A. Spaulding, and George Simpson. (1897) 1966. *Suicide: A Study in Sociology*. 1st Free Press paperback ed. New York: Free Press.

Eagleton, Terry. 1991. *Ideology: An Introduction*. London and New York: Verso.

———. 2015. *Hope without Optimism*. Charlottesville: University of Virginia Press.

Eder, Mine. 2015. "Turkey's Neoliberal Transformation and Changing Migration Regime: The Case of Female Migrant Workers." In *Social Transformation and Migration*, edited by S. Castles, D. Ozkul, and M. A. Cubas. Migration, Diasporas, and Citizenship Series. London: Palgrave Macmillan.

Eder, Mine, and Derya Özkul. 2016. "Editors' Introduction: Precarious Lives and Syrian Refugees in Turkey." *New Perspectives on Turkey* 54:1–8. https://doi.org/10.1017/npt.2016.5.

Ekmekçioğlu, Lerna. 2016. *Recovering Armenia: The Limits of Belonging in Post-Genocide Turkey*. Stanford: Stanford University Press.

Eminov, Ali. 1997. *Turkish and Other Muslim Minorities in Bulgaria*. London: Hurst.

———. 2000. "Turks and Tatars in Bulgaria and the Balkans." *Nationalities Papers* 28 (1): 129–64. https://doi.org/10.1080/00905990050002489.

Erder, Sema. 2007. "Yabancısız Kurgulanan Ülkenin 'Yabancıları.'" In *Türkiye'de Yabancı İşçiler: Uluslararası Göç, İşgücü ve Nüfus Hareketleri*, edited by F. Aylan Arı, 1–83. İstanbul: Derin.

———. 2011. "Zor Ziyaret: Nataşa mı? Döviz Getiren Bavul mu? Eski Doğu Bloğu Ülkelerinden Gelen Kadınların Emek Piyasasına Girişi." In *Birkaç Arpa Boyu: 21. Yüzyıla Girerken Türkiye'de Feminist Çalışmalar*, edited by Serpil Sancar, 191–219. İstanbul: Koç Üniversitesi Yayınları.

———. 2014a. "Balkan Göçmenleri Ve Değişen Uygulamalar: İskan Kurumunun Dostları, and Türkiye'de Değişen Siyasal Konjonktür, Değişen Göç Ve İskan Politikaları." *Türkiye'nin Uluslararası Göç Politikaları, 1923–2023*. İstanbul: Koç University, Migration Research Center. https://mirekoc.ku.edu.tr/wp-content/uploads/sites/22/2017/01/Tu%CC%88rkiyenin-Uluslararas%C4%B1-Go%CC%88c%CC%A7-Politikalar%C4%B1-1923-2023_-.pdf.

———. 2014b. "Türkiye'de Değişen Siyasal Konjonktür, Değişen Göç ve İskan Politikaları." In *Türkiye'nin Uluslararası Göç Politikaları (1923–2023): Ulus-Devlet*

Oluşumundan Ulus-Ötesi Dönüşümlere, edited by Ahmet İçduygu, Sema Erder, and Ömer Faruk Gençkaya, 77–138. İstanbul: Koç Üniversitesi Göç Araştırmaları Merkezi.

Erder, Sema, and Selmin Kaska. 2003. "Irregular Migration and Trafficking in Women: The Case of Turkey." Geneva: International Organization of Migration.

———. 2012. *Turkey in the New Migration Era: Migrants between Regularity and Irregularity*. Vol. 5. Edition HWWI. Hamburg University Press.

Erdoğan, M. Murat. 2015. *Türkiye'deki Suriyeliler Toplumsal Kabul ve Uyum*. Istanbul: İstanbul Bilgi Üniversitesi Yayınları.

Eren, Halit. 1993. *Balkanlarda Türk ve diğer Müslüman Toplumları ve Göç Olgusu*. Istanbul: Ortadoğu ve Balkan İncelemeleri Vakfı.

Ergin, Murat. 2017. *Is the Turk a White Man? Race and Modernity in the Making of Turkish Identity*. Leiden and Boston: Brill.

Erikson, Erik H. 2000. *The Erik Erikson Reader*. New York: W. W. Norton.

Fassin, Didier. 2001. "The Biopolitics of Otherness: Undocumented Foreigners and Racial Discrimination in French Public Debate." *Anthropology Today* 17 (1): 3–7.

———. 2005. "Compassion and Repression: The Moral Economy of Immigration Policies in France." *Cultural Anthropology* 20 (3): 362–87.

———. 2011a. *Humanitarian Reason: A Moral History of the Present*. Berkeley: University of California Press.

———. 2011b. "Policing Borders, Producing Boundaries: The Governmentality of Immigration in Dark Times." *Annual Review of Anthropology* 40:213–26.

———. 2011c. "Racialization: How to Do Races with Bodies." In *A Companion to the Anthropology of the Body and Embodiment*, edited by Frances Mascia-Lees, 419–34. Malden, MA: Wiley-Blackwell.

———. 2014. Introduction to Didier Fassin and Samuel Lézé, eds., *Moral Anthropology: A Critical Reader*. London: Routledge.

Favell, Adrian. 2008. "The New Face of East-West Migration in Europe." *Journal of Ethnic and Migration Studies* 34 (5): 699–841. Special issue, guest-edited by Adrian Favell and Tim Elrick.

Feldman, Ilana. 2016. "Reaction, Experimentation, and Refusal: Palestinian Refugees Confront the Future." *History and Anthropology* 27 (4): 411–29.

———. 2018. *Life Lived in Relief: Humanitarian Predicaments and Palestinian Refugee Politics*. Berkeley: University of California Press.

Fernando, Mayanthi, and Cristiana Giordano. 2016. "Refugees and the Crisis of Europe." Hot Spots. *Cultural Anthropology*. https:culanth.org/fieldsights/911-refugees-and-the-crisis-of-europe.

Fırat, Begüm Özden. 2011. "Adaletin Kağıtsız Halleri: Sorular, Sorunlar ve Feminist Siyaset." *Amargi Feminist Dergi*. http://www.amargidergi.com/yeni/?p=586.

Foucault, Michel. 1981. *The Tanner Lectures on Human Values*. Vol. 2, edited by Sterling M. McMurrin. Cambridge: Cambridge University Press.

Fox, Jon. 2003. "National Identities on the Move: Translyvanian Hungarian Labour Migrants in Hungary." *Journal of Ethnic and Migration Studies* 29 (3): 449–66.

Frederiksen, M. D. 2014. "To Russia with Love: Hope, Confinement, and Virtuality among Youth on the Georgian Black Sea Coast." *Focaal—Journal of Global and Historical Anthropology* 70:26–36.

Frelick, Bill. 2008. *Stuck in a Revolving Door: Iraqis and Other Asylum Seekers and Migrants at the Greece/Turkey Entrance to the European Union.* New York: Human Rights Watch. https://www.hrw.org/sites/default/files/reports/greeceturkey 1108_webwcover.pdf.

Gable, Eric. 2011. *Anthropology and Egalitarianism: Ethnographic Encounters from Monticello to Guinea-Bissau.* Bloomington: Indiana University Press.

Gadamer, Hans-Georg. (1975) 2013. *Truth and Method.* Translated by Joel Weinsheimer and Donald G. Marshall. London: Bloomsbury.

Gal, Susan, and Gail Kligman. 2000. *The Politics of Gender after Socialism.* Princeton, NJ: Princeton University Press.

Ganev, Georgy. 2005. "Where Has Marxism Gone? Gauging the Impact of Alternative Ideas in Transition Bulgaria." *East European Politics and Societies* 19 (3): 443–62.

Genç, Fırat. 2017. "Migration as a Site of Political Struggle: An Evaluation of the Istanbul Migrant Solidarity Network." *Movements. Journal for Critical Migration and Border Regime Studies* 3 (2): 117–32.

Ghodsee, Kristen. 2004a. "Feminism by Design: Emerging Capitalisms, Cultural Feminism, and Women's Nongovernmental Organization in Postsocialist Eastern Europe." *Signs* 29 (3): 727–53.

———. 2004b. "Red Nostalgia? Communism, Women's Emancipation, and Economic Transformation in Bulgaria." *L'Homme: Europäische Zeitschrift für feministische Geschichtswissenschaft* 15 (1): 23–36.

———. 2005. *The Red Riviera: Gender, Tourism, and Postsocialism on the Black Sea.* Durham, NC: Duke University Press.

———. 2010. *Muslim Lives in Eastern Europe: Gender, Ethnicity, and the Transformation of Islam in Postsocialist Bulgaria.* Princeton Studies in Muslim Politics. Princeton, NJ: Princeton University Press.

———. 2011. *Lost in Transition: Ethnographies of Everyday Life after Communism.* Durham, NC: Duke University Press.

Gibson-Graham, J. K. 2006. *A Postcapitalist Politics.* Minneapolis: University of Minnesota Press.

Glick Schiller, Nina, Linda Basch, and Cristina Blanc-Szanton. 1992. "Transnationalism: A New Analytic Framework for Understanding Migration." *Annals of the New York Academy of Sciences* 645: 1–24.

Glick Schiller, Nina, and Ayse Çağlar. 2010. *Locating Migration: Rescaling Cities and Migrants.* Ithaca, NY: Cornell University Press.

Glick Schiller, Nina, and Georges Fouron. 1998. "Transnational Lives and National Identities: The Identity Politics of Haitian Immigrants." In *Transnationalism from Below,* edited by Michael Peter Smith and Luis Eduardo Guarnizo, 128–60. New Brunswick, NJ: Transaction Publishers.

Grant, Bruce. 1995. *In the Soviet House of Culture: A Century of Perestroikas.* Princeton, NJ: Princeton University Press.

Greenberg, Jessica. 2014. *After the Revolution: Youth, Democracy, and the Politics of Disappointment in Serbia.* Stanford: Stanford University Press

———. 2016. "Being and Doing Politics: Moral Ontologies and Ethical Ways of Knowing at the End of the Cold War." In *Impulse to Act: A New Anthropology of Resistance and Social Life,* edited by Othon Alexandrakis, 19–40. Bloomington: Indiana University Press.

Grossberg, Lawrence. 1992. *We Gotta Get Out of This Place: Popular Conservatism and Postmodern Culture.* New York: Routledge.

Gulcur, Leyla, and Pınar İlkkaracan. 2002. "The 'Natasha' Experience: Migrant Sex Workers from the Former Soviet Union and Eastern Europe in Turkey." *Women's Studies International Forum* 25 (4): 411–21.

Gündoğan, Azat Zana. 2018. "Divergent Responses to Urban Transformation Projects in Turkey: Common Sense and State Affinity in Community Mobilization." *Urban Geography,* 1–25.

Hage, Ghassan. 2002. "'On the Side of Life'—Joy and the Capacity of Being—[interview] with Ghassan Hage." In *Hope: New Philosophies for Change,* edited by Mary Zournazi, 150–71. Annandale, NSW: Pluto Press Australia.

———. 2003. *Against Paranoid Nationalism: Searching for Hope in a Shrinking Society.* Annandale, NSW: Pluto Press Australia and Merlin.

———. 2009. "Waiting Out the Crisis: On Stuckedness and Governmentality." In *Waiting,* edited by Ghassan Hage, 97–106. Melbourne: Melbourne University Press.

———. 2016. "Questions concerning a Future-Politics." *History and Anthropology* 27 (4): 465–67.

Hage, Ghassan, and Dmitris Papadopoulos. 2004. "Migration, Hope, and the Making of Subjectivity in Transnational Capitalism." *International Journal for Critical Psychology* 12: 107–21.

Hakyemez, Serra. 2018. "Waiting with Hope and Doubt in the Trials of Terror." Presentation at the London School of Economics conference "Politics in Emotion in Turkey," January 9–12, 2018.

Hammarberg, Thomas. 2009. *The Report on Human Rights of Asylum Seekers and Refugees by the Commissioner for Human Rights of the Council of Europe, following His Visit to Turkey on 28 June–3 July 2009.* Available from: https://wcd.coe.int /ViewDoc.jsp?id=1511197&Site=CommDH&BackColorInternet=FEC65B&Back ColorIntranet=FEC65B&BackColorLogged=FFC679.

Han, Clara. 2011. "Symptoms of Another Life: Time, Possibility, and Domestic Relations in Chile's Credit Economy." *Cultural Anthropology* 26 (1): 7–32.

Haney, Lynne. 1999. "'But We Are Still Mothers': Gender, the State, and the Construction of Need in Postsocialist Hungary." In *Uncertain Transition: Ethnographies of Change in the Post-Socialist World,* edited by Michael Burawoy and Katherine Verdery, 151–88. Lanham, MD: Rowman and Littlefield.

Harvey, David. 2000. *Spaces of Hope*. Berkeley: University of California Press.

Hobbes, Thomas. (1651) 1981. *Leviathan*. New York: Penguin Books.

Hobbes, Thomas, and J. C. Gaskin. (1651) 1998. *Leviathan*. Oxford World's Classics. Oxford and New York: Oxford University Press.

Honig, Bonnie. 2015. "The Antigone-Effect and the Oedipal Curse: Toward a Promiscuous Natality." *philoSOPHIA* 5 (1): 41–49.

Hürriyet Daily News. 2016. "Syrian Children Employed to Produce Fake Life Jackets in Izmir Factory." www.hurriyetdailynews.com/syrian-children-employed-to -produce-life-jackets-in -izmir-factory.aspx?

İçduygu, A., Y. Çolak, and N. Soyarık. 1999. "What Is the Matter with Citizenship? A Turkish Debate." *Middle Eastern Studies* 35 (4): 187–208.

Iğsız, Aslı. 2018. *Humanism in Ruins: Entangled Legacies of the Greek-Turkish Population Exchange*. Stanford: Stanford University Press.

İkizoglu Erensu, Aslı, and Zeynep Kaşlı. 2016. "A Tale of Two Cities: Multiple Practices of Bordering and Degrees of 'Transit' and through Turkey." *Journal of Refugee Studies* 29 (4): 528–48. https://doi.org/10.1093/jrs/few037.

İlkkaracan, Pınar. 2007. "Reforming the Penal Code in Turkey: The Campaign for the Reform of the Turkish Penal Code from a Gender Perspective." Institute of Development Studies. https://www.ids.ac.uk/files/dmfile/PinarIlkkaracanGaventaMay 2007final.doc.

IOM. 2008. *Migration in Turkey: A Country Profile*. http://www.turkey.iom.int/docu ments/migration_profile_turkey.pdf?entryId=10260.

Işın, Engin F. 2004. "The Neurotic Citizen." *Citizenship Studies* 8 (3): 217–35.

Ivy, Marilyn. 1995. *Discourses of the Vanishing: Modernity, Phantasm, Japan*. Chicago: University of Chicago Press.

Jackson, Michael. 2011. *Life within Limits: Well-being in a World of Want*. Durham, NC: Duke University Press.

Jameson, Fredric. 1974. *Marxism and Form: 20th-Century Dialectical Theories of Literature*. Princeton, NJ: Princeton University Press.

Kaczor, C. 2008. *Thomas Aquinas on Faith, Hope, and Love: Edited and Explained for Everyone*. Ave Maria, FL: Sapientia Press of Ave Maria University

Kadirbeyoğlu, Zeynep. 2007. "National Transnationalism: Dual Citizenship in Turkey." In *Dual Citizenship in Europe: From Nationhood to Societal Integration*, edited by T. Faist, 127–46. Aldershot: Ashgate.

———. 2009. "Changing Conceptions of Citizenship in Turkey." In *Citizenship Policies in the New Europe*, edited by R. Bauböck, B. Perchinig, and W. Sievers. Amsterdam: Amsterdam University Press.

———. 2010. *Country Report: Turkey*. Online. EUDO Citizenship Observatory. European University Institute.

Kalfa, A. 2008. "Ex-Eastern European Countries Origin Trafficking and Women Working in the Sex Sector." Master's thesis, Ankara University.

Karpat, Kemal H. 1985. "Ottoman Urbanism: The Crimean Emigration to Dobruca and the Founding of Mecidiye, 1856–1878." *International Journal of Turkish Studies* 3 (1): 1–26.

———. 1990. *The Turks of Bulgaria: The History, Culture, and Political Fate of Minority.* İstanbul: Isis Press.

———. 2004. *Balkanlarda Osmanlı Mirası ve Ulusçuluk.* Ankara: İmge Yayınları.

Kars Gazetesi 772. "Irkdaşlarımız Hoşgeldi." August 25, 1939.

Kasaba, Reşat. 1998. "Göç ve Devlet: Bir Imparatorluk-Cumhuriyet Karşılaştırması." In *Osmanlı'dan Cumhuriyete Problemler, Araştırmalar, Tartışmalar Sempozyumu* 1003, edited by Hamdi Can Tuner, 336–43. Istanbul: Tarih Vakfı Yurt Yayınları.

Kaşlı, Zeynep. 2016. "Who Do Migrant Associations Represent? The Role of 'Ethnic Deservingness' and Legal Capital in Migrants' Rights Claims in Turkey." *Journal of Ethnic and Migration Studies* 42 (12): 1996–2012.

Kaşlı, Zeynep, and Aslı İkizoğlu Erensu. 2016. "A Tale of Two Cities: Multiple Practices of Bordering and Degrees of 'Transit' in and through Turkey." *Journal of Refugee Studies* 29 (4): 528–48.

Kaşlı, Zeynep, and Ayşe Parla. 2009. "Broken Lines of Il/legality and the Reproduction of State Sovereignty: The Impact of Visa Policies on Immigrants to Turkey from Bulgaria." *Alternatives: Global, Local, Political* 34 (2): 203–27.

Keane, Webb. 2007. *Christian Moderns: Freedom and Fetish in the Mission Encounter.* Berkeley: University of California Press.

Kelly, Tobias. 2006. "Documented Lives: Fear and the Uncertainties of Law during the Second Palestinian Intifada." *Journal of the Royal Anthropological Institute* 11 (1): 89–107.

Keough, Leyla J. 2006. "Globalizing 'Postsocialism': Mobile Mothers and Neoliberalism on the Margins of Europe." *Anthropological Quarterly* 79 (3): 431–61.

Kévorkian, Raymond. 2011. *The Armenian Genocide: A Complete History.* London: I. B. Taurus.

Keyder, Çağlar. 2004. "The Consequences of the Exchange of Populations for Turkey." In *Crossing the Aegean: Turkish-Greek Forced Population Exchange*, edited by R. Hirschon, 39–52. New York: Berghahn.

———. 2005. "A History and Geography of Turkish Nationalism." In *Citizenship and the Nation-state in Greece and Turkey*, edited by F. Birtek and T. Dragonas, 3–17. London: Routledge.

Khosravi, Shahram. 2010. "An Ethnography of Migrant 'Illegality' in Sweden: Included Yet Excluded?" *Journal of International Political Theory* 6 (1).

Kirişçi, Kemal. 1996. "Refugees of Turkish Origin: 'Coerced Immigrants' to Turkey since 1945." *International Migration* 34:385–412.

———. 2000. "Disaggregating Turkish Citizenship and Immigration Practices." *Middle Eastern Studies* 36 (3): 1–22.

———. 2012. "Turkey's New Draft Law on Asylum: What to Make of It?" In *Turkey, Migration and the EU*, edited by S. Paçaci-Elitok and T. Straubhaar, 63–83. Hamburg: Hamburg University Press.

Kleist, Nauja, and Stef Jansen. 2016. "Introduction: Hope over Time: Crisis, Immobility, and Future-Making." *History and Anthropology* 27 (4): 373–92. https://doi.org/10.1080/02757206.2016.1207636.

Kleist, Nauja, and D. Thorsen, eds. 2017. *Hope and Uncertainty in Contemporary African Migration.* London: Routledge.

Koğacıoğlu, Dicle. 2004. "The Tradition Effect: Framing Honor Crimes in Turkey." *Differences: A Journal of Feminist Cultural Studies* 15 (2): 118–52.

———. 2007. "Gelenek Söylemleri ve İktidarın Doğallaşması: Namus Cinayetleri Örneği." *Kultur ve Siyasette Feminist Yaklasimlar.* http://www.feministyaklasimlar.org/index.php?act=in.

Konukman, Ercüment. 1990. *Tarihi Belgeler Işığında Büyük Göç ve Anavatan (Bulgaristan'da Nedenleri, Boyutları, Sonuçları).* Ankara: Türk Basın Birliği.

Kotzeva, Tatyana. 1999. "Re-imaging Bulgarian Women: The Marxist Legacy and Women's Self-Identity." In *Gender and Identity in Central and Eastern Europe,* edited by Chris Corrin, 83–98. London: Frank Cass.

Lambek, Michael. 2010. *Ordinary Ethics: Anthropology, Language, and Action.* New York: Fordham University Press.

———. 2015. *The Ethical Condition: Essays on Action, Person, and Value.* Chicago: University of Chicago Press.

Lear, Jonathan. 2006. *Radical Hope: Ethics in the Face of Cultural Devastation.* Cambridge, MA: Harvard University Press.

Leavitt, John. 1996. "Meaning and Feeling in the Anthropology of Emotions." *American Ethnologist* 23 (3): 514–39.

Leys, Ruth. 2011. "The Turn to Affect: A Critique." *Critical Inquiry* 37 (3): 434–72.

Lutz, Catherine. 1988. *Unnatural Emotions: Everyday Sentiments on a Micronesian Atoll and Their Challenge to Western Theory.* Chicago: University of Chicago Press.

———. 2017. "What Matters." *Cultural Anthropology* 32 (2): 181–91.

Lutz, Catherine, and Lila Abu-Lughod. 1990. *Language and the Politics of Emotion.* Studies in Emotion and Social Interaction. Cambridge: Cambridge University Press; Paris: Editions de la Maison des Sciences de l'homme.

Lutz, Catherine, and Geoffrey M. White. 1986. "The Anthropology of Emotions." *Annual Review of Anthropology* 15:405–36.

MacIntyre, Alasdair. 1984. *After Virtue: A Study in Moral Theory.* Notre Dame, IN: University of Notre Dame Press.

Maksudyan, Nazan. 2005. *Türklüğü Ölçmek: Bilimkurgusal Antropoloji ve Türk Milliyetçiliğinin Irkçı Çehresi (1925–1939).* İstanbul: Metis.

Malkki, L. 1992. "National Geographic: The Rooting of Peoples and the Territorialisation of National Identity amongst Scholars and Refugees." *Cultural Anthropology* 7 (1): 22–44.

———. 1995. "Refugees and Exile: From 'Refugee Studies to the National Order of Things.'" *Annual Review of Anthropology* 24:495–523.

Mardin, Şerif. 1962. *The Genesis of Young Ottoman Thought*. Princeton, NJ: Princeton University Press.

Marichelar, Pascal. 2018. *Qui a tué les verriers de Givors?* Paris: La Découverte.

Martin, Emily. 2013. "The Potentiality of Ethnography and the Limits of Affect Theory." *Current Anthropology* 54 (7): 149–58.

Marx, Karl. 1852. "The Eighteenth Brumaire of Louis Bonaparte." *Die Revolution*. New York.

Massumi, Brian. 1995. "The Autonomy of Affect." *Cultural Critique* 31:83–109.

———. 2002. *Parables for the Virtual: Movement, Affect, Sensation*. Durham, NC: Duke University Press.

Mattingly, Cheryl. 2010. *The Paradox of Hope: Journeys through a Clinical Borderland*. Berkeley: University of California Press.

———. 2014. *Moral Laboratories: Family Peril and the Struggle for a Good Life*. Berkeley: University of California Press.

Mazzarella, William. 2009. "Affect: What Is It Good For?" In *Enchantments of Modernity: Empire, Nation, Globalization*, edited by Saurabh Dube, 291–309. London: Routledge.

Mbembe, Achille, and Sarah Nuttall. 2004. "Writing the World from an African Metropolis." *Public Culture* 16 (3): 347–72.

McGranahan, Carole. 2016. "Theorizing Refusal: An Introduction." *Cultural Anthropology* 31 (3): 319–25. https://doi.org/10.14506/ca31.3.01.

McNevin, Anne. 2006. "Political Belonging in a Neoliberal Era: The Struggle of the Sans-Papiers." *Citizenship Studies* 10 (2): 135–51.

Millar, Kathleen. 2014. "The Precarious Present: Wageless Labor and Disrupted Life in Rio de Janeiro, Brazil." *Cultural Anthropology* 29 (1): 32–53.

———. 2015. "The Tempo of Wageless Work: E. P. Thompson's Time-Sense at the Edges of Rio de Janeiro." *Focaal: Journal of Global and Historical Anthropology* 73:28–40.

Mishkova, Diana. 1994. "Literacy and Nation-Building in Bulgaria, 1878–1912." *East European Quarterly* 28 (1): 63–93.

Miyazaki, Hirokazu. 2004. *The Method of Hope: Anthropology, Philosophy, and Fijian Knowledge*. Stanford: Stanford University Press.

———. 2017a. "The Economy of Hope: An Introduction." In *The Economy of Hope*, edited by Miyazaki Hirokazu and Richard Swedberg, 1–36. Philadelphia: University of Pennsylvania Press.

———. 2017b. "Obama's Hope: An Economy of Belief and Substance." In *The Economy of Hope*, edited by Miyazaki Hirokazu and Richard Swedberg, 172–90. Philadelphia: University of Pennsylvania Press.

Miyazaki, Hirokazu, and Richard Swedberg, eds. 2017. *The Economy of Hope*. Philadelphia: University of Pennsylvania Press.

Mole, Noelle. 2010. "Living It on the Skin: Italian States, Working Illness." *American Ethnologist* 35 (2): 189–210.

Muehlebach, Andrea. 2012. *The Moral Neoliberal: Welfare and Citizenship in Italy.* Chicago: University of Chicago Press.

———. 2013. "On Precariousness and the Ethical Imagination: The Year 2012 in Sociocultural Anthropology." *American Anthropologist* 115:297–311.

Muehlebach, Andrea, and Nitzan Shoshan. 2012. "Introduction." *Anthropological Quarterly* 85 (2): 317–44.

Muñoz, José Esteban. 2009. *Cruising Utopia: The Then and There of Queer Futurity.* New York: New York University Press.

Münz, Rainer, and Rainer Ohliger, eds. 2003. *Diasporas and Ethnic Migrants: Germany, Israel, and Post-Soviet Successor States in Comparative Perspective.* London and Portland: Frank Cass.

Myers, Fred. 1986. *Pintupi Country, Pintupi Self: Sentiment, Place, and Politics among Western Desert Aborigines.* Berkeley: University of California Press.

Nadkarni, Maya, and Olga Shevchenko. 2004. "The Politics of Nostalgia: A Case for Comparative Analysis of Post-Socialist Practices." *Ab Imperio* 2:487–519.

Narayan, Kirin. 1993. "How Native Is a 'Native' Anthropologist?" *American Anthropologist* 95 (3): 671–86.

Narayan, Kirin, and Kenneth M. George. 2012. "Stories about Getting Stories." In *SAGE Handbook of Interview Research: The Complexity of the Craft,* edited by Jaber F. Gubrium, James Holstein, Amir B. Marvasti, and Karyn D. McKinney, 367–81. 2nd ed. Thousand Oaks, CA: SAGE Publications.

Navaro-Yashin, Yael. 2002. *Faces of the State: Secularism and Public Life in Turkey.* Princeton, NJ: Princeton University Press.

———. 2012. *The Make-Believe Space: Affective Geography in a Postwar Polity.* Durham, NC: Duke University Press.

Nehamas, Alexander. 1998. *The Art of Living: Socratic Reflections from Plato to Foucault.* Berkeley: University of California Press.

Ngai, Sianne. 2005. *Ugly Feelings.* Cambridge, MA: Harvard University Press.

Nietzsche, Friedrich Wilhelm. (1878) 1986. *Human, All Too Human: A Book for Free Spirits.* Translated by R. J. Hollingdale. Cambridge: Cambridge University Press.

Ochs, Elinor, and Lisa Capps. 1996. "Narrating the Self." *Annual Review of Anthropology* 25 (1): 19–43.

Ochs, Elinor, and Bambi Schieffelin. 1989. "Language Has a Heart." *Text—Interdisciplinary Journal for the Study of Discourse* 9 (1): 7–25.

Ong, Aihwa. 1996. "Cultural Citizenship as Subject-Making." *Current Anthropology* 37 (5): 737–62.

———. 1999. *Flexible Citizenship: The Cultural Logics of Transnationality.* Durham, NC: Duke University Press.

———. 2000. "Graduated Sovereignty in South-East Asia." *Theory, Culture, and Society* 17 (4): 55–75.

———. 2006. *Neoliberalism as Exception: Mutations in Citizenship and Sovereignty.* Durham, NC: Duke University Press.

O'Reilly, Karen. 2004. *Ethnographic Methods*. London: Routledge.

Özbay, Ferhunde, and Banu Yücel. 2001. "Türkiye'de Göç Hareketleri, Devlet Politikaları ve Demografik Yapı." In *Nüfus Kalkınma, Göç, Eğitim, Demokrasi ve Yaşam Kalitesi*, edited by Ferhunde Özbay et al., 1–68. Ankara: Hacettepe Üniversitesi Nüfus Etütleri Enstitütüsü.

Özgür, K., and R. Çavuş. 2011. "Bulgaristan Göçmenlerinin Temel Sorunları ve Çözüm Yolları." İzmir Balkan Göçmenleri Kültür ve Dayanışma Derneği. http://www.balgocizmir.org.tr/sorun.asp.

Özgür-Baklacıoğlu, Nurcan. 2006a. "Dual Citizenship, Extraterritorial Elections, and National Policies: Turkish Dual Citizens in the Bulgarian-Turkish Political Sphere." In *Beyond Sovereignty: From Status Law to Transnational Citizenship*, 319–58.

———. 2006b. "Türkiye'nin Balkan Politikasında Rumeli ve Balkan Göçmen Dernekleri." *Sivil Toplum ve Dış Politika: Yeni Sorunlar, Yeni Aktörler*, edited by S. C. Mazlum and E. Doğan, 77–117. Istanbul: Bağlam.

Özinian, Aline. 2009. "Identifying the State of Armenian Migrants in Turkey." Report for Eurasia Partnership Foundation.

Öztürk, Osman, and Aziz Çelik. 2008. *Soysal Guvenlikte Hak Kaybı Donemi*. Ankara: Türk Tabipler Birliği Yayınları.

Özyeğin, Gül. 2000. *Untidy Gender: Domestic Service in Turkey*. Philadelphia: Temple University Press.

Özyürek, Esra. 2006. *Nostalgia for the Modern: State Secularism and Everyday Politics in Turkey*. Durham, NC: Duke University Press.

———. 2009. "Christian and Turkish: Secularist Fears of a Converted Nation." *Comparative Studies of South Asia, Africa, and the Middle East* 29 (3): 398–412.

———. 2018. "Rethinking Empathy: Emotions Triggered by the Holocaust among Muslim-Minority in Germany." *Anthropological Theory*. http://eprints.lse.ac.uk/87798/.

Parla, Ayşe. 2001. "The 'Honor' of the State: Virginity Examinations in Turkey." *Feminist Studies* 27 (1): 65–88.

———. 2003. "Marking Time along the Bulgarian-Turkish Border." *Ethnography* 4 (4): 561–75.

———. 2006. "Longing, Belonging, and Locations of Homeland among Turkish Immigrants from Bulgaria." *Journal of Southeastern Europe and the Black Sea Studies* 6 (4): 543–57.

———. 2007. "Irregular Workers or Ethnic Kin? Post-1990s Labour Migration from Bulgaria to Turkey." *International Migration* 45 (3): 157–81.

———. 2009. "Remembering across the Border: Postsocialist Nostalgia among Turkish Immigrants from Bulgaria." *American Ethnologist* 36 (4): 750–67.

———. 2011. "Labor Migration, Ethnic Kinship, and the Conundrum of Citizenship in Turke." *Citizenship Studies* 15 (3–4): 457–70.

———. 2016. "'For Us, Migration Is Ordinary': Post-1989 Labour Migration from

Bulgaria to Turkey." In *Migration in the Southern Balkans: From Ottoman Territory to Globalized Nation States*, edited by Hans Vermeulen, Martin Baldwin-Edwards, and Riki van Boeschoten, 105–22. New York: Springer Open.

———. 2017. "The Complicity of Hope." *Political and Legal Anthropology Review.* https://politicalandlegalanthro.org/2017/05/03/the-complicity-of-hope/.

———. Forthcoming. "Critique without a Politics of Hope?" In *A Time for Critique*, edited by Didier Fassin and Bernard Harcourt. New York: Columbia University Press.

Parla, Ayşe, and Ceren Özgül. 2016. "Property, Dispossession, and Citizenship in Turkey; or, the History of the Gezi Uprising Starts in the Surp Hagop Armenian Cemetery." *Public Culture* 28 (3): 617–53.

Parla, Taha. 1991. *Türkiye'de Siyasal Kültürün Resmi Kaynakları*. Vols. 1 and 2. İstanbul: İletişim.

———. 2016. *Türkiye'de Anayasalar: Tarih, İdeoloji, Rejim (1921–2016)*. İstanbul: Metis.

Parla, Taha, and Andrew Davison. 2004. *Corporatist Ideology in Kemalist Turkey: Progress or Order?* Syracuse, NY: Syracuse University Press.

Parreñas, R. S. 2012. "The Indentured Mobility of Migrant Women: How Gendered Protectionist Laws Lead Hostesses to Forced Sexual Labor." *Journal of Workplace Rights* 15 (3–4): 327–39.

Partridge, Damani J. 2012. *Hypersexuality and Headscarves: Race, Sex, and Citizenship in the New Germany*. New Anthropologies of Europe, edited by Matti Bunzl and Michael Herzfeld. Bloomington: University of Indiana Press.

Patico, Jennifer. 2005. "To Be Happy in a Mercedes: Tropes of Value and Ambivalent Visions of Marketization." *American Ethnologist* 32 (3): 479– 96.

Petryna, Adriana, and Karolina Follis. 2015. "Risks of Citizenship and Fault Lines of Survival." *Annual Review of Anthropology* 44: 401–17.

Pilbrow, Tim. 2010. "Dignity in Transition: History, Teachers, and the Nation-State in Post-1989 Bulgaria." In *Post-Communist Nostalgia*, edited by Maria Todorova and Zsuzsa Gille, 84–95. New York: Berghahn Books.

Polatel, Mehmet. 2009. "Turkish State Formation and the Distribution of the Armenian Abandoned Properties from the Ottoman Empire to the Republic of Turkey (1915–1930)." Master's thesis, Koç University, İstanbul.

Polkinghorne, Donald E. 1995. "Narrative Configuration in Qualitative Analysis." *International Journal of Qualitative Studies in Education* 8 (1): 5–23.

Potuoğlu-Cook, Öykü. 2006. "Beyond the Glitter: Belly Dance and Neoliberal Gentrification in Istanbul." *Cultural Anthropology* 21 (4): 633–60.

Rafael, Vicente. 1997. "'Your Grief Is Our Gossip': Overseas Filipinos and Other Spectral Presences." *Public Culture* 9 (2): 267–91.

Ralph, Laurence. 2014. *Renegade Dreams: Living through Injury in Gangland Chicago*. Chicago and London: University of Chicago Press

Rapp, Rayna. 2000. *Testing Women, Testing the Fetus: The Social Impact of Amniocentesis in America*. Anthropology of Everyday Life. Abingdon, UK: Routledge.

Redfield, Peter. 2013. *Life in Crisis: The Ethical Journey of Doctors without Borders*. Berkeley: University of California Press.

Ricoeur, Paul. 1980. *Essays on Biblical Interpretation*. Minneapolis: Fortress Press.

Riles, Annelise. 2017. "Is the Law Hopeful?" In *The Economy of Hope*, edited by Miyazaki Hirokazu and Richard Swedberg. Philadelphia: University of Pennsylvania Press.

Robbins, Bruce. 2016. "Hope." *Political Concepts* 3. https://www.politicalconcepts.org/hope-bruce-robbins/4.

Rofel, Lisa. 1999. *Other Modernities: Gendered Yearnings in China after Socialism*. Berkeley: University of California Press.

Rosaldo, Michelle. 1984. "Toward an Anthropology of Self and Feeling." In *Culture Theory: Essays on Mind, Self, and Emotion*, edited by R. A. Schweder and R. Levine. Cambridge: Cambridge University Press.

Rose, Nikolas. 2007. *The Politics of Life Itself: Biomedicine, Power, and Subjectivity in the Twenty-First Century*. Princeton, NJ: Princeton University Press.

Rousseau, Jean-Jacques. (1762) 2003. *On the Social Contract*. Mineola, NY: Dover Publications.

Salter, Mark. 2006. "The Global Visa Regime and Political Technologies of the International Self: Borders, Bodies, Biopolitics." *Alternatives: Global, Local, Political* 2:167–89.

Şanlı, Ayşe. 2018. "Quotidian Boundaries and How to Circumvent Them: An Inquiry into a Syrian Community in Istanbul." Master's thesis, Sabancı University, Istanbul.

Sarat, Austin, and Thomas Kearns. 1993. *Law in Everyday Life*. Ann Arbor: University of Michigan Press.

Sarı, Elif, and Cemile Gizem Dinçer. 2017. "Toward a New Asylum Regime in Turkey." *Movements. Journal for Critical Migration and Border Regime Studies* 3 (2): 59–79.

Sassen, Saskia. 1998. *Globalization and Its Discontents*. New York: New Press.

Şaul, Mahir. 2014. "A Different *Kargo*: Sub-Saharan Migrants in Istanbul and African Commerce." *Urban Anthropology and Studies of Cultural Systems and World Economic Development* 43 (1–3): 143–203.

Scheper-Hughes, Nancy. (1989) 1992. *Death without Weeping: The Violence of Everyday Life in Brazil*. Berkeley: University of California Press.

Schopenhauer, Arthur. (1818) 2010. *The World as Will and Representation*, vol. 1. Translated by Judith Norman, Alistair Welchman, and Christopher Janaway. Cambridge: Cambridge University Press.

Scott, Joan. 1986. "Gender: A Useful Category of Historical Analysis." *American Historical Review* 91 (5): 1053–75.

Sedgwick, Eve Kosofsky. 2003. *Touching Feeling: Affect, Pedagogy, Performativity*. Durham, NC: Duke University Press.

Sennett, Richard. 1998. *The Corrosion of Character: The Personal Consequences of Work in the New Capitalism*. New York: Norton.

Shaw, Jennifer E., and Darren Byler. 2016. "Precarity." Curated Collections. *Cultural Anthropology.* https://culanth.org/curated_collections/21-precarity.

Shouse, Eric. 2005. "Feeling, Emotion, Affect." *M/C Journal,* 8 (6). http://journal.media-culture.org.au/0512/03-shouse.php.

Silverstein, Paul A. 2004. *Algeria in France: Transpolitics, Race, and Nation.* New Anthropologies of Europe. Bloomington: University of Indiana Press.

Şimşir, Bilal N. 1986. *Bulgaristan Türkleri,* Ankara: Bilgi.

———. 1990. *The Turks of Bulgaria in International Fora: Documents.* Vol. 2. Ankara: Atatürk Supreme Council for Culture, Language, and History Publications of Turkish Historical Society.

Smith, Nicholas H. 2005. "Hope and Critical Theory." *Critical Horizons* 6 (1): 45–61.

———. 2008. "Analysing Hope." *Critical Horizons* 9 (1): 5–23.

Soykan, Cavidan. 2012. "The New Draft Law on Foreigners and International Protection in Turkey." *Oxford Monitor of Forced Migration* 2 (2): 38–47.

Speri, Alice. 2014. "Afghan Asylum Seekers in Turkey Are Sewing Their Lips Together in Protest." *Vice News.*

Spinoza, Baruch. (1677) 2000. *Ethics.* Oxford Philosophical Texts. Edited and translated by G. H. R. Parkinson. Oxford: Oxford University Press.

Spinoza, Benedict de. 1994. *A Spinoza Reader: The Ethics and Other Works.* Edited and translated by Edwin Curley. Princeton, NJ: Princeton University Press.

Stahl, Titus, and Claudia Blöser. 2017. "Hope." In *The Stanford Encyclopedia of Philosophy* (Spring 2017), edited by Edward N. Zalta. https://plato.stanford.edu/archives/spr2017/entries/hope.

Stengers, Isabelle. 2002. "A Cosmo-Politics: Risk, Hope, Change." In *Hope: New Philosophies for Change,* edited by Mary Zournazi. New York: Routledge.

Stewart, Kathleen. 2007. *Ordinary Affects.* Durham, NC: Duke University Press.

Strathern, Marilyn. (1986) 2004. *Partial Connections.* Lanham, MD: Rowman Altamira.

Suciyan, Talin. 2015. *The Armenians in Modern Turkey: Post-Genocide Society, Politics, and History.* London: I. B. Tauris.

Swedberg, Richard. 2017. "A Sociological Approach to Hope in the Economy." In *The Economy of Hope,* edited by Miyazaki Hirokazu and Richard Swedberg, 37–50. Philadelphia: University of Pennsylvania Press.

Tadeusz, Rachwal. 2016. *Precarity and Loss: On Certain and Uncertain Properties of Life and Work.* Wiesbaden: Springer VS.

Tambar, Kabir. 2014. *The Reckoning of Pluralism: Political Belonging and the Demands of History in Turkey.* Redwood City, CA: Stanford University Press.

———. 2016. "Brotherhood in Dispossession: State Violence and the Ethics of Expectation in Turkey." *Cultural Anthropology* 31 (1): 30–55.

Tekeli, İlhan. 1990. "Osmanlı İmparatorluğundan Günümüze Nüfusun Zorunlu Yer Değiştirmesi ve İskan Sorunu." *Toplum ve Bilim* 50:49–72.

———. 2002. "Osmanlı İmparatorluğundan Günümüzün Nufusun Zorunlu Yer Değiştirmesi ve İskan Sorunu." In *Ilhan Tekeli Toplu Eserleri* 3:141–70. İstanbul: Tarih Vakfı Yurt Yayınları,

TBMM (Türkiye Büyük Millet Meclisi) Zabıt Ceridesi, 1934. Cilt 23. Ankara: TBMM.

Thorkelson, Eli. 2016. "Precarity Outside: The Political Unconscious of French Academic Labor." *American Ethnologist* 43:475–87. https://doi.org/10.1111/amet.12340.

Thrift, Nigel. 2007. *Non-representational Theory: Space, Politics, Affect.* London: Routledge.

Throop, C. Jason. 2015. "Ambivalent Happiness and Virtuous Suffering." *HAU: Journal of Ethnographic Theory* 5 (3): 45–68.

Ticktin, Miriam I. 2006. "Where Ethics and Politics Meet." *American Ethnologist: Journal of the American Ethnological Society* 33 (1): 33–49.

———. 2011. *Casualties of Care: Immigration and the Politics of Humanitarianism in France.* Berkeley: University of California Press.

Todorova, Maria. 2014. *Remembering Communism: Private and Public Recollections of Lived Experience in Southeast Europe.* Budapest: Central European University Press.

———., ed. 2010. *Remembering Communism: Genres of Representation.* New York: Social Science Research Council.

Toğrol, Beylan. 1991. *Direniş: Bulgaristan Türklerinin 114 yıllık Onur Mücadelesinin Karşılaştırmalı Psikolojik İncelemesi.* İstanbul: Boğaziçi Universitesi Matbaası.

Toksöz, Gülay, and Çağla Ünlütürk-Ulutaş . 2011. "Göç Kadınlaşıyor mu? Türkiye'ye Yönelen Düzensiz Göçe İlişkin Yazına Toplumsal Cinsiyet ve Etnisite Temelinde Bakış." In *Birkaç Arpa Boyu: 21. Yüzyıla Girerken Türkiye'de Feminist Çalışmalar.* Edited by Serpil Sancar. İstanbul: Koç Üniversitesi Yayınları, 157–79.

———. 2012. "Is Migration Feminized? A Gender- and Ethnicity-Based Review of the Literature on Irregular Migration to Turkey." In *Turkey, Migration, and the EU: Potentials, Challenges, and Opportunities*, edited by S. Paçacı-Elitok and T. ve Straubhaar, 85–113. Hamburg: Hamburg University Press,

Tokuzlu, Bertan. 2013. "Yabancılar Ve Uluslararası Koruma Kanun'nun Yasal Belirlilik İlkesi Konusunda Türk Uygulamasına Katkısı Üzerine Bir Değerlendirme." www.academia.edu.

Tolay, Juliette. 2010. "Turkey's Other Multicultural Debate: Lessons for the EU." Paper, recipient of the first prize of the 2010 Sakıp Sabancı International Research Award.

Tomkins, Silvan. 1962. *Affect, Imagery, Consciousness.* Vol. 1, *The Positive Affects.* New York: Springer.

———. 1995. *Exploring Affect: The Selected Writings of Silvan S. Tomkins.* Edited by Virginia E. Demos. Cambridge: Cambridge University Press.

Tsing, Anna L. 2005. *Friction: An Ethnography of Global Connection.* Princeton, NJ: Princeton University Press.

———. 2015. *The Mushroom at the End of the World: On the Possibility of Life in Capitalist Ruins.* Princeton, NJ: Princeton University Press

Tsuda, Takeyuki. *Strangers in the Ethnic Homeland: Japanese Brazilian Return Migration in Transnational Perspective*. New York: Columbia University Press, 2003.

Tuğal, Cihan. 2009. *Passive Revolution: Absorbing the Islamic Challenge to Capitalism*. Stanford: Stanford University Press.

Turam, Berna. 2007. *Between Islam and the State: The Politics of Engagement*. Stanford: Stanford University Press.

Turan, Ömer. 1998. *The Turkish Minority in Bulgaria (1878–1908)*. Ankara: Türk Tarih Kurumu Yayınları.

Turner, Simon. 2014. "'We Wait for Miracles' : Ideas of Hope and Future among Clandestine Burundian Refugees in Nairobi." In *Ethnographies of Uncertainty in Africa*, edited by David Pratten and Elizabeth Cooper, 1:173–93. Basingstoke, UK: Palgrave Macmillan.

Turner, Terence. 1980. "The Social Skin." In *Not Work Alone: A Cross-Cultural View of Activities Superfluous to Survival*, edited by Jeremy Cherfas and Roger Lewin, 112–40. London: Temple Smith.

Uğur, Üngör, and Mehmet Polatel. 2011. *Confiscation and Destruction: The Young Turk Seizure of Armenian Property*. London: Continuum International.

UNHCR (United Nations High Commissioner for Refugees). 2015. "State Parties to the 1951 Convention relating to the Status of Refugees and the 1967 Protocol." http://www.unhcr.org/protect/PROTECTION/3b73b0d63.pdf.

Ünlü, Barış. 2014. *Türkük Sözleşmesinin İmzalanışı (1915–1925)*. Mülkiye Dergisi 38 (3): 47–81.

van Bruinessen, Martin. "Ismail Beşikçi: Turkish Sociologist, Critic of Kemalism, and Kurdologist." *Journal of Kurdish Studies* 5 (2003–04): 19–34.

Vasileva, D. 1992. "Bulgarian Turkish Emigration and Return." *International Migration Review* 26 (2): 342–52.

Verdery, Katherine. 1996. *What Was Socialism and What Comes Next?* Princeton, NJ: Princeton University Press.

Vogt, Katja Maria. "Imagining Good Future States: Hope and Truth in Plato's *Philebus*." In *Selfhood and the Soul*, 33–48. Oxford: Oxford University Press, 2017. http://www.oxfordscholarship.com.ezp-prod1.hul.harvard.edu/view/10.1093/acprof:oso/9780198777250.001.0001/acprof-9780198777250-chapter-3.

Waite, Louise. 2009. "A Place and Space for a Critical Geography of Precarity?" *Geography Compass* 3 (1): 412–33.

White, Daniel. 2017. "Affect: An Introduction." *Cultural Anthropology* 32 (2): 175–80.

Whyte, Susan. 2005. "Uncertain Undertakings: Practicing Health Care in the Subjunctive Mood." In *Managing Uncertainty: Ethnographic Studies of Illness, Risk, and the Struggle for Control*, edited by Steffen Vibeke, Richard Jenkins, and Hanne Jessen, 245–64. Copenhagen: Museum Tusculanum.

———. 2009. "Epilogue." In *Dealing with Uncertainty in Contemporary African Lives*, edited by L. Haram and B. Yamba, 213–16. Uppsala, Sweden: Nordiska Afrika-Institutet.

Willen, Sarah. 2007. "Toward a Critical Phenomenology of 'Illegality': State Power,

Criminalization, and Abjectivity among Undocumented Migrant Workers in Tel Aviv, Israel." *International Migration* 45 (3): 8–38.

———. 2012. "Migration, 'Illegality,' and Health: Mapping Embodied Vulnerability and Debating Health-Related Deservingness." *Social Science and Medicine* 74 (6): 805–11.

Williams, Patricia J. 1991. *The Alchemy of Race and Rights*. Cambridge, MA: Harvard University Press.

Williams, Raymond. 1965. *The Long Revolution*. London: Penguin Books.

———. 1977. *Marxism and Literature*. Marxist Introductions. Oxford: Oxford University Press.

———. 1979. *Politics and Letters*. New York: Schocken Books.

Wimmer, Andreas. 2008. "The Making and Unmaking of Ethnic Boundaries: A Multilevel Process Theory." *American Journal of Sociology* 113 (4): 970–1022.

Yeats, W. B. 1933. "Death." In *The Winding Stair and Other Poems*. New York: Simon and Schuster.

Yeğen, Mesut. 2009. "'Prospective-Turks' or 'Pseudo-Citizens': Kurds in Turkey." *Middle East Journal* 63 (4): 597–615.

Yıldız, Ahmet. 2001. *Ne mutlu Türküm diyebilene: Türk Ulusal Kimliğinin Etno-Seküler Sınırları (1919–1938)*. İstanbul: İletişim.

Yükseker, Deniz. 2003. *Laleli-Moskova Mekiği: Kayıtdışı Ticaret ve Cinsiyet İlişkileri*. İstanbul: İletişim Yayınları.

Yükseker, Deniz, and Kelly Brewer. 2010. "İstanbul'daki Afrikalı Göçmen ve Sığınmacıların Yaşam Koşulları." In *Türkiye'ye Uluslararası Göç*, edited by Barbara Pusch and Tomas Wilkoszewski, 297–320. İstanbul: Kitap Yayınevi.

Zahariev, Bozhidar. 2004. "The Treatment of Ethnic Turks by the Bulgarian Communist Party and Their Status Quo." New York: Ithaca College Catalogs.

Zerilli, Linda M. G. 2015. "The Turn to Affect and the Problem of Judgment." *New Literary History* 46 (2): 261–86.

Zhelyazkova, A. 1998. *Between Adaptation and Nostalgia: The Bulgarian Turks in Turkey*. Sofia: International Centre for Minority Research and International Relations.

Zigon, Jarrett. 2009. "Hope Dies Last: Two Aspects of Hope in Contemporary Moscow." *Anthropological Theory* 9 (3): 253–71.

Zournazi, Mary, Chantal Mouffe, and Ernesto Laclau. 2003. "Hope, Passion, and Politics: A Conversation with Chantal Mouffe and Ernesto Laclau." In *Hope: New Philosophies for Change*, edited by Mary Zournazi, 122–48. New York: Routledge.

INDEX